# The
# MAN WHO DIDN'T
# FIT IN

Also by Dick North

*The Lost Patrol*
*Trackdown*
*The Mad Trapper of Rat River*
*Arctic Exodus*

*Dick North*

# The
# MAN WHO DIDN'T FIT IN

*How Canada's Most Wanted Outlaw
Began His Life of Crime*

Dick North

*For Stein Kruse,
Steve Leonard of your company,
who is a long time friend of mine,
suggested I send this to you. The
lad whom it's about came from
Norway & North Dakota.
all the best
Dick*

**THE LYONS PRESS**
Guilford, Connecticut
An imprint of The Globe Pequot Press

*P.O. Box 971
Dawson City, YT, Y0B1G0
Canada*

The Lyons Press is an imprint of The Globe Pequot Press.

10 9 8 7 6 5 4 3 2 1

Printed in The United States of America

Library of Congress Cataloging-in-Publication Data

North, Dick.
  The man who didn't fit in : how Canada's most wanted outlaw began his life of crime / Dick North.
    p. cm.
  ISBN 1-59228-838-3
  1. Delker, Burt. 2. Outlaws—Canada—Biography. I. Title.
HV6248.D365N67 2005
364.15'52092—dc22

2005027307

In memory of Governor William Egan and Commissioner Emory Chapple, and for Deputy Commissioner James P. Wellington. They hired the author as the first full-time public information officer for Alaska's Department of Public Safety in 1972.

*There's a race of men that don't fit in,*
*A race that can't stay still;*
*So they break the hearts of kith and kin,*
*And they roam the world at will.*

*They range the field and they rove the flood,*
*And they climb the mountain's crest;*
*Theirs is the curse of the gypsy blood,*
*And they don't know how to rest.*

—from "The Men That Don't Fit In"
by Robert Service,

*The Spell of the Yukon*

# Contents

# Chapter 1

# THE FARM

**B**urt Delker thundered his objections over Magnor's plan to rob a bank. "It ain't like rustlin' horses," he bellowed, and emphasized the point by slamming his gnarled fist down hard on the hewn plank table. Coffee mugs rocked precariously, spoons and forks rattled, and a rummaging pack rat ran for its life.

Johnny Johnson lurched slightly where he rested on a cot behind his two companions. He opened one eye, looked at Delker, then closed it again. Only sixteen years old, Johnny was not included in Magnor's plans to rescue the Johnson family from debt, a situation that was not unique in North Dakota in 1915.

The three men were in Delker's sod house, warm against the wintry blasts of a blue norther raging outside. A potbellied stove, glowing cherry red in the center of the one-room hut, provided heat for the structure. The light from an oil lamp resting on the table flickered weakly off the walls, with the flame itself seemingly threatened by the darkness surrounding it.

Dimly visible in the light of the lantern were the faces of Johnny's two companions as they leaned forward in serious discussion. Delker's features displayed the lines of middle age biting into his temples and the corner of his eyes. He had a broad, open look about him that belied his years spent as a rustler. Johnny's half brother, Magnor Hanson, whose handsome, blond features underscored his youth, seemed less sinister in the periphery of light provided by the lamp. Magnor's gray eyes took on a curious sapphire hue as he and Delker debated Magnor's scheme to relieve the family farm of financial burdens incurred by a heavy double mortgage. The date was fast approaching when the loans would be called in, and all the care and sweat and toil over the foregoing decade would go for naught if they could not come up with the necessary funds.

The hard times of the Johnson family were by no means unique among immigrants to North Dakota, but this fact did not serve to make living any easier—especially since the newcomers were almost as bad off in the new land as they were in their old home in northern Norway. The vista of Johnny's life flashed across his mind. Raised in Bardu, he was six in 1904 when his pa and ma emigrated. Yet he recalled the clear air of the old country, and the mountains and the wild deer, and fishing at Lake Altevatn. As young as he was, Johnny's travels had spanned two continents and an ocean, and as yet, he had seen nothing but abject poverty. Now it was 1915, and his sister Signe and her baby were dead as the result of a fouled-up childbirth. She had been Delker's wife for only a year. Johnny often wondered if she really loved Delker when she married, or went with him to get away from the poverty of the farm, and his pa's drinking. Helga, his older sister, had fled, he knew not where. Johnny figured it was to escape the depressing conditions at home. That left his younger sister, Olga; Magnor; and his ma, Petra, still there with his pa, Anders.

The rock in the family was his half brother, Magnor. Anders's sour temperament never seemed to get under Magnor's skin like it did Johnny's. Somehow, his brother kept things going, yet even for him the constant demand for cash to pay off the loans was like feeding worms to a bird. The bank never stopped demanding. Johnny and Magnor broke horses until they could not stand or walk or sit down. At fifty cents a head it was one way to put together some cash, but more often than not the customer wanted to barter food in return for the service. It reached a point where the boys would ask for money before they broke the horse. Nobody had cash, and the bank payments were as inevitable as the morning sun.

This never-ending demand resulted in Magnor and Johnny occasionally running with a gang of horse thieves whose members included Delker and his friend, Ki Mathews. This network of rustlers pursued their trade from the Canadian border fifty miles north of the Johnson home in the community of Gladys, south to Deadwood in the Black Hills of South Dakota. Rustling was, at best, a poor answer to their money woes. It took a long time to bring off a rustling job and there were always too many others involved in divvying up the take. The gain was small for the energy expended. And this was the crux of the discussion between Magnor and Delker. Magnor wanted to rob a bank to settle the family financial problems. Delker did not think much of the scheme. He had his reasons and they were good ones.

Burt drew a slug of coffee, and looking at Magnor he said, "Yer a fool if you go ahead with robbin' a bank. They'll get you one way or the other."

Magnor stiffened at the heat of the older man's argument. Delker was not in a plight like his father and mother.

"Maybe not, but the folks' mortgage will never get paid up rustling a few ponies now and then," he said. Magnor, in his farmer's overalls, did not look much like a bank robber or even a rustler.

Burt tried another tack. "The next job will get us a hundred nags. That's twenty grand."

Magnor laughed derisively. "You said the same thing the last time, Burt, and we ended up with seven crow-hoppers not fit for a glue factory."

"Different situation," Delker mumbled, embarrassed by the remembrance.

Magnor pressed his advantage. "What's the difference between robbing a bank and stealing horses? In the eyes of the law it's still grand larceny, isn't it?"

Burt paused to roll a cigarette, then answered. "There's a big difference."

"I don't see it. Jail term's the same," Magnor said.

The old rustler slowly, deliberately lit his cigarette over the top of the oil lamp, and then spoke. "That ain't the point. Robbin' a bank is like kickin' the law in the teeth. They'll pull out all stops to get you."

"You don't hang for it."

"Yes you do, if you shoot somebody."

"I don't plan on shooting anyone."

"You'd better if yer gonna pull a gun."

"Okay, okay," Magnor replied impatiently. "You reformed crooks are worse than drunks. I'm still going ahead with it, Burt. Are you with me?"

"No," Delker replied emphatically.

*Once bit, twice shy* was an apropos maxim concerning Delker, who was at best a paradoxical figure. He was born Marinus B. Mortensen in Denmark in 1875. Emigrating with relatives as an infant, he was raised in the West, and unlike the Johnson boys, recalled nothing of the land of his birth. By the age of fifteen he had thrown his horse's reins over hitching rails from the badlands of the Dakotas to the distant Rocky Mountains. This included Lander, Wyoming, the home of his sister, Hanna Hejde. Robert Parker (alias Butch Cassidy), another man with equal propensity for acquiring things illegally, also lived there. Delker often ran with the same crowd as the popular Cassidy, but was luckier. He was eighteen when Cassidy, at twenty-seven, was thrown into a Wyoming penitentiary for rustling.

Delker drifted from Wyoming to North Dakota, and then to Montana as a typical cowpoke who was not against picking up an illegal dollar if the occasion presented itself. The law finally caught up with the lanky cowboy. He was put on trial in Glasgow, Montana, for stealing a passel of horses from one J. M. Smith. He was convicted and sentenced to eight years in prison for the deed. As steep as it was, the sentence could have been worse. Another man on the same docket, J. Markell, was given twelve years for a similar offense.

Delker served four of the eight years before being paroled from the state penitentiary at Deer Lodge in 1910. He managed to avoid further jail time, and took up residence next to the Johnson place in North Dakota. He was not disliked in the neighborhood, and on more than one occasion helped neighbors in need by giving them a cow or a horse. However, he was not a person gentle folk cuddled up to anymore than they would a sleeping rattler. For one thing, he was never without his .44 revolver, which hung ominously on his narrow hips, and for another, he was a hard guy to find, his comings and goings viewed suspiciously by other settlers of the countryside.

Therefore, when Delker talked about crime, he was speaking from the podium of experience. His own travails had been bad enough. He stood up and walked to the coal box and removed several large chunks. He dumped them into the stove and returned to the table where Magnor waited anxiously. He decided on another approach with Magnor, who looked up to him as a nephew would his uncle. "For one thing, Magnor, you got no idea of how to go about a bank robbery," he said.

The younger man tried to interrupt, but the old rustler kept on speaking. "What'll you do, hit the bank alone?"

Magnor had thought of that. "I'll get Ki Mathews," he said.

Burt shook his head. "Forget him. He's been through the mill same as me."

"Well, there must be someone around," said Magnor.

"Sure, but no one you can trust."

Johnny, half asleep on the cot, came off his daydream. Robbing a bank suddenly appealed to him, but not wholly for Magnor's reasons. He could use some of the money for himself. He could buy presents for his girl, Thora Hermansen, who had lost her father at a young age and was being raised by her mother. They and another brother and sister had fought hard to keep their farm.

The Hermansens were of hardy fiber and prevailed under adversity. Compared with the Johnson home theirs was one of peace and tranquility.

Johnny often sought refuge there, not only to see Thora, but to get away from the chaos at his own place. Though they were the same age, Thora had grown to womanhood while Johnny was still stumbling through the pitfalls of youth. Johnny knew he wanted Thora, but possessed neither the judgment nor the patience to bend his shoulder to the plow for the years needed to win her favor. The bank holdup could be the answer to all of his problems if Magnor would cut him in.

"*Jeg er med dig*, Magnor," Johnny said sitting up.

Though Johnny said it in Norwegian, Delker knew the kid was offering his services to Magnor. The younger Johnson fit the mold of a gunman more than his older brother. A look at him pointed up certain characteristics supporting this assumption. For one thing, Johnny's icy blue eyes were colder than the depths of a mountain lake, and just as unfathomable. There was little warmth in them like in Magnor's. Delker noted an inner hostility in Johnny that boiled under the surface like a dormant volcano. Outwardly, though stoic, he was not unsociable. He looked much like his older brother with unusually wide shoulders and a narrow waist. And he was blond like Magnor, and dressed in overalls, but there the similarity ended. Johnny, at five feet eight, was almost three inches taller than his half brother. Where Magnor displayed an open personality, Johnny tended to be more skeptical.

Magnor looked at his kid brother as though he were seeing him for the first time and quickly dismissed the thought of the teenager accompanying him. Johnny was only halfway through his sixteenth year, decidedly no age to embark on something as extreme as a stickup. Someone had to stay behind to look after the farm. It was enough for one brother to cast his lot onto the storm-tossed waters of a bank robber's life, let alone two.

"Nah, Johnny, it wouldn't work," he said.

"Why not?" Johnny replied hotly.

"Who'll watch after the farm?"

"What farm? Even crows got to pack rations when they fly over ours."

Magnor grimaced. His kid brother was not so easily put aside. He had talents that could be of considerable help in time of need, one being his ability with a six-gun and rifle. Magnor knew Johnny could outshoot him with both.

"Good or bad, it's still a farm," Magnor said. "You know the old man can't run it."

"He could if he'd sober up once in a while," Johnny said.

"Fat chance, he's never recovered from the shock of leaving Norway," Magnor counseled.

"C'mon, Magnor," Johnny retorted, "there's nothing to look after. The drought this summer took care of the wheat crop. We've sold our cows, the horses are gone. The bank's got everything, even our guns. So what does the old man need me for?"

Magnor had to admit to himself that what Johnny said was true. Considering the disastrous situation at home, it really made little difference. Without quick cash the farm would go under come what may.

Magnor turned to Delker. "Johnny might have something. It doesn't leave much in the way of choices."

The old rustler pondered the question while studying the two youths. Though they were immigrants, experience had honed them into typical American cowboys, hard as nails, and inured to difficulty. These boys looked up to Delker like an uncle, and he had taught them much in the way of handling horses, but so had their father, who trained horses in Norway and introduced the boys to busting broncs. Delker had to admit to himself he had not been a great help instructing the boys in the art of stealing horses. Rustling was a dangerous business, but its value began to pale with the increasing popularity of the "horseless carriage." The horse was rapidly taking on a minor role in the marketplace. Stealing cayuses that were often little more than wild, unbranded mustangs was not likely to raise people's eyebrows. But banks were another matter. It was an extreme venture that invited disaster.

Burt held up his hands, palms out. "Wait a minute," he said, "Let me tell you what yer in for. So you rob a bank. That's just the beginnin' of yer troubles; from then on yer runnin' for yer life. Runnin' from shadows, no sleep, yer guts rubbed raw by the money belt you gotta hide somewhere. Every turn in the road brings a problem or a reckoned problem. And you know there's years rottin' behind bars if they catch you."

"I don't plan on getting caught," Magnor said, then turned to Johnny, "Okay, you're in. We knock off a bank."

Johnny was all ears, but he was not without a brain. "What bank?" he asked.

Magnor was plainly surprised by their readiness. "I don't know," he replied.

"How about Farmers in Medicine Lake," Johnny said. "That bank's got lots of money and they don't know us very well."

Magnor had not figured out that aspect of the pending robbery.

With this Delker threw up his hands in frustration. He walked to the stove and stood before it, stretching his hands to the warmth of the fire, his back to the two youths. Then he turned to face them.

"Fine and dandy," he said sarcastically, "you just up and rob a bank. How about yer getaway? Where are you gonna get fresh horses? Who'll put you up if you gotta hide out?"

Magnor and Johnny had obviously not looked into the practical sides of the venture.

Delker rambled on, "How about a telephone? One call can trip you up. And don't be surprised if they crank up an automobile to chase you. . . . By golly someday they'll even use them new aeroplanes to track you down." He paused to see if the boys were paying attention to him. And this time they were not.

"You won't listen, will you," he said, exasperated.

"Seems like we've been listening for ten years," Magnor said.

Delker pondered the determination of Magnor and Johnny for some minutes before he arrived at a decision concerning them. Satisfied they were hard-nosed in their plans to go ahead with the holdup even over his own objections, he felt obligated to assist them—if not by his physical presence, at least by offering advice.

"You boys best likely take on somethin' not so heavy as a bank. Try robbin' the hardware store over in Bainville," he said, then turned, and dug into a sack hanging from a nail in the wall of the sod house. When he faced the two boys again he had a gun in his hand. "Here's a six-gun for you," he said, giving it to Magnor. "You'll need more guns. Use this and you'll get 'em at the hardware store."

Magnor and Johnny were both acquainted with Bainville and accepted Delker's directive with little comment.

"Okay," Magnor said. "Now let's turn in."

Outside, the wind wailed and howled, lambasting the sod hut. After a day of rest and preparation, Magnor and Johnny rode for Bainville.

# Chapter 2

# THE BAINVILLE HOAX

Johnny sensed tidal-like currents were sweeping him forward in a surge that he could not swim against. Fate had one course for him and its heavy-handed inevitability prodded him on. He could not, would not, deny the adventurous strains of his ancestral past. The hot blood of Viking warriors raced through Johnny's veins, and he was constantly conscious of this legacy of his forefathers, who terrorized the people of Europe with their exciting, bloody raids. Johnny had played the part of a Viking in childhood games. It was the warrior's dream, and like thousands of youngsters before and since, he relived all of the glory in his make-believe world. But Johnny had other heroes, much closer, thus more ominous than the Vikings of so many centuries past.

These were the adventurers of the New World who trod the very soil his family now tilled, sailed the rivers, and hunted the endless plains where he, too, hunted and fought imaginary battles over ground they walked upon. Johnny's mind, as he rode toward Bainville, was an overlay of images of the giants of the western frontier. Now he, too, was embarking on the danger trail, and he silently vowed to live up to the hand-me-downs they had left behind.

How many times had he played the part of Captain Keogh who had ridden out from nearby Fort Buford to die bravely with Custer on the Little Big Horn? The Sioux and the Cheyenne Indians had paid the captain their highest compliment in refusing to desecrate his body. More than once Johnny and Magnor, while gathering wood in the Missouri River breaks, had sloughed off to build a raft and drift several miles with the current. At such times they pretended they were Lewis and Clark on their historic journey of exploration, or imagined they were the voyageur Mike Fink, ready to challenge an enemy at a moment's notice.

Johnny often sat on a bluff by his father's farm and looked west imagining the Rocky Mountains, which he could not see but knew were there. The peaks lured him like the sea did a migrating lemming. His idols were Sublette, Glass, Carson, Colter, and other courageous men of a drifting clan of free trappers who had once roamed the length and breadth of those peaks in their search for beaver, mink, and otter, and other fur bearers important to their way of life.

There were others he admired, no less valiant, but of a different stamp. They were the trail drivers who rammed giant herds of cattle northward through storms and floods and marauding Indians to establish mammoth cattle ranches in Montana and North Dakota. These cowboys were just as fickle in nature and dangerous as the vicious longhorns they herded. They were callous to such trail hazards as rattlesnakes, lightning bolts, and stampedes that could render a bloodied mess of a man if he was unlucky enough to fall in front of a panic-stricken herd.

The toughness of the cowboys carried over into other pursuits. At best their pay was poor, which led the impatient ones to look for the "fast buck" through horse and cattle rustling and more serious crimes such as robbing banks and trains. This, in turn, gave rise to the "hero bandit" who stole from the large corporations that were already unpopular with the public. Such men as Butch Cassidy, Sundance Longabaugh, the Logan brothers, and other men of the "Wild Bunch" became an inspiration for many impressionable youngsters raised in the 1890s and early 1900s, years that saw the names of the bandits constantly in the headlines.

This fact was one reason Johnny looked up to Burt Delker. Delker knew the men of the Wild Bunch and had even ridden with them. Many a night Delker had cast a spell on Johnny with his stories of the "owl hoot trail" where the rustlers were one step ahead of the law in running to such places as Robbers' Roost, the Hole in the Wall, Brown's Hole, Starr Valley, and other hideouts soon buried in the memories of the adventurous past. Johnny respected Delker for treating him as an equal. Delker did not hassle him, and he taught by example. He was lean and hard, fearless to the point of recklessness, and unparalleled in his ability to live off the land. Delker was the man who honed Johnny's skills with a six-gun into a machinelike maneuver.

"Just point the gun like it's part of yer finger and the bullet will take care of itself," Delker often told him.

Johnny had dutifully followed Delker's lead for years, but this time, led by Magnor's acceptance of him as a partner, he chose go against the older man's wishes, mainly for the money.

Johnny held his half brother equally high in esteem. Magnor did not get easily flustered. He was an uncomplaining individual who bore pain and hardships silently. Once he set his shoulder to a task it would get done. Johnny could trust Magnor's judgment anywhere.

Conscious of what they were doing, Johnny spoke out.

"Magnor?"

"What?"

"Remember Ma's Lapp yarn about two brothers and the northern lights?"

Magnor frowned. "You mean Samis," he replied, referring to the actual name for the Lapps.

"Yeah," said Johnny, "Can you tell it?"

"Sure. The younger one kept teasing the northern lights. His older brother told him to stop or he'd regret it. You follow me?"

"I think so," Johnny said.

"Well he didn't stop and the gods gave him the shaft."

"The shaft?" Johnny said quizzically.

"Yes," replied Magnor, "a shaft of light that killed him. Get the moral?"

"Yeah."

After three cold hours in the saddle, they reached Bainville. Winter's early dark had set in and lanterns winked sleepily in the gelid blackness. Johnny and Magnor knew the hardware store's location, and saw immediately why Delker had chosen it for their first robbery. The store was only a hop, skip, and a jump from the railroad and the northern boundary of the community. Their getaway would be easy, if they managed their task properly. They dismounted in front of the store, noting the cold had driven the residents of Bainville indoors. No people lingered around the front of the saloons as they would have in warmer weather. The lights of the hardware store were on, indicating it was still open for business.

Magnor and Johnny looked at one another, and Johnny put his hand on Magnor's shoulder. "Let me handle it, okay?" he said.

Magnor gave him a skeptical look. "Why?" he asked, "I'm the one who has the gun." He carried the .41 given to him by Delker at the last minute. He loosened his sheepskin coat to bring it out.

Ignoring the offered gun, Johnny said, "Just let me handle it." He had no qualms about what he was about to do, realizing the plan was as much a test of his guts as it was anything else. He knew his youth was a handicap as far as his brother and Delker were concerned.

The proprietors of the hardware store were Walter Von Eschen and Louis Haefner. Von Eschen had gone home for the night, leaving his partner in charge. Business was slow at that time of the year, so each extra dime the store could muster by remaining open for longer hours was worth the effort.

Every implement imaginable that could be used on a farm or ranch could be seen in the room—which was cluttered from floor to ceiling.

Haefner was tidying up the shelves when he heard the door open, and turned around. He saw two youths enter. They were dressed in overalls, sheepskin coats, and hobnail boots. Wide-brimmed hats were pulled down low over their eyes. Their attire was no different from hundreds of others worn by customers Haefner and his partner served throughout the year. True, he did not know them, but with the increased mobility of the population, he often found himself waiting on strangers passing through. He walked to the counter and asked the young men what he could do for them.

Johnny was the first to pass through the door and the first to stand in front of the counter. Magnor, still wondering what Johnny was up to, joined him in a matter of a few seconds. Both were shivering from the extreme cold outside and perhaps from plain ordinary fear, once inside. Johnny put his hands under his armpits and stomped his feet, at the same time mumbling warmer weather would be a welcome order to be filled.

Haefner smiled. He noticed the lads were clean-cut looking. The thought of making a sale so engrossed him it voided any suspicion, and he responded in a friendly manner.

"What can I do for you?" he asked.

"We want to buy some guns," Johnny replied.

Haefner noticed the lad who did the talking was quite young—couldn't be over seventeen. Obviously he had had some schooling as he spoke well, though with a Scandinavian accent.

"Rifles or short guns?" the storekeeper queried.

"Short," Magnor broke in.

The storekeeper eyed the older of the two, and noted they looked somewhat alike. Probably brothers, he thought.

"What caliber?"

"Forty-fours or .45s ought to be enough, eh, Magnor?" Johnny said.

Magnor nodded and noted Johnny was nervous or he would never have mentioned him by name. There was nothing he could do about it now. It was just water over the dam.

Haefner was so elated over the idea of making a sale, the name slipped by him. He fumbled with the sliding panel under the counter and finally drew out three .44s. If he sold them it would amount to more money than he and Von Eschen had made in a week. He placed the guns on the counter.

"Here you are," said the storekeeper.

Johnny picked one up and hefted it in his hands. It had been three months since he and Magnor hocked their guns, and for a cowboy to go around without one was like a carpenter without his hammer. He turned the revolver over in his hands, tested the trigger pull, and put it back down on the counter.

"I reckon it's out of balance," Johnny said. "Would you mind loading it for me?"

If Haefner had not been so inclined to make a sale he would have given the request deeper thought, but times were not that good, nor had he ever experienced anything untoward when filling unorthodox requests from other unfamiliar customers. In addition, he was proud of his own dexterity with a gun and welcomed the chance to demonstrate it. He took out five bullets, expertly loaded the gun, twirled it, and laid it back down on the counter.

"Not bad," Johnny said.

"You fellows want anything else?" the storekeeper asked.

"Yeah, a couple of boxes of ammunition," Johnny said.

Haefner placed them on the counter. "That it?" he asked.

"That'll do, I guess," Johnny replied, and turned to Magnor. "What do you think?"

Magnor nodded. "Okay."

Johnny picked up the loaded gun and twirled it expertly to point it directly at the storekeeper. "Nice weight. Balance is good."

"You're pointing it at me," Haefner said.

"That's right," Johnny said with his eyes hardening, "we'll take these on credit."

Haefner, though not what one would call a robust person, had plenty of guts. He had been around long enough to judge a man's intent by looking into his eyes. Haefner did this and was jolted. What he saw were cerulean beads reflecting like reverberating rays in a prism. The color and wildness of those eyes was enough to sober up the most astute of men. Transfixed, Haefner nodded, and said, "Yeah, sure, I get you."

Magnor was sufficiently impressed by his brother's performance to discard any doubts as to his dependability, but wondered why Johnny went to all the trouble.

Magnor took over. He drew his own gun and covered the storekeeper. "Tie him up," he said brusquely to Johnny.

There was no shortage of rope in the hardware store. Johnny grabbed a coil and bound Haefner and gagged him. "Like roping a calf," he said when he had completed the job.

The youths now had the run of the place. They scooped up the three guns and boxes of ammunition and hastily rummaged through the store goods on their way out the door. They did not bother to look for cash, figuring there would be little around at that hour.

"This guy's got everything," Johnny said picking up a homemade sign.

"What do you mean?" asked Magnor.

"Look at this!" Johnny exclaimed and held it up.

Magnor read it and laughed. "Stick it on the door; it might keep eyes away from the place for a while."

Johnny grabbed a tack and put it up. It read: OUT TO LUNCH!

The two brothers with a muffled whoop and a holler vaulted onto their horses and sped toward the breaks between Bainville and Delker's place. That night they made a cold camp.

Magnor wondered if Johnny enjoyed the heist a bit more than he should have. He was proud of his brother's guts, but he'd never seen the kid's eyes glow like they did after the holdup.

John Duggan, sheriff of Sheridan County, the farthest east in the state of Montana, was working late in his office at the county seat of Plentywood when the phone rang. The call was from Haefner, who had been discovered and freed less than an hour after the robbery. He reported the details to Duggan, who guessed immediately that the guns were taken for another purpose, probably another holdup.

Duggan was a fixture in Sheridan County, having been reelected a number of times to his job as sheriff. He was a conscientious man, albeit a political one. He was elected by his constituents. This oddity of the system had its advantages and disadvantages. The former meant a man must do his job satisfactorily or he could be removed by popular vote. This made the sheriff acutely susceptible to any headline-making violation that he failed to account for or solve. The disadvantages inherent in the system made it possible for a man to be elected on the basis of popularity, but with little in the way of competence or training to back it up. In other words, if the party in power was swept out in a landslide of votes, an untrained or inexperienced man could end up as sheriff. As a consequence of the system, Duggan, who was competent, found that he devoted at least part of each term in office to being reelected, or to worrying about it.

This was an election year. He deliberated whether to send one of his deputies, Walter Mathews, a competent man, on this case, but then decided against it. He'd go himself. He called Mathews and told him to cover the office and then took the next train south.

# Chapter 3

# BANK HEIST

Johnny and Magnor saddled their horses at dawn and cantered back to Delker's ranch, arriving there on Wednesday morning. They rested during the day and that night, with fresh horses provided by Delker, set out for Medicine Lake. They were dressed for the cold, having their sheepskin coats turned up around their necks, and scarves wrapped around their ears. Mittens covered their hands. Riding at a leisurely pace through the blackness of a North Dakota winter's night, they skirted the town of Dagmar, which sat halfway between Delker's place and Medicine Lake. Since Dagmar was along their projected escape route they spent some time looking for the telephone line. Magnor found it and reined up in front of one of the poles.

"There's the line," he mumbled.

"I see it," Johnny enjoined.

"You got the wire cutters from home?" Magnor asked.

Johnny reached into his saddlebag and patted it. "Right here," he said.

"Well, what are you waiting for?"

"What do you mean, what am I waiting for?"

"Get up the pole and take care of it," Magnor retorted.

Johnny felt the wind whistling by his ears. Climbing the pole under the conditions at hand would not be pleasant.

"Why don't you climb the pole?" he said.

"I'm the oldest," Magnor retorted.

"So what!"

"Don't be an idiot. You got the cutters, you do it."

Johnny shrugged. "I got a better way," he said taking out his .44 at the same time, and without seeming to aim fired two shots in rapid succession to blast the two insulators on the pole into a thousand pieces. "Beats climbing," he added as the wind-blown wires writhed like snakes on the frozen ground.

Johnny's abrupt solution to their bickering with nary a thought for the consequences—someone could have heard the shots—took Magnor by surprise. He had expected to have the last word on this task, as Johnny, in the past, had always deferred to his judgment. Now Magnor wondered even more if his kid brother would solve his problems by shooting them away.

"I know what you're thinking Magnor. See those rocks over there?"

Magnor peered into the night. Sure enough, there was a line of rocks that looked like they were piled up by a rancher. The rocks resembled a wall more than anything else.

"Yeah, I see it."

"There isn't even a hut within five miles of us."

Magnor had to smile. The kid was a natural. "Well," he said, "you haven't lost your touch. You've got possibilities."

"One thing, Magnor, what did I shoot?"

Magnor wondered that himself. Was it a telephone line? If not, and they only nipped the telegraph line, it could spell disaster for them when they made their getaway.

"I'm not sure," he said as they rode on.

The sun was just peeking over the horizon when the town of Medicine Lake seemed to rise up out of the barren expanse of plains like a mirage in a desert. It was the kind of blustery winter morning where the eerie light refracted the bleakness of the town—a characteristically western hodgepodge of weatherworn, false-fronted buildings.

Magnor whistled unenthusiastically on viewing the place. He had been there before, but had never looked at it from the perspective of a bank robber. He judged the community was so poor a church mouse would have scowled at it. He could count the ribs of a droopy-tailed cur that slinked across a street in front of them. He wondered if he was peering at a ghost town. It was not so far-fetched, as villages boomed and died on the approach of a railroad. If the steel rails veered away from it, a community could become deserted overnight. As if to accent Magnor's thoughts, the cur sat down on his haunches and howled forlornly. By the looks of the hamlet, its inhabitants were unacquainted with paint, and carpenters had gone the way of the buffalo. Shutters were loose and askew, banging loudly under the onslaught of the ever-present gale that swept down from Canada. Clapboard shacks shook, and they seemed to shiver in the face of the norther.

The brothers reined up in front of a dilapidated building that appeared to lean into the wind. Dimly visible from years of pummeling by dust and sand were the words FARMERS STATE BANK.

"This is it," Johnny said, and added, "It does look kinda poor."

Magnor waved his hand at their bleak surroundings. Not a soul was to be seen. "You sure this isn't a ghost town?"

"Last time I was here it wasn't."

"How long was that?"

"A couple of months."

Magnor pointed at the sign. "Is that really the bank?"

Johnny became defensive as he was the one who suggested the Medicine Lake bank.

"It doesn't have to look nice as long as it's got plenty of cash."

"Let's hitch our horses in front of the store," Magnor suggested. "It wouldn't look too good with the only horses in town in front of the bank."

They walked their horses to Stubban's store, tied them loosely, and ambled back to the bank.

Magnor took out a pocket watch he had borrowed from Delker and checked the time. It was nine o'clock. He and Johnny attempted looking through the front window of the bank, but it was covered with frost.

They went to the door, tried it, and saw that it was open. Magnor walked in, with Johnny following behind. The inside of the structure was not as broken down as it was outside, but it had seen better days. A counter with two teller's cages stretched for half the length of the left side of the front room. To the rear of the commercial area was a railing that separated it from a door leading to what was presumably the bank manager's office. Several desks were immediately in front of the two men. A telephone rested on one and a typewriter on the other. There appeared to be no one in the bank. Johnny leaned forward and tapped the key of the typewriter and dust flew up.

Magnor looked at his brother and scowled. "Are you sure this is still a bank? There's no one here."

Johnny shrugged. "There's got to be. Whoever heard of a place like this having its' doors open with no one in it?"

"Maybe it's not a bank anymore," Magnor offered.

Meanwhile the vice president, H. G. Anderson, and the cashier, S. C. Faaborg, were in the rear office brewing a pot of coffee. One could not blame the bankers for being careless, especially with a blue norther engulfing the town with so cold a wind no one in his right mind would venture out in it. The two men heard the brothers conversing and walked into the front room.

Johnny and Magnor were startled by the sudden appearance of the bankers who wore the typical uniform of dark pants and suspenders and white shirts with high, starched collars. Faaborg, with a motion of his hand, waved an invitation. "Come on back and have some coffee. We just brewed it."

Neither Magnor nor Johnny was expecting so cordial a welcome. It came as something of a shock to receive such an invitation while ponderously encumbered with four revolvers loaded for the purpose of robbing one's hosts. However, Magnor and Johnny were too far down the road to turn back. This applied particularly to Magnor. Since he had been the one to wonder about the intestinal fortitude of his younger brother, there was no way that he could pull out on the deal without earning Delker's disrespect. Magnor accepted the invitation, and he and Johnny followed the bankers into the back room.

Anderson poured coffee for Johnny and Magnor and then stepped back a space, taking a sharp look at both of them, particularly Johnny.

"You're Johnson's boys, aren't you?" he asked. "What brings you here?"

Johnny was normally a quick-thinking individual, but it was impossible to deny the family resemblance. His only recourse was silence.

Magnor figured it best to change the subject. "If this is still a bank, when are you open for business?" he asked.

Anderson smiled. "In a few minutes."

It was easy for Johnny to suppose that he and Magnor had fallen into a trap. Everything seemed too pat.

"Help yourself," Anderson added as he stepped out of the back room to help his boss.

"We might just do that," Magnor chimed in.

After only a short interval, Anderson was back.

"Okay boys, we're officially open."

The two youths took deep breaths, hitched up their heavily laden overalls, followed Anderson into the forward area, and drew their guns.

"Now you're officially closed," Magnor said, and lowering his voice an octave to show he meant business, added "Put 'em up."

Surprise registered on the face of the vice president. Thinking it was a prank, he was slow in obeying the command, but when Magnor jammed his Colts into the banker's ribs, Anderson quickly raised his hands aloft.

Johnny, on his own initiative, vaulted over the railing in front of the teller's cage and routed out Faaborg, ordering him to stand next to Anderson.

"While you're at it, lock the front door," Magnor said.

Johnny took care of that task. "We'd better tie these guys up," he said to Magnor.

They looked around for a rope but could not find one. "I got it," Magnor said. "Tie 'em up with their suspenders."

Johnny accomplished the mission quickly, ordering the bankers to lie down on the floor and looping them like calves ready for branding. That done, he and Magnor plundered the cash boxes and the safe, which was open. They stuffed money into bags and a money belt Johnny had stolen from the hardware store. Johnny was surprised at the weight of the belt, which held mostly gold and silver pieces.

When the task at hand was completed the two cowboys backed out of the bank; Magnor carried a bag filled with the overflow from Johnny's money belt. For the moment luck was on their side. There was not one person to be seen between them and the east end of town, which the main street pointed to like an arrow in the direction they wanted to go.

Magnor and Johnny walked to their horses, mounted up, and, to avoid suspicion, paced them slowly until they reached the outskirts of Medicine Lake, and from there headed east at a gallop. Once out of town, the bank robbers spurred their mounts along the Dagmar road heading for the Sand Hills that constituted the breaks along the Montana–North Dakota border. After riding hard for half an hour, they reined up for a breather.

"Sure was easy," Johnny said.

Magnor frowned and said, "Yeah, too easy."

Back at the bank, Faaborg was the first to free himself from his bonds. He untied the suspenders that bound Anderson and picked up the phone. To his relief it had not been tampered with. He called Sheriff Duggan's office in Plentywood and received word that the lawman was in Medicine Lake. Smiling, he hung up.

"We're in luck. The sheriff's here," he said.

"Good, but where?" Anderson asked.

"The place across the street," Faaborg said.

Faaborg picked up the phone again and called the hotel where the sheriff was staying.

The clerk answered.

"Sheriff Duggan, please," Faaborg said hurriedly.

"He's asleep."

"Get him up. It's an emergency."

The sheriff was groggy and not a little cranky over being awakened so early after a night of traveling.

"Yes," he said.

"Sheriff Duggan?"

"That's right."

"This is Faaborg at the bank. We've been robbed."

The law enforcement side of the sheriff's mind was always prepared for the unplanned and the unusual, but the political side was another matter. He never knew when some sort of event could ambush him and destroy his vote-gathering potential.

"What happened?" he asked.

"Two kids held us up. Hell, we know 'em! Johnson's boys from over in Climax township, North Dakota."

Outwardly, the sheriff was calm, but inwardly he was seething. The report, if true, was a worst-case scenario. It was rotten luck on his part. He'd been doing his job, and only an odd twist of fortune brought him into a town where a bank heist occurred right under his nose. No matter what the facts were in the case, newspapers supporting the other political party would hold him accountable. One thing you could not ignore as a career police officer was a bank heist.

"You know which way they went?"

"No, but they could have headed for their old man's place."

The sheriff thought it over. The robbers certainly were not pros. Any characters dumb enough to hold up someone they knew were capable of doing what the banker suggested.

"How much did they get?"

"Anderson's trying to sort it out right now," Faaborg replied. "He says between three and four thousand."

The sheriff whistled. "That's big haul for a little bank."

"I know what you're thinking," said Faaborg. "We didn't pad it."

The sheriff laughed. "Well, they don't pay you fellows much. You insured?"

"We're bonded, and the bank is insured against theft."

"Glad to hear it," the sheriff replied and hung up. He was a progressive thinker and well aware of the advantages of employing new procedures in tracking down criminals. He picked up the phone and got the operator, whom he knew by name. It paid to groom such acquaintances.

"Hilda?"

"Yes."

"This is Sheriff Duggan."

"Yes, Jack."

"Get me Peter Grossgaard in Dagmar," he said knowing full well that most of the farm and ranch families along the route would pick up their phones to listen in on the call—the whole county hookup was a party line. That way he and Grossgaard, the sheriff of Dagmar, could muster a posse in a hurry. He smiled as he heard at least five clicks before Grossgaard answered the phone.

"Pete, this is Jack Duggan. I'm in Medicine Lake."

"What can I do for you, Sheriff?"

"Muster a blocking posse as quick as you can."

"Holdup?"

"Yeah, the Farmers State Bank here."

"How many men are there?"

"Only two, and my guess is they'd be heading for Climax."

"How do you figure?" Grossgaard asked.

"We know 'em. They're Johnson's boys."

"Okay, they've got to come pretty close to us."

"Is there anybody on the line?" the sheriff asked, speaking into the phone.

Numerous residents answered in the affirmative.

"This is Grossgaard. We've got a sleigh and some fast horses. I want you men to show up at the city hall as quick as you can get here. We'll load up and head south. Bring your rifles," said Grossgaard. "Are you still on, Jack?"

"Yes, I appreciate that, Pete. I'll round up a posse here as soon as possible."

"Anything else?"

"Yeah, Pete. I guess you know the younger Johnson kid can hit a crow on the wing at one hundred yards with a rifle."

"Yeah, he's not too bad with a pistol either," Grossgaard answered. "A pal of his sister's said he can knock a rock off a fence post riding full tilt firing under a horse's neck."

"Okay, I'll see you in an hour or so, with any luck," Duggan said, then hung up the phone. Thanking the clerk, he went back to his room. He quickly dressed in his warmest clothing and then walked across the street to the butcher shop. The proprietor, Gerry Leonard, was cutting meat when he walked in.

"Gerry, I need horses and yourself and anyone else you can get to go out on a posse."

Normally Leonard would have been an enthusiastic volunteer, but not in a blue norther.

"Sheriff, glad to see you," he said, putting down a meat cleaver. "But I ain't going anywhere in weather like this."

"What's your bank?" Sheriff Duggan asked.

"Farmers State, why?"

"Two holdup men got three thousand out of there an hour ago."

The butcher scratched his head. "That tends to put a different light on things. Some of that is my money. Okay, I'll get a couple of horses, but I doubt you'll get anybody else. Not in this weather, no matter what the bank is."

Sheriff Duggan tried to raise a posse, but Leonard was right. No one was available.

The butcher quickly closed shop and rounded up two horses. He and the sheriff set out immediately, tracking the two robbers due east along the main street, and then through the backyards of a few homes to angle into the Dagmar road.

Duggan's use of the phone proved to be effective, and within forty minutes Grossgaard, with two outriders and a sleigh with four fully armed men on it, had set out and deployed across the Dagmar road at a point where an old wagon trail headed straight east. Even at that, it was difficult for Grossgaard to convince himself that Johnson's boys were dangerous. He had known them since they were children. The men, though well bundled up in buffalo robes, shivered as they waited for the robbers to appear.

Magnor and Johnny reached a crest on the road and standing in their stirrups, spotted the posse waiting for them across a swale several miles distant. Looking back, they could see another group of horsemen cantering toward them. Sheriff Duggan had managed to add several more men he and Leonard had picked up along the way. In all, at least a dozen men seemed to have hemmed the brothers into the hastily formed trap.

The blood stirred in Johnny's veins. Adrenalin pumped through his body, bringing on a strange elation. He was drunk with excitement. The sensation was such that it dissipated any fear. He was on a high inspired by danger. And though the lad could not explain it himself, this lift was almost as addictive as that received through drugs or alcohol, and was probably as good an explanation of any of why men have fought wars throughout the history of mankind—they enjoyed the tingle of danger.

"I guess we missed something," Johnny said.

Magnor nodded. "We must have got the telegraph, but not the telephone."

"Should be around here somewhere," Johnny said.

"Isn't going to do us much good now," Magnor added. "It looks like we're the nut in the cracker."

"Yeah, lead or prison," Johnny responded. "Any suggestions?"

"We could give up," Magnor said.

"After all the trouble getting this," Johnny replied, patting his money belt at the same time.

"Well, we have to do something," said Magnor.

"I got an idea," said Johnny, "let's act like we're going to give up, then run right by 'em."

If the suggestion went against Magnor's better judgment, he did not comment on it. He nodded.

The two men put their horses into a leisurely jog and approached the blocking posse.

As soon as he saw the brothers' pace slow down, Sheriff Grossgaard ordered his men to hold their fire. It seemed to him that the young bank robbers had had enough excitement for one day. "They're coming in," he ventured, "I don't think they'll be any trouble."

Duggan, too, was as equally optimistic on seeing the robbers' slower pace and was elated over the fact the capture would be easy. A quick resolution of the case would look good in the papers. He would easily take the next election.

Magnor and Johnny paced their steeds until they were close enough to see the frozen breath of the men and horses of the posse as they waited for them to surrender.

Magnor turned for a look at his kid brother. He'd led him into this mess. The only chance they had of avoiding injury was sheer luck or poor shooting on the part of the posse because of the cold or the fact that the men lined up might not want to kill them. Otherwise he would not give a plugged nickel for either his life or Johnny's.

"Well Johnny, it's now or never," he said and kicked his horse's flanks with his boots.

Johnny reacted quickly, and the two bolted past the posse, whose smiles turned sour and then to rage when they knew they had been duped. Pumping like jockeys, the two galloped toward the protection of the breaks.

The stunned deputies took an instant to recover, and Magnor and Johnny had almost made it out of sight, when a rifle slug slammed into Magnor's shoulder. Gasping, he grabbed the saddle horn and tried to hang on as he and Johnny crossed the brow of a hill. Magnor managed to keep to his saddle for another mile before he tumbled to the ground, feeble from the loss of blood.

Johnny reined up and dismounted to kneel next to his brother. He yanked off his bandanna and stuffed it into the wound.

Magnor, though in pain, had managed to fling his saddlebags onto the ground. "Take my share and git," Magnor said hoarsely.

"Nah, I'll stay with you."

"Don't be a damned fool. Either way you get the same sentence, so git."

Johnny hadn't thought of that sort of logic. "Okay, brother, I'm gone."

Johnny was mounted when Magnor spoke again. "Remember that speed horse you liked?"

"Yeah, sure."

"Buy it with my share," Magnor said, and dismissed his brother by closing his eyes.

Johnny smacked his horse and galloped off. Magnor's suggestion lingered in his mind. The speed horse was between him and Delker. Maybe he could pick it up on the way.

# Chapter 4

# BUYING THE SPEED HORSE

Peter Grossgaard was more saddened than startled by the sudden turn of events. There was nothing a lawman hated more than to see youngsters of his own neighborhood go bad. Sheriff Duggan caught up with Grossgaard in a matter of minutes, and Peter gave him the news. "They got by us," he said.

The merged posse lit out after the robbers, following their trail across the snowy landscape, and soon came upon Magnor.

"Which one is he?" Duggan asked as they dismounted.

"Magnor," Grossgaard answered.

Both sheriffs kneeled down to look at the wounded man.

Duggan turned to his deputy. "A shoulder wound. Gerry, bandage him up and get him back to Medicine Lake."

Duggan anticipated his deputy's thoughts. "Peter," he said, "can we borrow your sled?"

The Dagmar sheriff nodded. "Okay," he responded.

The Medicine Lake butcher, Leonard, helped by Grossgaard and Duggan, loaded the wounded man onto the sleigh and set the horses into a trot for Medicine Lake.

"We'll need three more horses for the men who were on the sled," Grossgaard advised, and sent a deputy to a nearby farm to round some up. They were back quickly and the merged posse headed out.

Their delay had helped Johnny stretch the distance between him and the posse. But now, even in the cold, his weary horse was collared in sweat. Resisting the temptation to continue riding, he dismounted and walked, leading his horse. The beast would have to last until he reached the Sand Hill breaks. There, Johnny figured, he might have a chance of getting away. He walked for half an hour and then remounted, coaxing the tired animal along until he found a jumble of rocks and boulders piled atop a rise that gave him a good view of the ground behind him. He placed the tired horse in a swale, safe there from gunfire, and turned to face the posse, which he figured would not be far behind. He waited longer than he expected he would have to, which was all the better. His horse, with a slight rest, might carry him out of range of the posse's fatigued animals.

Johnny was now on his own for the first time. Magnor, the rock on whom he often depended, was gone. The decisions were completely his to make, and the necessity for them could not have come at a more demanding moment. The posse was in view and approaching fast. He laid out his ammunition on a rock, picked up his guns, and started firing. His shots were selective in order to drive his pursuers into cover and keep them pinned down. To get away, he'd have to stall them 'til nightfall.

Duggan was a brave man, but not a foolish one. As soon as Johnny's bullets hummed past the posse, he ordered the men to hole up until there was something to shoot at. They did this, but could not give a good accounting as Johnny seemed to anticipate their moves. The stalemate became a siege as Sheriff Duggan waited for the youth to make some mistake. While they waited, Grossgaard filled Duggan in on the younger man's background, correctly surmising what Johnny barely knew himself.

"The kid's after excitement," Peter told the sheriff. "It's his form of Halloween."

Duggan nodded in agreement. "We'll bide our time."

Johnny fretted impatiently in his stronghold. If he waited too long, they would flank him. He was just about to expose himself to fire in an effort to withdraw when he saw a fog bank rolling toward him like a giant tidal wave. It engulfed everything in its path. If he could hold out until the curtain of mist enshrouded the posse, his escape would be assured.

Finally, the fog swirled in as silent as an apparition, and as effective as the darkness of the night. Johnny walked silently to his horse, mounted up, and stole away in the mists.

"Of all the fool luck!" Duggan exclaimed. "We might as well make camp."

Moving along at a trot, Johnny rode in the direction of the ranch of Andrew Gilbertson who lived across the North Dakota state line. He made camp in the breaks, knowing it would take some time for Duggan to summon a posse from that side of the Montana border. The next morning Johnny rose early and made his way to the Gilbertson ranch. The old guy was working in the corral when Johnny rode up.

"Good morning, Mr. Gilbertson," he said.

Gilbertson leaned on his rake. "You're up and around early, Johnny."

"I've come a long way," Johnny said, aware that news of the bank robbery had not as yet reached Gilbertson's isolated place.

Gilbertson nodded toward Johnny's horse. "I noticed," he said. "Where've you been?"

"Medicine Lake."

"Medicine Lake?"

"Had some banking business."

"What can I do for you?"

Johnny scanned the horses in the corral. Then spoke. "You know that speed horse," he said pointing to the stallion. "I'd like to buy him. What's the price?"

"Same as before. Two hundred and fifty," the rancher replied.

"Okay, I'll take him."

The rancher looked with wonderment at Johnny and then walked to get the horse. Johnny took advantage of the rancher's preoccupation to grab a handful of ten-dollar gold pieces out of his money belt, and counted out twenty-five coins for the rancher when he came back.

"What did you do, rob that bank?"

Johnny grinned. "Why, sure," he said.

There was a pause and then Gilbertson looked at Johnny and then laughed. "For a minute I thought you were serious."

Johnny slipped a noose over the speed horse's head and led him away without a look back.

He later passed the ranch owned by the Vigs, who were old friends from Climax. The owners invited him in for coffee, but Johnny declined, saying he was looking for strays. He rode on as though intensely occupied with this task, only to circle and pick his way through a series of connecting draws to reach Delker's sod house, which was up a gully a few hundred yards from the Johnson spread. He hadn't slept in twenty-four hours, and just as Delker had predicted, the money belt was beginning to chafe his belly.

The posse, too, headed out early in the morning. Following Johnny's trail they quickly crossed the border into North Dakota.

"You know we've left Montana now," Grossgaard offered.

Duggan nodded. "Yeah, but I'd like to get a line on him. We'll go a little farther on, then head back."

"Gilbertson's farm is just up the road a piece," Grossgaard advised, "maybe he saw 'im."

The posse shortly thereafter came upon the Gilbertson ranch.

Gilbertson was still working in the corral and greeted them. "Sheriff, you looking for anyone?"

Grossgaard nodded. "Yeah, we're looking for Johnny Johnson. You see him?"

Ranchers by nature and instinct tended to protect their own, but Gilbertson realized to lie would do no one any good. The tracks of Johnny's horse in the snow were there for all to see.

"Yup," the rancher said, "went through here a couple of hours ago," Gilbertson said, fudging the time. In lieu of this he figured he might as well give them something. "I even sold him a horse," he added.

"A horse?" Sheriff Duggan asked.

"Yeah, the fastest one I got."

"Pay you?"

"Yeah, in gold coins."

"Didn't you think it a bit strange?" Duggan asked.

Gilbertson tipped his Stetson back on his head. "Yeah, I did. I says, 'What did you do, rob a bank?'"

"What'd he say?"

"Something like 'Why sure I did' and grinned. Naturally, I didn't believe him."

Duggan spoke to Grossgaard. "Peter, that boy's got more brains than I give him credit for."

"Yeah, he's a pretty cool customer."

Rancher Gilbertson grimaced. "What's this all about?"

"He told you the truth," said Duggan.

"You mean about robbin' the bank?"

"That's right."

Gilbertson rubbed his chin pensively. "By gum," he said, "that Johnny's got an honest face at that."

Duggan and Grossgaard looked at each other quizzically, and laughed. "Looks like the joke's on all of us," Grossgaard said philosophically. The two lawmen had seen everything to do with human nature in their stints and were not without a sense of humor—a quality a man needed to last in their business.

"You're Gilbertson?" Duggan asked.

"That's right, why?"

"You got a phone?" Duggan importuned, ignoring the question.

"No."

"Thanks for your cooperation, Mr. Gilbertson. We'll be on our way."

Sheriff Duggan eyed his fellow lawman, Grossgaard, and said, "We've lost him for now. Better head back."

"Sounds logical," Grossgaard said.

"It's gonna cost me," Duggan volunteered.

"How do you mean?"

"Votes," Duggan said, and they rode out.

Delker waved Johnny into the hut. "Where's Magnor?" he asked.

"Hit," Johnny said and took off his sheepskin coat, then threw the money belt onto the coarse plank table.

"Bad?"

"Shoulder shot. He'll live."

"Where's he at?"

"I don't know for sure, but I'd guess the posse got him."

Delker shook his head. "You guys wouldn't listen."

Johnny looked at him, hurt by the comment.

"Hey, it wasn't my idea. I got the money, didn't I?"

"You care about your brother?"

Johnny gave Delker a cold stare. "Jesus, Burt, what am I supposed to do, lie down on the floor and bawl?"

Delker was taken aback by the verbal slap in the face.

"Forget it," he said.

"Blame yourself. You taught me the ropes."

"I said forget it," Delker retorted. "Now we got to get you outta here. How far's the posse behind you?"

"Half a day or more. Maybe not at all since I crossed the state line."

"That don't make any difference to some lawmen I've met," Delker commented. "All right, head for the breaks, then work your way southwest to Ki Mathews's place. He'll have a plan for you."

"How'd he know?"

"I got word to him you might need some help."

Ki could be trusted, and if anyone knew the route Johnny should take in effecting an escape it was he.

"Okay."

"You got any future plans if you ever get out of this mess?"

That was an easy question for John Conrad Johnson to answer. For most of his life he had lived in the lengthy shadow cast by the distant Rocky Mountains, and that was where he wanted to go. He sought the peace provided by being alone and the freshness of the mountain wilderness. Though he had never been to the Rockies, his experiences as a child in Norway were not forgotten. The dim memories created an insatiable longing for lofty peaks, tumbling brooks, and lakes bountiful with fish that could be caught with the dabbling of a hook.

"What I always wanted. Buy an outfit and head for the mountains to hunt and trap."

"Where?"

"You mentioned Wyoming, remember?"

"Yeah, it's good country."

Delker looked at Johnny in a resigned manner. Suddenly Johnny had matured, and he wondered about the man he had helped to mold.

Johnny dug into the money belt and counted out twelve hundred dollars. "Here's a thousand for Ma and Pa and two hundred for you."

"How much you get?"

"I don't rightly know. Probably about three?"

Delker stood up. "You better get goin'."

Johnny strapped on his money belt, and put his sheepskin coat on.

"You need a horse?" Delker asked.

"Nah. I bought the fastest one around here."

"That one at Gilbertson's?"

"Yeah."

Delker was taken by surprise. Johnny was proving to be pretty clever. Maybe too clever. "I'd say if you get through this, Johnny, play it straight."

Johnny laughed. "Yeah, sure, Burt."

The older man opened the door and accompanied Johnny to his horse. Johnny mounted and departed. Delker waved to him, but the gesture was wasted. Johnny never looked back.

Thora Hermansen had emigrated with her mother and younger brother from Norway after losing her father and was now a young lady of seventeen years. They had managed to carve a working farm out of their homestead acres about six miles southwest of the Johnsons'. She was blonde, blue-eyed, and attractive. Despite giving off an impression of being soft and gentle, she held a strong determination honed by the harsh years of a homesteader's life. She and Johnny had been friends since the first grade, and from that time the relationship had grown into something more than that, though Johnny tended to be more enamored with Thora then she was with him.

Johnny weaved his horse up a swale to the Hermansen farm, carefully circling a hill on the southwest side. From this point, he could clearly see the Lutheran church's spire that loomed on a ridge three miles north of the house. The view from the hill also gave him a view of his back trail. All was clear. Johnny decided to risk seeing Thora for the simple reason that he liked her, but also there was a distant possibility that he might be able to talk her into going with him. He was basically shy, but not with Thora. He could at least give it a try.

He rode up to the front of the house, dismounted, and knocked on the door.

Thora opened the door and was pleasantly surprised to see him, though Johnny's visit was nothing really unusual. "Hello, Johnny," she said in greeting. "Would you like to come in?"

"Not this time, Thora, I'm in a bit of a hurry. Can I talk to you alone for minute?"

"Sure," she said and asked, "anything wrong?"

"No, no, just get your coat and come out."

"All right," she said.

They walked down the swale, which ran eastward from the house. Johnny was nervous and fidgety and kept looking around. Finally, he stopped and turned and faced her. He was mesmerized by the thought of running away with her, and without any preliminaries, blurted out his point. "Thora, I've got a little money and I'm leaving the country. Would you like to go with me?"

Thora was taken aback by Johnny's question. "Now?" she asked, then added, "You must be kidding."

Johnny shook his head. "No, no. Let's go now."

Thora stood wide-eyed in disbelief. "But why run away?" she asked.

"It's less complicated," he said, and put his hands on her shoulders. "I have plenty of money. We can go west to the mountains, and we'll—"

"I don't understand all this," she said, interrupting him. She knew full well that the Johnson family bordered on poverty. "Where did you get the money to do this?"

"It doesn't matter. I have enough to get us outta here."

"How about the farm and your folks?"

"That is all I hear about is the farm, the farm! What the buzzards and the blizzards didn't take, my father has drunk away. So what's left?"

Thora had known Johnny most of her life. She sensed that something was not quite right. "You're not telling me everything. What happened?" she asked.

"I love you," he said, surprised at his own outburst. "I thought you loved me. That's all."

"Oh, I do. But I can't—"

Johnny stepped forward and held her face between his hands and kissed her gently on the mouth, then ran his fingers through her hair and caressed her, as if to calm her fear of the unknown. "Can't?" he said.

Thora was thoroughly confused. Emotions were tugging at her from all directions and she tried to get them under control. "No," she said, "I can't."

"You could if you cared."

She pushed herself away from him and stood back. "It isn't that."

"Then what is it?"

"With Papa gone my mother's all alone."

"We won't be away forever."

"Then why hurry now?"

Johnny looked around. He was like the taut string on a crossbow. He did not dare take any more time. "You won't come?"

Thora shook her head. "No, Johnny."

"All right then, it's just as well I know how you feel."

"You're being cruel," Thora said.

"Am I, or is it you?" Johnny said and whirled around and walked back to his horse. He was disturbed over being turned down. It seemed like his whole life had been that way. He mounted up and yanked the roan's reins.

"Good-bye, Thora," he said harshly.

Thora watched him ride away. She was flattered by it all, yet dismayed. He did not understand that she rejected his plan, but she did not reject him.

Johnny reached Mathews's frame house and barn undetected. The sudden descent of a prairie blizzard helped. Since the area was swarming with deputies from two counties in two states looking for him, he figured he was lucky to get as far as Mathews's place.

Though cold and tired, Johnny felt relieved to have reached friendly hands. Mathews was a lanky cowboy in the mold of Delker with rugged features and a clean appearance. He escorted Johnny to the barn, where they sponged down Johnny's horse and fed him.

"Fine looking animal you got there," Mathews said. "Built for speed. I never heard Burt mention such a horse."

"Good reason. I just bought him."

"Bought him?" Mathews repeated and laughed. "By gum, it makes sense."

They walked back to the house where Mathews ushered Johnny into the kitchen and helped him pull off his boots. A pot of stew bubbled invitingly on the stove. Mathews ladled victuals onto a plate and set it on the table in front of his guest, who wolfed down the grub.

"I was expecting you earlier. Anyone on your tail?" Mathews asked.

"I don't think so."

"Good."

"I've hardly slept for two days," Johnny said.

"I'll fix up a place for you to sleep."

"Thanks."

Mathews grabbed up a bunch of newspapers and laid them out on the table. "Kid," he said phlegmatically, "you've bought yourself a pack of trouble. Read 'em."

Half awake, Johnny scanned the journals. A huge headline emblazoned the holdup on the front page of the *Medicine Lake Wave*, and a smaller caption described how daring bandits had gotten away with three thousand dollars. He looked for reports on Magnor and read in the *Plentywood Herald* that his brother had been captured and was in the Williston hospital. He'd be okay. Another account gave him a laugh. The *Sheridan County News* reported that he had been nabbed near the Canadian border. That was an option he might consider one day.

Another article was grimmer. It said Sheriff Duggan would dog his trail until he brought him in.

Mathews emerged from the canvas-draped alcove off the kitchen. He sat down, hesitated briefly, and proffered still another newspaper. "I wasn't gonna show it to you, but I figured you'd better know."

The journal was the *Searchlight of Culbertson*. Johnny had broken horses there the previous fall. Mathews had underlined several sentences that quoted Johnny's father. The words seemed to rise up off the page and smack Johnny between the eyes: "I hope you fellows kill the boy before he gets a chance to kill you, as he is a bad boy and better off dead." That was his old man's gratitude for years spent bronco busting, clearing ditches, wielding a pitchfork until he couldn't lift his arms, babying calves at thirty below zero, hacking away at the woodpile, and digging coal in Thull's rattlesnake-infested coal mine? He crumpled up the newspaper in his hand, slammed his fist down on the table, and wept, albeit silently. He could not recall his father ever once telling him he'd done a good job. Not one compliment in sixteen years of his life. Shaking his head, and embarrassed by this display of emotion, he rubbed the moisture from his eyes and stood up.

"Johnny, you ain't the only one who ever had an old man like that," Mathews empathized.

Johnny nodded. He went into the alcove, flopped down on the straw tick mattress, and was asleep in a matter of seconds.

# Chapter 5

# GETAWAY

Mathews put away the newspapers, then flipped the canvas curtain behind him and walked to the stove. He drained hot water into a bucket from the stove's storage compartment. Then he put the soiled tableware into a wash pan and, picking up the bucket, poured its contents into the pan. No sooner had he finished washing the dishes when he heard a loud "Hello" followed by a knock on the front door.

Mathews opened the door and immediately recognized Walter "Matt" Mathews, an old acquaintance but not a relative. He was one of Sheriff Duggan's deputies. Ki was not a man prone to panic. If he was, he would have landed in jail a long time ago.

"Hello Matt," he said genially. "C'mon in and get warm."

"Don't mind if I do," his visitor said easily.

Matt was a veteran of twelve years of law enforcement. He was a man of consummate wisdom gathered from years of patient observation of human behavior. In a sense, he was not only a lawman, but he was also a judge—a judge of character. Unlike a magistrate who presided over a court and could ponder his decisions for hours or even days, at times Matt was forced to make his in a split second. He had feelings but was not at liberty to vent them. And, as a veteran, he had long since learned that by keeping his own counsel he too could invoke justice.

Matt followed Ki to the kitchen and sat down at the table while his host poured out two cups of coffee. He had noted moisture on the floor in the shape of a perfect footprint. It was too small to be Ki's boots.

"Have someone with you?" he asked, looking steadily at Ki.

Ki did not flinch. He was prepared for the question. "Just a kid doin' the chores," he said casually. The explanation seemed to satisfy the lawman. "What's up?"

Matt took a draught of coffee. "We got a call from Sheriff Duggan. He said to keep an eye out for a bank robber. That's what I'm doing."

Ki knew that this was the nadir of their conversation. Whatever he came up with now would have to be good enough to lure his visitor off Johnny's trail. There was no other way to handle the situation than to throw the house open to the deputy. Any weaseling on Ki's part would be a surefire tip-off that the kid with him was the bank robber.

"Matt, it's gettin' pretty late. You might as well stay until morning," Ki said congenially.

"Sounds good, but Duggan wants me to go down to the Missouri breaks and watch the river crossings."

"You can't do that at night. I'll rustle up some grub for you," Ki said.

A gust of wind from the norther raging outside slapped the shutters and rattled the windows, as if to emphasize just how bad it was out.

The deputy had no desire to spend the night wandering through a prairie storm. He sat back and lit up a cigar. "It sounds good," he said. "Rustling grub and otherwise, you're always proficient at what you do, Ki."

"Hey, that was years ago," Ki commented, knowing full well the remark was an indirect reference to his horse rustlings of the past. "I'll get the boy to take your horse to the stable."

Ki realized it was a big gamble, but if he was going to put the deputy up for the night there was no sense in being shy about including Johnny in the chores that had to be done. To do otherwise would cast suspicion. The ball would soon be in Johnny's hands. One mistake on the lad's part and Johnny would be in jail for a long time, and so might he, Ki reflected.

Ki stepped behind the curtain and woke up Johnny, holding his finger over his lips in the time-honored signal for silence. Ki realized it would do no good to whisper because the cubbyhole was right off the kitchen. Making sure Johnny got the signal, he spoke out in a normal tone.

"Come on, kid, your chores ain't finished yet."

Johnny nodded.

"Get the deputy's horse, and take it to the barn."

Johnny's eyes widened when he heard the word "sheriff" and he came wide awake. He quickly recognized the role he would have to play and nodded to his host. "Okay," he said.

Ki eased his way around the canvas and returned to the kitchen where the lawman sat comfortably, chewing on his cigar. He could hear Johnny putting on his boots behind the canvas. "The kid will have your horse unsaddled and groomed in a jiffy," Ki offered.

"Fine," Deputy Mathews responded.

A guilty conscience works in unusual ways. After years of dealing with the ranks of the deceitful, an experienced lawman can spot patterns that are not obvious to the average citizen. Thus, one little out-of-character remark, or untoward glance, or nervous expression can spell disaster.

Fear gnawed at the pit of Johnny's stomach like a rat eating cheese. He thought of the advice Delker had once given him wherein he explained that a sweaty palm was a red flag to a policeman. Fear incurred the sweat, which in turn pointed to the man with the guilt. Johnny carefully wiped his hands dry and walked, gloves in hand, into the kitchen. He was icy calm as he blinked the sleep from his eyes.

"Okay, if I can have some coffee first?" Johnny asked.

Ki, who had been watching Johnny with the acute eyes of a drama coach appraising an actor, felt like standing up and yelling his approval at Johnny's bold approach.

"Sure, sit down," Ki said.

Johnny, trying to act natural, glanced at the visitor and saw that he was giving him the once-over. However, his gaze, at least to Johnny, did not seem to be a professional observation, though he could not tell for sure. One thing in Johnny's favor was that he looked much younger than his age. Fuzzy-cheeked and fair, he appeared more the boy than the young man.

"Where are you from, son?" Matt asked.

"Minot," Johnny said. He had relatives there.

"What's your name?"

Johnny was edgy, but judged the man was making normal questions that anyone in a similar situation would ask. "Johnny Nelson," he said.

"How long you been here?"

"About six months."

"Well, Ki can use a good hand," the deputy said.

Ki nodded and added approvingly, "He's a big help."

Johnny finished his coffee and stood up. "Thanks for the coffee," he said.

"Speaking of coffee," Ki said, "we don't have enough for breakfast, so when you finish with the sheriff's horse, ride up to Peterson's and get some, and if the weather stays bad, spend the night there and come back early in the morning."

Ki's afterthought came as an inspiration. The suggestion was so logical his guest seemed to ignore it completely. Ki was silently congratulating himself after Johnny had left, when Matt suddenly straightened up.

"Come back," he yelled.

Johnny had his hand on the front door latch, and the command froze him in terror. He wanted to bolt right then and there, but knew it would be a wasted gesture. He would have to tough it out. He returned to the kitchen.

The deputy pointed to Johnny's gloves, which rested on the counter by the pantry. "You forgot 'em," he said, and smiled.

Johnny was so overwhelmed by the gesture, he wanted to slap the deputy on the back and thank him, but on looking into the lawman's eyes, he saw a twinkle as if the deputy knew all along what was going on. The tension went out of Johnny like air out of a deflated balloon. He picked up his gloves. "Thanks," he said calmly, and left.

"You're gonna stay the night aren't you?" Ki asked the deputy sheriff, hoping he had not changed his mind.

Mathews yawned. "Yeah, sure. I don't think Duggan will lose any votes if I get a good night's sleep."

"Votes?" Ki said.

"Yeah, votes. Bank robbers should know better than to pull off a job right before an election."

"By golly, you're right. I never thought of that."

"Who knows, I might even run for the office myself," Matt said.

Ki eyed his guest suspiciously.

Matt caught the look and laughed.

Then Ki comprehended the meaning and grinned. Sometimes lawmen were almost human.

Johnny did not need hand-written directions to know what to do. After taking care of the deputy's horse, he rode for Peterson's place. Peterson, on opening the door, did not seem to be overly surprised when Johnny explained who he was, and invited him into the house. Peterson oozed refinement and education and by the looks of his place had mustered more than a few dollars in his lifetime. Johnny explained the jam he was in.

"You do have problems," Peterson said, at the same time silently cursing Ki for not being more explicit. This was big time. He paced the floor trying to figure a way out for Johnny. Finally, he disappeared into a room and came back out with a dress in his hand.

"My late wife's," he said, "put this on and I can get you aboard the seven o'clock train heading west tomorrow morning." He handed it to Johnny who dropped it like a hot potato.

"No sir, not me," Johnny mumbled in disgust. "I'm not gonna wear it."

Peterson was patient with him. "Look," said Peterson, "nowhere in the world is a woman safer than in the American West. This code is the key to your escape. Few lawmen ever have the guts to check and see, er, if a woman is really a woman. Either you wear this dress for a couple of hours, or you spend ten years in jail."

"I can run for it."

"Where? By tomorrow every road will be under a lawman's gaze. Your only chance is to catch a train. That's the one way you have of getting beyond the local circles of the men chasing you. Once beyond that, you're home free—that is, if you don't get into more trouble."

After weighing the alternatives, Johnny agreed to give it a try. He retrieved the garment from the floor and put it on. Fortunately, the dress covered his legs, or Johnny's muscular build would have been a dead giveaway. Peterson rummaged around and came up with shoes and a bonnet, which Johnny dutifully put on. He took two steps in his newly endowed feet and fell flat on his face.

Peterson was amused. "You have all night to practice," he said, and took another look at Johnny. "You know, you're pretty good looking."

Johnny didn't smile. He was too worked up for any humor.

The next morning the two men reached the railroad station at Bainville without incident. Johnny carried his gear in a carpetbag supplied by Peterson. However, he kept his money belt strapped around his waist. It was beginning to rub and it irritated him, but he dared not stow the cash in any other place.

The lady's woolen cape given to him by Peterson served well to hide his bulky waistline.

Peterson's timing was good. The train was already in the station, its steam engine hissing in the cold, when they pulled up in Peterson's buggy. One man stood on the station platform. He turned around and looked at them curiously. A badge was clearly visible on the man's coat.

Johnny started to climb down from the buggy, but Peterson retrained him by grabbing his arm. "Hold up," he said, and walked around to Johnny's side and offered him his arm.

"What the hell!" Johnny muttered.

"You're a woman, remember?" Peterson growled.

Johnny stepped down from the rig and almost immediately turned his ankle and stumbled. Peterson kept him from falling. Luckily the deputy was looking down the tracks at the train and did not see the incident.

They managed to walk the rest of the way to the boarding platform without notice, but once there, the deputy approached them.

"It's the deputy, let me handle it," Peterson said out of the side of his mouth.

"Cold day, mister," the lawman said.

"Yeah, too cold to be up and around."

"Going anywhere?"

"No, but my niece here is."

The deputy, whose name was Walker, had been told to look for a blond-haired youth of around sixteen years. More than likely, according to Duggan's office, the robber—if he was with anybody—would be with Ki Mathews. Walker did not know Peterson, and he did not see any man matching the description of Johnny. The deputy tipped his hat to the two, and walked off without comment.

Fortunately Johnny was not called on to say anything. Peterson went into the station house and came back with a ticket, which he gave to Johnny, along with the carpetbag, as the lad stepped onto the train.

Johnny walked into the railroad car and immediately sat down. He did not want to expose himself to the public any more than he had to. The coach was not unlike the one he had ridden west in a little over a decade earlier. The windows were square and there was a potbellied stove located at each end of the railroad car. The seats were straw-backed. The "iron horse" was an adventure in itself, down to the toilets that emptied directly onto the railroad track.

Johnny eased back and tried to relax as the wheels churned and the train gathered momentum. There were only a few people in the car. He noticed that the man across the aisle looked at him with keen interest. At first, he thought the gazer was a deputy, but then it dawned on him that the man was admiring him, thinking he was a woman. Johnny wished he could get out of the disguise, and wondered if he would have trouble with the leering character across the aisle.

The conductor collected Johnny's ticket without comment, merely repeating the name of his destination, punching the ticket, and handing it back to him.

Fortunately, after a few hours, the aisle man got off the train, thus solving Johnny's problem on that score. But now he was presented with another problem, and that was getting out of his clothes. If he changed them on the train, the conductor might be suspicious. If he wore them when he got off the train, he could foresee exposure every time he opened his mouth. He pondered his choices all night, then elected to take his chances on the train.

Nearing his destination, he toted his carpetbag to a restroom located in the rear of the car behind his, and changed. He stuffed the dress, shoes, bonnet, and cape into the toilet and shoved them clear through so they fell onto the tracks. Then he moved to yet another car and sat down, happy to be dressed normally. Fortunately, a bunch of cowboys got onto the train just after he'd tossed away his disguise, and when he flashed the ticket stub, the conductor, taking him for one of the cowboys, failed to notice the change. John Conrad Johnson stepped off the train an hour later in Rock Springs, Wyoming, well beyond the area under search by the law.

Johnny chanced checking into a local hotel, which he accomplished using the alias of Bill Peterson. His preoccupations at that moment were the women in his life, and how he was going to make his escape.

Knowing his mother might be adverse to taking "blood money," Johnny bound up one thousand dollars in a package the next day and addressed it to his sister Olga, asking her to spend it any way she could to help pay the farm's debts. He also wrapped another package containing a gold watch he bought for Thora, and mailed the two parcels from Rock Springs. In addition, he purchased traps, guns, two horses, a tent, supplies, and with five hundred dollars remaining in his money belt, headed north.

Both packages were intercepted by the sheriff's department in Williston, North Dakota, but were allowed to go through after the postmark was identified.

"There's probably cash in one of the parcels," a deputy warned Sheriff John Erickson of Williston. The sheriff was a practical man, and not unaware of the hardships of so many of the farmers in his constituency. "Don't worry about it," Erickson advised his aid: "The National Security Company will take care of the bank's losses."


Occurring at 9:30 a.m. on a Thursday, the Medicine Lake bank holdup was early enough to make most of the weekly newspapers of the area, thereby launching a month-long journalistic hurricane with Sheriff Jack Duggan writhing in its eye.

Charges and countercharges were hurled about with impunity, and the political reverberations so shook the office of the sheriff, he called in his deputies and told them if they wanted their jobs come next election they'd have to bring in the fugitive. It was as simple as that. His reputation was on the line, and being in an elective capacity, if he went out of office, they all did. A wanted poster was quickly put together and printed. The sheriff advised that the circular be sent to every last two-bit jail in the West, because he figured the boy would end up in one of them sooner or later.

Meanwhile press barbs were being hurled at Duggan, frequently finding their mark. As is often the case, the least justified criticism was played up the most.

The sheriff, in an unguarded moment—for he seldom gave local scribes fodder to chew on—had told the editor of the Antelope, Montana, newspaper that he could have done a better job if he had ridden a faster horse—by this he meant his own.

Somehow the editor turned this around to report Duggan's disgust over not being able to procure a decent horse in Medicine Lake.

Editor Doolin of the *Medicine Lake Wave* leaped to defend the "honor" of his community. He succinctly pointed out that the Bowman ranch was only five minutes' walk from the hotel that housed the sheriff at the time of the robbery, and by going there, Duggan could have leased a string of the best saddle horses in the country. Being of a different political persuasion than the sheriff, Doolin then proceeded to twist the lion's tail even more by deprecating Duggan's lone success in the case. He wrote: "If any of those papers wish to learn the facts, we refer them to a number of Dagmar farmers who done [*sic*] the real capturing [of Magnor Hanson], and to whom all credit for so doing belongs, absolutely."

This prompted yet another publication, the *Dooley Sun*, to inject its comments into the caustic free-for-all when it blasted the *Wave* for its curt remarks concerning Sheriff Duggan. The *Sun* said that humans were apt to make mistakes, and if the editor of the *Wave* knew so much about Duggan's office, he should take the job.

The *Sun*'s riposte gave the sheriff a shudder—with friends like that, who needed enemies? Duggan writhed even more when Doolin took another stab at him in his rebuttal to the *Sun*. Doolin thanked his lucky stars that he was not occupying the sheriff's place in the minds of the citizens of Sheridan County.

While this battle of words was raging, Magnor was recovering from his shoulder wound under the guard of the Williams County Sheriff's Department at a hospital in Williston. When he was well enough, Duggan sent one of his men to bring the prisoner back to Plentywood to stand trial for his part in the bank holdup. Ironically, the money stolen by Magnor to bail out the farm never served the intended purpose. Instead, his mother, Petra, used the funds Olga had received in the mail from Johnny to retain a well-known attorney, Alphonse Braatelien, who defended Magnor in the district court. There was little dickering, though Braatelien did his best to convince the judge of Magnor's remorse. He pleaded guilty and was sentenced to "from three to ten years at hard labor" in the state penitentiary.

The backlash did not stop there. Delker began to worry about his part in planning the robbery, and called on the postmaster in nearby Gladys explaining that he had in his possession two hundred dollars given to him by Johnny. The postmaster called Sheriff Erickson on the phone and advised him of Delker's anxiety. Erickson reiterated what he earlier told his deputy. "Tell the damned fool to forget it. The bank was insured."

The real loser in the case was the National Security Company, insurer of Farmers State Bank. Its officials wasted no time in hiring Pinkerton detectives to track down Johnson, but the "Pinks" were unsuccessful.

It did not take long for the lawmen to trace Johnny's trail, but they were always two or three steps behind him until he disappeared altogether.

Chapter 6

# THE WOLF HUNT

Johnny whistled a tune as he rode north along the road to Big Piney, Wyoming. It was a beautiful March day, and the cold air was crisp and invigorating. Young Johnny held a tight rein on his horse and trailing packhorse, for occasionally he was approached and passed by an automobile. The animals were shy of the iron monsters. Johnny rounded a bend and spotted a lanky man of about his brother's age leading a lame horse. He reined up in front of the man.

"Hello," Johnny said.

The man looked up and stared at Johnny. "You mind taking me along?" he asked.

Johnny felt expansive. "Sure, why not. Hop aboard. Tie your horse to the horn."

The man climbed up behind him, and grabbed hold of his waist. "Where you headed?" he asked.

"Big Piney," Johnny replied. "How about you?"

"Same, my horse threw a shoe."

"What's your name?"

"Dan Creedon, what's yours?"

"Bill," Johnny said, then added, "Bill Hoffner."

"You ain't from these parts," Creedon commented.

Creedon had grown up in southwestern Wyoming and considered himself an authority on who came and went in the area. He was a shifty character who had more run-ins with the law than railroads had crack-ups, and that was considerable. He was a thief and a braggart, yet with enough qualifications to back up the brag. For one, he was a good street fighter, and for another, he either had absolutely no fear or was too reckless to understand the meaning of the word. He was also shrewd and a fair judge of character. Seeing this kid and noting that he was packing a brand new outfit made Creedon wonder, then he felt the bulging money belt under Johnny's coat. This was going to be easy pickings.

"Looks like you plan on spendin' some time in the high country," Creedon said.

"Might," Johnny replied.

"You need a guide?"

"Not sure."

"A man goes to the high country for only three things: to hunt and trap and prospect. You plan on any of those?"

"Might," Johnny replied.

"You got any relatives in these parts?

"No."

"Don't know a soul, huh?"

"That's right."

Creedon found that pumping the kid was difficult because he was not much of a talker. But he surmised two things: the stranger knew no one in the vicinity, and he wanted to go trapping. If he could weasel himself into that venture, the kid's money was as good as in his pocket.

"I can help you."

"How?"

"Well, for one, I know a good spot for wolves."

"Where?"

Creedon pointed to the west. "See them peaks?"

"Yeah."

"They're loaded with wolves.

"They are?"

"Yeah, I could be your guide."

"How much?"

Creedon figured he had the kid hooked. He dared not overcharge as he might scare him off. "A few bucks a day."

Johnny thought about the offer. He couldn't see any holes in it because he had met his newly found acquaintance on the road. There was no chance that this Creedon could be a lawman, and though he was a little on the seedy side, his horse and saddle were first rate. He did not visualize Creedon as a crook. "I'll think about it," he commented.

In silence, the two rode north.

The scenery was breathtaking. Barely recalling mountains of Norway in his youth, he had longed for the high country and now he was in it, or almost. Delker had told him about it. On their left rose the pinnacles of the rugged Salt River Mountains where Butch Cassidy and Sundance Kid Longabaugh had prowled fifteen years before. To the northeast, barely visible through a purple haze, was the snow-capped Wind River Range, and to the east, in stark contrast, were the barren rocks of the Little Colorado desert. Immediately next to the road flowed the Green River, where at the headwaters additional idols of Johnny's dreams, the free trappers of the old West, had held their annual rendezvous. Johnny wanted nothing more than their style of independence. The way to get it was to head into the mountains to trap and in so doing detach himself from the outside world. Creedon could be a big help in getting him off on the right foot.

They rode on to Big Piney, where they stopped in a café of the same name and ordered a sandwich.

Johnny had made up his mind. "All right, I'll hire you for a couple of bucks a day, and food, but you got to supply your own outfit."

Creedon's mind worked swiftly. There was no sense arguing with the kid over the particulars, because he might back out, and he knew better than to nix a golden opportunity like this. The only gamble was that he did not know how much money the kid had stuffed in his money belt, but he guessed it would be worth more than the time involved to go out to his pa's ranch and pick up a sleeping bag and a rifle and some grub. Being a crook himself, Creedon's instincts told him the kid had come by his riches dishonestly, and consequently, it would be much easier for him to take them from this newcomer. Hoffner, or whatever his name was, would have a difficult time complaining about a theft knowing full well it was stolen money.

"Sounds okay to me," Creedon said quietly. "I'll head out to my pa's ranch and meet you at the livery in two hours."

"Livery?"

"I gotta get my horse shoed," he said.

Johnny nodded. "Where's that?

"Black's. You can't miss it."

Later they joined up and camped at the rim of the town.

The next day Johnny and Creedon rode westward fifteen miles until they reached a trail winding up into the mountains. The air thinned perceptibly as they gained high ground above the town. From here Johnny could view the endless forest of spruce, aspen, and pine welling up from the wall of mountains that sealed off the arid desert below. Never before had he ridden into the high country of North America. Here he could see the world with the same perspective as the mighty eagle. Sparse clouds floated lazily below him, and the houses of Big Piney looked like a scattering of matchboxes. The clean mountain air honed his senses like no other place he had ever been, and brought him peace he had never felt before. For the moment he forgot his precarious position as a hunted man.

Creedon led the way as they rode up the path. "You heard of the Oregon Trail?"

"Sure."

"We're on it," Creedon said. Notching a leg over the saddle, he pointed back the way they had come.

"See that faint line across the desert? That's where the wagon trains crossed."

Johnny looked in awe at the panorama stretching as far as the eye could see. The desert was a seemingly unending wasteland, and the fact that anyone had ventured to cross it was hard to believe. "Up here, it's like bein' an eagle," he commented.

"Yeah, come to think of it you're right. We're probably two thousand feet above the desert right now," Creedon said.

With Creedon leading the way they climbed steadily, now and then crossing the Gray River. Snow now lay over the ground. At one point they rode around a bend in the trail and almost ran right into a moose snipping willow tips. Creedon held up until the animal drifted off into the forest.

"Even bigger'n I thought they'd be," Johnny said.

"Good eatin' too," Creedon said.

Creedon led them on, going ever deeper into the forest. Finally, they made camp in a copse of spruce overlooking a frozen alpine lake. Creedon had had enough foresight to bring snowshoes along. Using them he shoveled out an area for the wall tent Johnny had purchased. He and Johnny put it up and then cut spruce boughs to provide a floor, warmth, and comfort for their sleeping bags.

They built a roaring fire outside the tent to break the evening chill and to cook supper.

"Tomorrow we'll go wolfin'," Creedon announced.

"Haven't seen any sign," Johnny said. He'd trapped a lot around his home, and though he'd never seen a full-blooded wolf, he'd spotted the tracks of plenty of coyotes and dogs and guessed a wolf track would be about the same, only bigger. Johnny was beginning to get a little leery of his partner.

Creedon laughed. "They don't run up to you like dogs do, you know."

Johnny shrugged and resisted comment.

"We gotta go back a little farther."

"You're the sawbones."

"There's a bounty on wolves," Creedon said, "a buck apiece."

To collect a bounty meant Johnny would have to go to the law, which he wanted none of. "You can have the bounty," he said. "I think I'll turn in."

Creedon nodded. "Okay," he said, "I'm gonna rustle up some more wood."

Johnny was so fatigued he could not keep his eyes open. He climbed over the assorted paraphernalia crammed into the tent—including food supplies, an ax, cooking utensils, saddles, saddle blankets, overcoats, spare clothing, a Swede saw—and laid out his sleeping bag. Carefully noting that Creedon was still sitting at the fire, he opened his shirt and removed the money belt from around his waist.

Overlooked by Johnny, the shadow cast by the flickering candle used to light the tent enabled Creedon to discern the money belt as Johnny took it off.

Johnny put his six-gun and rifle under his bedroll, and tucking his precious burden under his feet, immediately fell asleep.

Creedon waited a long time by the fire, then cautiously ventured into the tent. He approached his companion while drawing his revolver. It would be a simple matter to kill the kid where he lay. He briefly deliberated doing this, then decided against it. There was no need. Creedon could steal his victim's horses and money and be long gone before he woke up. The kid would spend at least four or five days struggling on the trail before reaching Big Piney. Even then, he would be reluctant to complain of a theft for fear he would be arrested.

Smiling at such easy pickings, Creedon deftly slid the money belt out from under his partner's feet. The poor kid was obviously so worn out from being on the lam, Creedon figured he could have run a truck out of there without waking him up. He also would have raked away the kid's guns, but dismissed that risk as unneeded. The lad would never see him again; he was positive of that.

Leading the kid's horses and his own, and packing away anything of value, including the grub box, he quietly stole out of camp, only mounting up when he was one hundred yards away. No sense being careless. He had gone a few hundred yards when he remembered the snowshoes. Briefly deliberating whether he should go back for them, and then discarding that idea, he kept on riding, pushing his horses into a jog. He'd check out the money belt down the line. He was already two horses ahead on the deal. Even the moon was cooperating. It was full and radiated light, making it easy for him to follow their return trail. He rode about a mile before he stopped, made a fire, and emptied the belt. He counted out almost five hundred dollars in silver and gold coins and paper money. Not only was it the biggest haul Creedon had ever made, it was the easiest.

The next morning, the first thing Johnny reached for was his money belt. It was gone. As sleepy as he was, the loss made him alert. He looked across the tent and there was no sign of Creedon or his gear. Johnny knew then his initial suspicions of Creedon had been well founded. He should have acted upon them when the first warning bell rang in his mind. Now it was too late. He jumped up and ran out of the tent. His horses were gone, too, and most of his supplies. His one chance of living the life he wanted had vanished with his guide. A man could exist without horses, but he could not be without an ax, food, ammunition, or traps.

Johnny had been tricked by the oldest swindle in the business, the old "snipe hunt" con, only the wolf was the sucker bait instead of the snipe. Cursing his fate, Johnny donned the snowshoes Creedon had forgotten, and set out to follow his partner's trail. It led, as Johnny suspected, right back the way they had come. Three days later he reached Big Piney looking for Creedon. His total funds were a few dollars, nickels, and dimes.

Johnny went to the same café that he had visited with Creedon. If he was going to find Creedon, the owners might know something about him. The waitress brought him some coffee and he asked her if she knew him.

"Sure, everyone around here does," she said.

"Have you seen him lately?"

"Yes," she said, "with you!"

"I mean in the last day or two."

"No."

"Is there anyone who might know?"

"Try the barber," she replied.

There were no customers in the barber shop when Johnny walked in. The barber was sitting in the barber chair reading a newspaper. He looked up.

"What can I do for you?" he asked.

"I'm looking for Dan Creedon, you seen him?"

"Yes, I did," he said. "Claimed he came up with a little windfall and was heading for Rock Springs to have some fun."

Johnny cursed himself again. If he wanted to salvage anything, he would have to catch up with Creedon, but without a horse, there wasn't much chance. Waiting for dark, he ambled down to the livery stable, and peeked in the door. The attendant, a bit of a rummy, was sound asleep. It was now or never as far as Johnny was concerned. He calmly walked by the drunk, saddled a chestnut, mounted up, and rode out leading a second horse.

Luck was with him. He managed to get clear of town and lit out at a gallop, hoping to reach Creedon before he blew the money. That night he camped along Dry Piney Creek near Mule Shoe Bridge south of Big Piney. The weather was bitterly cold, forcing him to build a fire from the debris found in the creek bed. He knew he was taking a chance at being discovered but it was either that or freeze. He picketed the horses back in the trees and sat in front of the fire holding out his hands to warm them.

Five hours later, the livery attendant woke up. Hung over, and walking through the stable with a sense of guilt because of his booze-induced sleep, he found two of the stalls empty. He knew he would have to report this and it could cost him his job. Finally, after delaying an hour, he went to Sheriff Mills's office, and knocked on the door calling out the sheriff's name.

Fortunately, the sheriff was there. "Yeah, come in," he said in a fit of irritation. It seemed that no matter what the hour, there was always something happening. Then he dismissed his negative thoughts. He was paid to be available.

"Sheriff, someone stole a roan and a sorrel out of the stable," the attendant said.

Sheriff Mills knew the livery keeper and was not surprised by the news. Smith was a rummy, and was paid more for fire watch, heaven forbid, than to guard against horses being stolen. If Smith had a first name, he had never heard it.

"When did this happen, Smitty?"

"Well . . . er, I don't rightly know."

The sheriff nodded. "That figures. Sleeping again?"

"Just a little ole catnap, Sheriff."

"I don't suppose you'd know in which direction the thief went?"

Spoor was the one and only thing that Smith did know for sure. "It looks to me like he headed south. There's a string of steaming dung heading in that direction."

"Well, Smitty," the sheriff said, "One thing is certain: you've shoveled enough of it to know the difference between that and plain old dirt."

"Thank you, Sheriff, thank you."

"How long since you traced it?"

"An hour or two."

"What the hell have you been doing? The livery's only a block from here."

"Well . . ."

"Never mind," said the sheriff, at the same time reaching for the telephone on his desk. "A couple of phone calls and we'll have a posse after 'em."

Sheriff Mills called the owner of the stable, Jim Black, and shortly afterward, with Black and some of his cowhands, he took the road south.


Johnny more or less expected to be caught. And in a sense it did not make any difference if he was, because without funds or an outfit and food, where could he go? And especially since he'd stolen the horses. Now he sat in front of the fire and rested without a plan.

Suddenly a voice boomed out of the thicket across from the fire. "Hold still, or you're a dead man."

Johnny went for his gun, but then held up, his hand twitching over the holster. He realized he was a perfect target standing in the light of his fire.

Four men emerged from the thicket. One of the men brought in the chestnut. Another put his gun into Johnny's back and relieved him of his .44.

"What's your name?" Sheriff Mills asked.

Johnny had to think fast, but he was new in the game of being a crook. He gave the same name he gave to Creedon, which happened to be a version of the moniker of the man he had robbed in Bainville. "Hoffner, Bill Hoffner," he said.

"That roan of yours was stolen last night."

Johnny decided to deny everything. "I bought it fair and square," he replied.

"You did?"

"Yeah."

Mills motioned for Black to come forward. "Jim, did you sell a horse to this jasper?"

Black shook his head. "I never saw this guy before in my life."

"I bought it from someone else," Johnny said defensively.

"You get a bill of sale?"

Johnny nodded. "It's in my pocket."

"Which one?"

"Left."

Mills dutifully checked his left pocket. "It's not there now," he said.

"Maybe I lost it," Johnny said in a last desperate chance to gain time to think.

"It's your tough luck if you did," Mills said. "I'm taking you in."

Mills snapped handcuffs on Johnny and they rode back to Big Piney.

Johnny had never given much thought about what it would be like to get caught. At sixteen years of age he could boast of pulling off two successful armed robberies. Yet here he was a prisoner, having put his faith—against his better judgment—in a partner he was inclined to mistrust almost from the start.

Now he was on the treadmill of the damned. He was arraigned before the magistrate in Big Piney. At this point in the legal process, he saw his chance to get even with Creedon by implicating him in the theft of the two horses from the livery. Johnny was intelligent and needed no one to tell him that his lying about Creedon would be ineffectual, but he was cornered like a rat and he had nothing to lose by trying.

A warrant was sworn out for the arrest of Johnny's "partner," and a search was launched. Black, who was deputized by Sheriff Mills, caught up with Creedon, who was hightailing it across the desert. Creedon was shot out of the saddle and captured. After recovering from a shoulder wound, he denied everything and chose a trial by jury. Later, he was acquitted.

Johnny's case was cut and dried because he pled guilty to the charge of "stealing livestock." The dehumanization of this sixteen-year-old boy commenced on June 7, 1915, when he entered the Wyoming Penitentiary at Rawlings shackled to three other men convicted at the same time. Shortly thereafter, his hair was cut off. In addition various statistics were amassed under what identification experts called the Bertillon system. This included measuring his head, fingers, and reach. Johnny's fingerprints were also taken. He was fitted out with a striped suit, and the big iron doors slammed shut behind him. His sentence was to be "not less than a year or more than eighteen months."

# Chapter 7

# KEMMERER JAIL

Johnny's incarceration brought him into contact with some of the most hardened criminals of the American West. Bank and train robbers, rustlers, and murderers and thieves were all part the company he would keep during the most impressionable period of his life.

He now felt the full import of what it was like to be an outcast—to be without hope, without friends, and without a family. His refuge was to retreat into a world of silence. This aspect of his personality was paradoxical compared with his innately bold and aggressive nature and led casual acquaintances to underestimate his capacity for violence. In prison, the fact that Johnny was a man who kept to himself tended to set him against those who did not know him well. His cellmates, Burt Long and George Powers, the former a sheep rustler and the latter a horse thief, advised Johnny to open up, but this he refused to do. He was curt to the point where others considered him insolent, but there was a certain look to Johnny's eyes that warded them off. Something in his makeup reflected danger. Long sensed this and said as much one day to Powers when the latter had commented on Johnny's silence. "He's a dormant volcano," Long said. "Let well enough alone."

One thing bothered Johnny. The story had circulated through prison that he'd escaped the law once by wearing women's clothes. He could expect trouble over that, and it was not long in coming. He was in the prison yard where the men were allowed an hour each day when another young inmate walked right up to him and broached the subject jaw to jaw. "I understand you wear ladies' clothes," he said with a sneer.

Johnny was not much of a talker, and knew it would do no good to waste words anyway. He turned as if to walk away—just enough to crook his right arm at the shoulder—then with a right cross caught the wise guy in the temple. The con went down like he was hit with a pole rather than a fist. The guards saw it all, and though they reported it, they did nothing. A man had to settle his own problems in that environment.

The incident served to focus Warden Alston's eyes on Johnny, and he was summoned to his office. While in prison Johnny had one hope, that the Wyoming people would not get wind of his connection with the bank robbery in Montana. If they did, he'd have that rap to deal with. Warden Alston told him to sit down. Johnny noticed he was a stern-looking man. In one hand the warden held what Johnny supposed were his records, and in the other, another sheet, the contents of which Johnny could only guess.

"You're Bill Hoffner?" the warden asked.

Johnny affirmed that he was.

"You're nineteen, of German descent, and from California?"

There was nothing Johnny could do now but to stick by his story. "Yes," he said.

The warden stood up, walked around his desk, and handed Johnny the other paper in his hands. One look and he knew what it was—a wanted poster.

"According to Sheriff Duggan of Sheridan County, Montana, you're somebody else," Alston said sourly. The situation was nothing new to Alston. Every convict in prison with another offense over his head gave an alias. But in this case the warden hoped he could head off a criminal career before it was barely started. "According to that notice," he said, pointing to the poster in Johnny's hands, "You're John Conrad Johnson, not Bill Hoffner; you're sixteen, not nineteen; you're a Norwegian by birth, not of German descent; and you are from North Dakota, not California."

Johnny was lacking options and said nothing.

Alton turned and pointed to a photo on the wall behind his desk. "You know who that is?"

Johnny shook his head.

"That's Douglas Preston, the attorney general of the state of Wyoming. When you were born he was Butch Cassidy's lawyer. You heard of Cassidy?"

Johnny nodded. Delker had told him a lot more about Cassidy than he wanted to admit knowing.

"Butch served time here. He was probably the most successful holdup man in the history of the West, but even he ended up shot to pieces—in Bolivia of all places. It's a one-way street, son. If you don't wise up now you'll end up the same way. Do you have anything to say for yourself?"

Johnny thought about it. Butch and he pursued different goals. Cassidy squandered his time on parties and nightlife in the big cities. Johnny wanted no part of that. All he wished to do was to trap and hunt and fish. He shrugged and shook his head. "No, I don't," he replied.

Alston took the records and the poster out of Johnny's hands and went back to his desk. He sat down and scanned Johnny's Wyoming prison records, shook his head, and looked up. "Hoffner, or Johnson, or whatever your name is, did you fill out this form?"

"No, the clerk did."

"It says here after 'Nativity' you told the clerk 'Nowhere.'"

Johnny recalled having almost answered "Montana," but realizing it might tip off the authorities about the bank robbery, he had mumbled, "Nowhere."

"I guess so," he replied.

Warden Alston rose from his chair and walked to the entrance to his secretary's office. "Sara," he said, "get the records clerk in here." Then he returned and sat back down in his swivel chair and repeated half to himself, "Nowhere."

The clerk appeared.

"Sit down, Jim," Alston growled. "Did you type this out?" He handed him the records.

The clerk scanned it, and nodded. "Yes, I did."

"What's this 'nowhere' crap?"

"That's what he said."

Alston looked at the prisoner and softened. "Son, what'd you mean by that?"

Johnny shrugged. "I don't know."

"Come on, you just can't say 'nowhere,'" the warden commented.

"Maybe, that's the way I feel."

"What way?"

"I'm a nobody from nowhere."

The warden had thirty years' experience dealing with criminals and their records, and he had never before heard of anything like this. He picked up a pen and scribbled something.

"You can go now."

As soon as the prisoner left the office, the clerk spoke out: "Well, chief, do you want me to change the form?"

Warden Alston thought for a moment, and shook his head. "No, Jim, let it stand. Maybe it's prophetic."

"What do you mean?"

The warden gazed out the window. His years in the business gave him considerable insight. Finally, he turned to the clerk. "You know, Jim, every so often there's a reason for things on this great disorderly planet of ours. Possibly some guy will come snooping around these records fifty years from now and give us the answer."

Johnny's sentence was up in August 1916, a little more than a year after he was first incarcerated. Sheriff Duggan of Montana sent Deputy Walter Mathews to pick Johnny up, and it turned out to be a reunion of sorts.

Mathews snapped handcuffs on Johnny, and they headed for the railroad station in the prison's buggy. Deputy Mathews had not forgotten the night he met the kid. However, now Johnny looked a thousand years older than before he went to jail. Mathews imagined that each day in the lockup was a year for Johnny. Once they climbed aboard the train heading back to Montana, the deputy took the opportunity to explore the kid's mind. "You made a clean getaway, kid. What happened?"

Johnny was surprised the lawman was not mad at him. He'd have reason enough to be, since he had wiggled past the deputy's fingertips to get away. He decided he would be honest with him. "I should have kept to myself," he said.

The answer was simple enough, but Mathews understood it completely. Johnny could have gotten directions from Creedon, but that was as far as it should have gone. He shouldn't have taken a stranger along.

"How'd you happen to get hung up with Creedon?" the deputy asked.

"Good turn," he said.

"Good turn?" Mathews repeated.

"Yeah, he had a lame horse and I picked him up and gave him a ride."

"Ride double?"

"Yeah."

"So that's how he knew you had a money belt?"

"That's the lick of it."

"He get the money?"

"Every cent."

"Well, kid, nothin's worth trading money for time in the pen for stealing money. Stay clear and you can live a good life."

"Yeah," Johnny said.


Sheriff Duggan had a much greater reason for being disgusted with Johnny than Mathews did. The damned kid had almost cost him an election, and by now, as far as he was concerned, the youngster would be so hardened he would be lost to society. He'd seen it too many times in the past to think Johnny would be any different. He had nothing good to say about Johnny in court.

Johnny was arraigned at the county seat in Plentywood where he again pleaded guilty, this time to the charge of bank robbery. Judge Frank Utter, the same man who had sentenced Johnny's brother, sent him to the Montana State Penitentiary at Deer Lodge for "three to ten years at hard labor."


No place was drearier and more forlorn than a prison rock pile. Here the convicts sentenced to hard labor passed their long, monotonous hours swinging sixteen-pound sledgehammers. Six months on the pile was enough to toughen up the weak (if they didn't break), and to turn the strong into men of iron. Johnny was one of the latter. He hacked at the rocks in stubborn silence, as if the continuous pounding would speed up the day when he could pick up where he left off—in the mountains.

Johnny's spirits would lift whenever he came across Magnor at the quarry and the two managed to exchange a few words. These were brief moments, as silence among the prisoners was a rule strictly enforced by the guards, and both Magnor and Johnny did not want to jeopardize their chance meetings.

A year went by, and the war in Europe, which had been going on for four years, loomed larger than ever. The Germans launched a huge attack against the French and British in March of 1917, cracking the line and driving deep into France. The Allies held, but just barely. The United States came into the war at this time, and immediately all of the National Guard and reserve troops were called up. The government was starved for manpower, and this fact was not lost on the men in jails throughout the country.

Another year went by and the Allies were desperate. The word got out quickly. Magnor broke the news to Johnny at the rock pile. "I've been called up," he muttered to Johnny over the handle of a sledgehammer.

Johnny was thrilled at the chance for Magnor to get out. He looked around at the guards. They hardly noticed him. Discipline had become lax during wartime. "Glad to hear it," Johnny said, not even bothering to whisper.

"Maybe you'll get out, too," Magnor said.

"Ain't old enough," Johnny countered.

Magnor nodded. "I hadn't thought of that. How old are you?"

"One hundred," Johnny replied with a straight face.

Magnor compressed a laugh into a smile. "I know what you mean."

"I'll be twenty July thirteenth."

"You'll probably get out quick like. They'll need you on the farm."

"The hell with the farm."

"What do you mean?"

"Dammit, Magnor, did you hear what the old man said about me?"

Magnor shrugged and looked around. Neither he nor Johnny was working and the guards were ignoring them. "No, I haven't."

"He said I was no good and better off dead."

"You sure?"

"It was in the newspaper."

Magnor thought about Johnny's relationship with his father, who was not Magnor's father. Johnny was inclined to get a lot hotter under the collar with the old man than he did. But if Johnny could curb his temper, he might be released from prison. "Listen to me, Johnny, and for God's sake pay attention. You are too young for the draft, but not too young to work on the farm. They are letting guys out to do just that. So if they ask you, go along with it."

Johnny boiled at the thought of his father's lack of loyalty to him, his own son. "I don't know," he said.

Magnor looked hard at his younger brother. "Just once pay attention to me. You got a sentence of three to ten years. As long as the war is on you got a chance to get out of prison. But if the war ends in the next year or two, they'll soon be back to their old ways, and you might have to serve the whole ten."

Johnny did not answer because he did not get the chance.

A guard cut them off. "You guys are out here to break rocks, not bread. Git back to work."

Magnor's parole came through in a matter of days, and he had no chance to talk with his brother. Three weeks later Magnor was inducted into the army. And by August he was in the front lines with the Eighty-Eighth Infantry Division. He wrote Johnny from a hospital where he was under care after being shot through the shoulder, the same one pierced by the posse bullet. He told Johnny that the money he had sent to Olga was used by the family to hire a lawyer to defend him, thus the funds had been expended without helping the old folks at all. It was a bitter pill for Johnny to swallow.

Magnor went on to say he was sorry he had not told Johnny before, but in view of his bitterness, he decided not to make things worse. Magnor also offered apologies for getting Johnny involved in the first place. He hoped Johnny would go straight once he was out of jail, as he himself was determined to do. Finally, he pleaded with his brother to save the farm, for their mother's sake, if for no other reason.

Johnny pondered the letter as the days rolled by, and Magnor's words began to sink in. Eating a little crow was better than battering away at rocks for ten years. The old man was seventy-two years old and maybe he was more than a little scared when the newspaper people talked with him. He reckoned if he got the chance to get out, he'd take it.

Two months later, Johnny was free, turned loose in time to care for foals and calves and for spring plowing and planting. He had been so engrossed in his tribulations with his father he'd never even thought about how he would be received by the farmers and ranchers around the township of Climax. Now as the train headed east, he wondered if anyone would even talk to him because of the bank robbery, and really did not much care. He was not a mixer to begin with, but he did wonder about Thora. She had never written to him, and he couldn't blame her. Could there be a thread of feeling left for him in her thoughts? He had been in prison exactly three years. Those usually awkward teenage years had been spent with some of the toughest criminals in the West. In a sense, now that he was out, he did not feel any different. These three years from then on would be a void in his life he would never refer to.

His sister Olga raced out to greet Johnny when he walked up the short path from the road to the homestead. He noticed the girl he had left behind had become a woman, and a good-looking one at that. He immediately saw how badly the place was run down. The grass of the front yard was uncut. The fields were weeds, the barn roof was in a state of disrepair, and even what pieces of farm equipment they had were in need of servicing. His father greeted him, reticently, as though he suffered from a guilty conscience. Johnny knew his pa was not the kind to apologize for anything he ever did, so he did not really expect it.

"You heard about Magnor," his father said in Norwegian. He had been over fifty when they immigrated, too old to master a new language.

Johnny nodded and spoke in Norwegian. "When's he coming home?"

"I don't know," his father replied, "maybe not at all. How long are you going to be here?"

The old man's pride would never bend as far as asking Johnny to stay. He knew that. At least his father was sober, and as long as he remained that way, Johnny figured he would stick around, but it did no good to say that. Typically, he knew it might set his old man off in exactly the opposite direction. Johnny would do what he could to save the farm from the bank. "I don't know," he said, "but long enough to get us out of debt."

The months went by and Johnny tried. He and his father worked hard, though at seventy-two the old man was a little slower than he had once been. They fixed up the machinery, broke new land to plant wheat, rebuilt the barn, and worked from dawn to dark trying to put the operation into the black. His mother and Olga also pitched in. His sister could ride almost as well as Johnny and occasionally got her friend Lena Stanley to move their tiny herd of cattle from one pasture to another. However, crops turned out to be poor. Wheat and meat prices were low, and as much as the Johnsons tried, debts kept piling up. Even then Johnny might have prevailed if it were not for his father's weakness for alcohol.

Often, when times are bleakest, alcoholics tend to fold, and Anders Johnson was no different. Frequently he went on a drunk in Medicine Lake, and returned asleep in the back of his wagon—a cow and ox having pulled him home. It happened so many times, the animals knew the way. Finally, Johnny decided to confront his father, though he suspected he'd be wasting his time.

Anders was clearing his head under the pump in the kitchen, and Johnny lashed out at him, "I see things really haven't changed much around here."

Anders, his head still under the pump, ignored Johnny's upbraiding remark. In his befuddled alcoholic mind he rejected criticism as easily as shutting a door in the face of an unwelcome visitor. Finally, the elder Johnson finished with the pump and faced his son. "What did you come back for, Johan?" Anders asked bitterly.

"To help you out," Johnny said.

"Some help. You shame your mother, and then have the guts to come back."

Johnny recoiled at his father's cryptic comment. He knew when it came to nagging, the old man was an expert, and could always get under his skin. "Someone had to save the farm," he replied.

His father laughed derisively. "When I needed you, you were in prison."

Johnny saw that no matter what he said, his father would turn the argument around until it was his fault. "You needed help long before that. You've had your head buried in the bottle so long you can't think straight," he said.

Anders's capacity to hurt was accentuated by his intractability. The power of the elder Johnson's reasoning lay in his irrational rhetoric. Anders saw his chance to destroy Johnny and took it. "We don't need you here, Johan. You don't fit. You never did and you never will. So get out."

Johnny had to force himself to refrain from hitting his father, and he stormed out of the kitchen. Magnor was still in France, and Delker had moved to Canada. Thora had married. The farm was beyond hope. He tossed his meager personal belongings into a duffel bag, bade good-bye to his sister and mother who were in tears, and left home for good.

Johnny joined hundreds of others from poor farms who drifted aimlessly, taking any job that gave them enough money to eat. He had mastered a specialty of breaking horses, which was more than most of the drifters. He went west to Nevada and approached the foreman of a ranch in the Smoke Creek Desert and asked for a job.

"You had much experience?" the foreman asked.

Johnny nodded. "Enough to get along."

"We'll see," the head wrangler said, and pointed to the corral. "I'll give you a buck for every one of those critters you can gentle."

Working with horses was a pleasure for Johnny, even though they could be the most ornery creatures that walked the globe. Maybe it was the smell of them, or their fractious nature, or the sensation of speed he obtained from spurring a fast horse, or the satisfaction gained from clinging to a crow-hopper until the "outlaw" was subdued, or maybe it was simply that he was good at what he did.

Johnny grabbed his lariat and walked to the corral. There, with the help of a hazer, he selected the nearest animal, roped him, and threw him violently to the ground. He put a saddle on the beast and each time the steed struggled, Johnny whacked him with a quirt. It did not permanently damage the animal, but it stung him. Finally, Johnny placed the bit in the horse's mouth, mounted him, and waited for him to buck. Every time the cayuse did so Johnny swatted him heavily. He kept this up until the horse finally realized his bucking was inviting a hurt, and he desisted. Johnny then pegged the horse using a long rope. A hackamore was placed over the animal's head, the reins being attached to the free end of the rope. As soon as Johnny let go, the horse took off running only to find his wind cut off by the hackamore and his escape violently shut down when he hit the end of the rope. The steed somersaulted, hitting the ground heavily, yet decidedly meeker than he was before.

The foreman watched with the eagle eye of a man who spent years on the range. "You'll do," he said when Johnny had gentled the first horse. "We got ten more for you, and after that we might have a pile of 'em, it depends on a contract we got lined up."

Over the next few weeks Johnny was in the air more than he was on a horse, but he got the job done. He grew to like the area, and figured he had found a place where he could put down some roots, but it was not to be.

The foreman paid Johnny the eleven dollars he had coming, then said, "That contract didn't come through. There're too many cars and tractors around. Even the army is getting rid of horses."

It seemed as though nothing ever worked right for Johnny. He packed his gear into his saddlebags and rode across the desert toward the distant Sierras, whose brilliant white peaks beckoned to him. It was a dry, dusty trip with only the occasional whir of a rattlesnake and bark of a coyote to break the monotony.

Eventually, he reached the foothills of the Sierras in Lassen County, California, and settled into an abandoned cabin he found on the road to Bieber, a jump-off point for a number of logging operations in the area. He was short of cash, so he sold his horse, his last remaining possession of value, and used the funds to buy hobnail boots he'd need in the woods.

Johnny pounded the logging roads and trails, seeking work as a logger, but he had no luck. Hearing there was work in Susanville, the Lassen County seat, he and another tramp paired up and walked sixty miles only to find out that the rumor was untrue. Johnny then headed back to the cabin where he had been a squatter, and the route took him past the Wood and Geiger slaughterhouse just outside of Susanville. It was late in the evening when he and his companion spotted two horses, a bay gelding and a roan mare, in the corral of the Sierra Packing Company. They also noticed two saddles on the corral's fence. The temptation was too much for Johnny. He was tuckered out. Why not "borrow" the horses for a while, he suggested. His itinerant pal was not adverse to the idea. They entered the corral, saddled up, and rode away. The whole thing was so easy Johnny and his companion did not even try to cover up their tracks.

About five miles out he and his partner split up—without his ever learning the tramp's name. Johnny continued on the road toward his shack, sometimes riding the bay gelding and sometimes leading him afoot. It was well past midnight when he stopped to make camp at Eagle Lake, thirty miles from his destination.

# Chapter 8

# CAUGHT STEALING HORSES

The morning of May 23, 1921, was typical for the town of Susanville, a place where it rarely rained in late spring and summer. A mantle of dew from the night had settled on the dust to compact it. Later in the day this would dry out, causing a person to kick up little dust swirls wherever he went.

Thomas H. Long, ruggedly built, authoritative, and his son, Goddard, a lad of about sixteen who was the image of his father, though more slender, went to the packing company yard that morning to feed their horses. They found them missing. Long cursed, and in the same breath blessed his luck for the dew-moistened sand, which offered clear samples of the footprints of both horses and the men who took them. "Better go find the sheriff," Long told his son. "Ask him if he can bring Baughman along. The old codger can track a deer on bare rock."

Goddard left and in a short time had rounded up Sheriff Church, a stocky man of forty who radiated a quiet confidence, and the tracker, Isaac Henry Baughman. "Henry," as he was called, was once an Indian fighter who had won esteem throughout the Sierras for his ability to track down people and wild animals.

Long was happy to see that the two men were available.

"Hello, Sheriff," he said. "We've lost a few horses and saddles."

"How'd that happen?" the sheriff asked, wondering immediately why the horses hadn't been put in the stable for the night.

"The bay's gone and so is the roan. Some of my cowhands left the horses in the corral and the saddles on the fence. Damned if I know why."

Church looked at Baughman who was already scanning the corral for tracks. He took little time in figuring out the scene of the previous night.

"Well," said the tracker, "there's a mess of hoss tracks and people tracks. One hoss's got only two shoes, and the other's barefoot."

"The roan's only got two shoes, and the bay's got none," Long affirmed, already admiring Baughman's talents.

Baughman squatted, carefully eyeing a rash of footprints. "Now the hombres who stole them hosses, one of 'em must have been a logger, cause he's wearing hobnailed boots. The right one got three nails missin'. The other guy's got smooth soles."

"You think you could follow them?" Sheriff Church asked.

"Well, I reckon so," Baughman replied, "let me take a look." He followed the tracks several hundred yards up the dirt road that ran by the corral before returning.

"Tom," said Church, "You've got an open automobile. We could use it."

Baughman looked perplexed. "An automobile?"

"Yeah, Henry, an automobile," Church said patiently.

"I ain't never tracked a critter from a machine."

Long smiled. "You'd be surprised, Henry. It has some advantages. Lights for example."

"Lights?"

"Yeah, headlights, you'll be able to work at night."

Baughman pursed his lips in thought, and then nodded. "Yup, it might work."

Long looked at Church. "We'll bring along horses just the same. Tie 'em to the rear bumper." He turned to Goddard. "Get three horses out of the barn. There might be three bedrolls there as well."

Goddard nodded and trotted off.

Sheriff Church knew the value of the footprints. "Tom, you'd better make sure you keep the corral clear, and cover up those prints with a canvas. We might need 'em for evidence."

The sheriff had seen plenty of changes in law enforcement but nothing to match those that had occurred in the last few years. He was a visionary and accepted change, though he knew there were plenty of lawmen who did not. To him, no scene could be more representative of the end of one era and the beginning of another than that of Baughman, an animal tracker sitting on the front fender of the car following a horse thief's trail. A decade earlier, the employment of an auto in such a chase was scarcely heard of; neither, for that matter, was a telephone. Of course, it was a double-edged sword. Already crooks were using autos to make their getaway. He grinned self-consciously and shook his head.

The road they proceeded on was part of a system of wagon paths and trails that went north, skirting Eagle Lake, to link up the towns of Bieber on the northwest and Madeline on the northeast. Baughman and Sheriff Church set out on foot when telltale tracks led them off the road and across Antelope Hill. Long continued on with the car, and when Baughman traced the imprints of the horse thieves across the brow of the hill and back to the road, Long met them there, and Church climbed back into the vehicle. Baughman resumed his seat on the fender of the car.

"As long as these birds keep to the road, it ain't half bad," Baughman said once he was back on the fender,

Scarcely had Baughman's words been uttered when the three-man posse met a number of cars and several horse-drawn wagons that had obliterated the faintly discernible tracks of the rustlers and raised a dense cloud of dust, causing Baughman to sputter and cough.

"Tarnation!" he exclaimed, "This is worse than ridin' drag on a cattle drive." He signaled for Long to stop the car. "I lost 'em."

"You think they doubled back?" Long asked.

The old tracker scratched his head. "Maybe and maybe not," he said.

Church intervened with a hunch, a hunch born of many years as a lawman. "Go as far as Willow Creek. If we don't find anything, we'll turn back."

"That's fifteen miles," Long said.

"I know," Church said, "it's a long way, but let's try it."

"All right with me," Long said, adding, "you're the doctor."

Baughman also agreed. "Good idea. If they water the horses, or take a drink we might find 'em at the crick."

Long put the car into gear and started out again.

They arrived at the creek and scanned its banks. In a short time Baughman had found tracks. "There's one of 'em," he said. "He's hobnailed with a coupla nails missin'. He's alone leadin' the barefoot horse. The other guy has skedaddled."

The three men followed the boot tracks up the road and again lost them, but decided to keep on, figuring the man had gone at least as far as Eagle Lake. Sure enough, Baughman found the boot mark with the missing nails.

"He seems to have one place in mind, I'd say," the old tracker suggested.

"How do you figure?" Long asked.

"The way he keeps to the road," Baughman said.

"Henry's right," Church added. "I wouldn't be surprised if he has a shack somewhere around here, or he would have taken off like the other guy did."

Darkness was closing in, but Sheriff Church urged them on, "We got the car lights, so why not take advantage of 'em."

Their progress was slow, as hoof prints made by other horsemen tended to obscure the tracks of the man and the horse. It grew dark, yet the three men maintained their diligent pace while using the lights of the car. Around midnight they lost the trail near Said Valley Reservoir, but continued along the road anyway, hoping their logic about the fugitive's homing tendencies was correct.

Johnny had been weary and slept so heavily that when he woke up at the lake camp and first saw the horse, he forgot that he had stolen it. He'd never even got the other guy's name. He sat up and did a retake on the horse. He jumped up, and fully clothed, rushed to the lake and washed the sleep out of his eyes. When the severity of the deed sank into his senses, he looked around furtively, then grabbed his pack, and mounting up, spurred the horse northward along the road. The horse was a good one, but in spite of the fact that he had stolen the animal, he could not bring himself to let go of it. Once in a while, a car went by, but no one showed the least interest in him.

Occasionally, he rode the horse off the road, never going more than a few hundred feet or attempting to hide his tracks in any way. He had no intention of keeping the horse, but its use was saving him a lot of walking. He was still on the road to Bieber when the sun went down. A full moon came up and since it was easy to follow the road in the moonlight, and there was virtually no traffic, he kept riding north. He had no inkling he was being followed until he heard the drone of an engine moving slowly behind him. He turned off the road and reined up among a stand of piñon trees. Peering at the road, awash with light from the moon, he saw two men on foot examining tracks under the glare of the headlights of a touring car being driven by a third man. Three horses were tethered to the car's rear bumper. He judged whoever was following him was good—too good— at tracking. He put his hand over the muzzle of the horse and waited. He watched as the searchers slowly worked their way past him to disappear over the next hill.

Johnny was in a quandary. He did not know the country and could only guess how many men were on his trail. The men with the car might be part of a larger posse that could be scouring the area looking for him. His only recourse was to get rid of the incriminating evidence, so he decided to let the horse go.

"Well, boy," he said, "I guess you and me better part company." He lifted the halter and saddle off the horse, and carried the gear farther back in the trees. He bedded down like a hibernating bear and slept four hours. When he got up, knowing the posse had long since bypassed him, he continued up the road following them.

Church and his posse had picked up the trail again and followed it for part of the night, then it disappeared.

"Looks like he gave us the slip," Church commented, dejected over their lack of success.

"He has so far," said tracker Baughman

Long looked at both of his companions. "What now?"

"We camp here. My guess is we went past him," said Baughman.

Sheriff Church always enjoyed seeing the tracker at work. He seldom missed anything. "How do you figure?" he asked.

"The tracks were fresh to the minute, and then gone. We might even see him on the road tomorrow."

"Without my horse?" Long asked.

"Of course," the tracker said.

They made camp and then hid the car in the bushes.

They broke camp at daybreak. They saddled up and proceeded to trace their steps on horseback, as horses were less noisy than the vehicle. Also, horses would be needed if the fugitive headed for the back country. The three men had only traveled a quarter of a mile in a southerly direction when they saw a man walking toward them. Even if the posse had not been looking for anyone, the stranger still would have attracted their attention. He was hiking along a road where there were no houses or other settlements for many miles in either direction. Mostly, people who traveled that stretch were either riding in a car or were astride a horse. Since the posse had no description of the rustler, Sheriff Church, in a low voice, advised them to ride right by him. "We have to connect the thief with the horse, or we got no case," he whispered.

As soon as the stranger was out of sight, Baughman dismounted, and kneeling in the road, examined the hiker's footprints. The hobnails of the man's boots stood out in the caked dust of the road.

"That's our man all right," he said straightening up.

"Yeah, Henry, but those tracks don't do me any good until you connect them with the horse," Church said.

Baughman remained afoot and they continued following the stranger's back trail.

Suddenly, the tracker stopped and held up his hand. "Look here," he said pointing down, "the tracks go off the road."

After a brief search in a copse of piñon trees, Baughman shouted. "Here we are."

Church and Long rode up and dismounted.

"You see the hobnailed imprints with the three nails missin'?"

Church and Long nodded.

"They're the same as the feller on the road," Baughman offered. "We must have been pressin' him pretty close last night."

"Now at least we know what he looks like," said Church.

"Okay, here's your barefoot horse, he ain't hard to tell."

"Yes, that's the bay," said Long.

"I'll bet if we follow these here horse tracks back a little farther in the trees we'll find your saddle and halter," Baughman said. "Maybe even the horse."

Church and Long eyed the tracker as a crow hopped along the trace of a trail. In a short time he had found the horse's paraphernalia, but not the horse.

"Good work, Henry," Church said. "That's all I need for an arrest."

"Yeah," said Baughman, "if we can find the hombre."

"What do mean?" Long asked.

Baughman grimaced. "By this time he knows we're after him. Wouldn't surprise me none if he parted with the road for a spell."

They returned to the road, and all being mounted, cantered up the stranger's trail.

Johnny, having recognized the three horsemen as his trackers of the night before, had walked boldly by them. He now realized how tight a situation he was in. He knew it would be only a matter of an hour or so before the posse would return. He thought that since the horse was gone there would be no way of tying him to the theft. Never once did he think his hobnailed boots were a dead give-away. To be on the safe side, he abandoned the road and descended a canyon too steep for the posse to follow. He continued north for a short time then doubled back, walking south toward Susanville.

Church, Baughman, and Long passed their well-hidden auto and followed the trail to where it left the road and terminated at the brink of a steep tree-lined canyon.

Baughman, who had dismounted again, shook his head in disgust. "Slip-perier than a rattler," he said.

"Well, old-timer, you've met your match this time," Church commented.

Baughman possessed an inexhaustible reserve of patience. If he gave up each time the trail became tedious and seemingly hopeless, he would never have been involved in the tracking craft to begin with.

"Maybe I have and maybe not. If we git the auto and we keep agoin' north, I'll betcha he'll come back to the road again."

"Why?" asked Long. "Seems to me he'd know we'd find him."

Baughman shook his wise old head. "It's funny about some people. They figure they're pretty cagey, but like animals they come up with habits they don't even know they have. He's got somethin' in mind, and like a beaver makin' for his house, he's just got to go there."

"It doesn't make sense," Long said.

Church smiled. "If he did make sense, he wouldn't have stolen the horse in the first place."

The men rode back, dismounted, and took to the car again, riding north at a slow pace. They went on for about an hour. During that time several vehi-cles, including a bus, passed them.

Baughman, who was atop the front fender, suddenly held his hand up, sig-naling Long to stop the car.

"Drat it!" he said. "I've been a fool. Pull off the road so's the auto can't be seen."

"What's up?" Long asked.

"Simple, I'll bet he doubled back like a mule deer does before he goes to bed."

They waited for an hour and saw no one other than a few riders and cars that went by in both directions.

Long was confused by the movements. "Where the hell is he now? So far when we first saw his tracks he was heading north. After that he camped off the road and let us by. Am I right so far?" he asked.

"Yeah," said Baughman.

Long continued, "We camped, and the next morning doubled back on our own tracks to head south. We passed the sonofagun who had again taken to the road going north, or was it south?"

"North," Baughman averred, "like you said, at that point we were headin' south."

"Okay," Long said. "We found his camp and the saddle and halter. He'd let the horse loose, then we turned around and went north following him."

"Yer right on," Baughman said, smiling.

"Now you figure he's behind us again," Long said.

"Yeah, he thought we'd catch up to him, so he doubled back behind us, and probably watched us go by."

Sheriff Church, though not the tracker Baughman was, comprehended the criminal mind just as well or even more so than Baughman. "He also might not be behind us," he said.

"What do you mean?" Long asked.

"What he means," Baughman broke in, "is that he mighta been aboard that there bus that passed us."

"So he could be north of us again?" Long asked.

"Yes," Sheriff Church said interrupting. "He could be halfway to Bieber by now, if that's where he's going."

"Funny guy," Long said.

"Yeah," said the sheriff, "he's been followed before."

Questioning people along the way, they found out a man answering their description had taken the bus to Bieber. They drove to Bieber only to find out from the stage driver that he had not picked up anyone.

Ever patient, they drove back to the spot they had last looked and continued their search for footprints. In a short time Baughman spotted faint marks and followed them until they left the road and descended into a flat where some old cabins were huddled together about a quarter of a mile away.

"That's the old Gehrig place," Church said.

Keeping to the trees, the posse approached the cluster of shacks to see smoke rising from the stovepipe of one.

"If my guess is right, we'll probably find our rustler in there," Baughman commented, pointing to the shack.

Church deputized the other two men. They drew their guns and advanced on the cabin from three sides.

Johnny had indeed returned to the cabin. Having let the horse go, he had not fathomed that he could be identified as the man who stole it. He decided that if anyone was caught it would be his erstwhile partner who had chosen to flee across country on the other horse.

Feeling secure in his shack, Johnny was brewing a mulligan stew with what little grub he had when the sound of a commanding voice caused him to lift his head in surprise.

"Come out with your hands up," Church ordered.

Having no guns to make a stand, Johnny did as he was ordered, quickly deciding his only recourse was to deny everything.

Church flashed his badge while Long and Baughman covered him.

"We're putting you under arrest for stealing a horse," Church said gruffly.

"I didn't steal a horse," Johnny said. "I've been here all day."

"We'll see," Church countered. "Take off your boots and we'll have a look."

Johnny reluctantly removed his boots. Baughman examined them and turned to the sheriff. "He's your man all right, count the hobnails."

Church looked grimly at Johnny and asked him his name.

"Charley Johnson," Johnny lied.

"Okay, Johnson, we'll have to take you in," Church said and turned to his deputies. "Check the cabin and see what you can find in the way of identification or anything else." In his own mind, the sheriff doubted they would find anything. The kid he was looking at was just one of literally hundreds of destitute drifters who were constantly passing through the country. They were not so much a menace as they were an aggravation. There was no work for them. They'd steal a horse just to get somewhere rather than sell it and make a profit. But the law did not differentiate as to purpose—a stolen horse was still a stolen horse. Even if the owner regained the steed, there was still a loss incurred looking for it.

Long and Baughman searched the cabin and found nothing more than a few old coats, but no papers.

"Just a drifter," the tracker said as he emerged from the cabin. "There's nothin' here."

Johnny was escorted back to Susanville and locked up in the Lassen County jail. The men of the posse noted that he was a man of few words, answering their questions only in monosyllables.

Sheriff Church and Long took his shoes to the Sierra Packing Company corral and compared them to the footprints made at the time of the theft and found they were the same. A little while later the bay gelding was brought in. At least Long had got one horse back. It had wandered onto the Anderson place near the foot of Hayden Hill on the road to Bieber. Long identified him as the same one that had been stolen. The net of circumstantial evidence drew tighter around Johnny, now in jail for the third time.

Long filed a complaint on May 28, 1921, charging Charles W. Johnson with grand larceny. Three days later, bail was set at $5,000 by M. R. Arnold, justice of the peace for Honey Lake Township.

Johnny remained confined because he could not put up bond money. A preliminary hearing was held on June 1.

Johnny felt like a ping-pong ball being whacked back and forth by the justice system. It was all beyond him, though he had learned one thing, and that was to admit to nothing. He was generally silent at the hearing other than to ask a few innocuous questions. Sufficient evidence was presented by the district attorney to indict him. Johnny elected to be tried by a jury, and since he was out of funds, an attorney was provided for him by the court. His attorney was unusually succinct in his observations and talents and earned Johnny a hung jury. He was tried again, and again the same attorney managed to prevail and won another hung jury. This was not good enough for Johnny and he asked for another lawyer, and on the third trial he was convicted. Application for probation was denied, and on August 12, 1921, Johnny was given an indeterminate sentence, the minimum time being one year.

The next day, Johnny, under the alias Charles W. Johnson, walked again into the corridors of another state penitentiary, this time San Quentin at San Anselmo, California. This lockup was only a few miles across the bay from San Francisco. He was there for a month, and was then transferred to Folsom State Prison, twenty-two miles southeast of the state capital, Sacramento.

Situated on the American River, Folsom Prison had been in operation for forty-two years when Johnny was incarcerated in the notorious Building Five, the first cell block built at the prison. It consisted of two wings that stood two stories high, with 162 cells in one wing and 166 cells in the other. Constructed entirely of granite blocks, the cells were seven feet by nine feet, with nine-foot ceilings. The doors to the cells were made of heavy iron, with a seven-inch slot that served for ventilation. Also a few holes had been drilled through the outside wall to allow for additional circulation of air. There were no sanitary facilities other than two wooden buckets, one for water, and the other for a toilet. Electric lights had been newly installed but were more off than on because of the inadequacy of the system, and frequently the prisoners reverted to the one kerosene lamp in the cell. If the prisoners ran out of their monthly supply of kerosene they spent the rest of the month in darkness.

Despite the fact that additional quarters had been opened by the time Johnny arrived there, Building Five was vastly overcrowded. He shared his cell with three other inmates. Their only relief from the oppression of the seven-by-nine cell was the alternative of working in the dreaded rock quarry. There the men broke rocks that were fed into a crusher, which supplied the California Department of Highways with construction material. The heat in the airless pit of the quarry was almost unbearable, but it was still better than rotting in Building Five.

Johnny was the "victim" of an indeterminate sentence, which meant that the state could prescribe the length of his jail time. The final sentencing was left up to the prison board, which could hold off levying it for a year or more. Johnny was wracked by the torment of not knowing what they were going to do for a whole year.

The agony of Folsom was too much for some. One man attempted suicide by drinking carbolic acid. Another placed his head under the rear wheel of a truck and let it pass over him, and a third took his own life by leaping off the fifth tier of Building Two.

Finally, Johnny was summoned to appear before the prison board, but by this time he had steeled himself to disappointment. He was prepared for the worst, but even he was not ready for the sentence that was handed out to him— seven and a half more years in jail! All for temporarily taking a horse that he had let go. His way of surviving such a jolt was, in effect, to die inside. From that instant on, he sheathed his personality—even his soul—in a protective shell of intransigence and stopped living for anyone else but himself. The agony of the imposed jail term prodded Johnny to plan an escape, but fortunately, before his plans came to fruition, he was paroled at Christmas, December 22, 1922.

# Chapter 9

# ANYOX, TELEGRAPH TRAIL, AND THE PONY

At the young age of twenty-three, Johnny was already sick of people. After having been crammed into prisons for almost five years, he was ready for a new start. He had heard that jobs were available in the mines of northern British Columbia, Canada's westernmost province. The huge undeveloped country hungered for men, therefore a general informality allowed for easy ingress to Canada. He eventually gained employment as a carpenter at Anyox, a copper mining camp that included a smelter. It was situated ninety miles up Observatory Inlet from the Pacific port city of Prince Rupert. Anyox was a "closed" camp of fifteen hundred souls, and a melting pot of Chinese, Australians, Finns, Swedes, Americans, New Zealanders, homegrown Canadians, and scores of other nationalities.

Johnny's first view of the mining camp was a disappointing one. The mine's smelter spewed forth smoke and fumes and made Anyox look like it had been under a perennial attack of mustard gas. Trees clinging to the surrounding mountains were no more than limp skeletons, and a fire that had swept the surrounding valley and hills created a wasteland that was hardly an improvement over the drab concrete of Folsom Prison.

Under the name Art Nelson, Johnny was hired as a carpenter and put to work on a gang repairing a trestle that supported a water pipeline to the mining community. Johnny worked steadily, keeping to himself most of the time, and accomplished his work with minimal conversation. He would pull his shift, go back to the bunkhouse provided for the men, eat, and go to bed. After being there three months he felt cooped up and miserable. It wasn't much different than his time in jail and he wanted out. During the nights, he planned his escape, as he had done many times when he was a prisoner, but now the way out was only limited by the amount of funds he needed to purchase an outfit so he could hunt and trap. Though he kept to himself most of the time, Johnny eventually became friendly with another carpenter who didn't pry into his business. This man, Swede Hutchings, often joined him at lunch hour. Johnny found out that

Hutchings was not really a Scandinavian at all, but because he was blond and blue-eyed, he had been tagged with the nickname. His first name was Oswald, and though he was about the same age as Johnny, he had many years' experience trapping, hunting, and prospecting in the interior.

One day over their lunch buckets, Johnny mentioned to his coworker his plans to head for the interior.

"Swede, you've been places I'd like to go. Could you give me a line on them?"

"Sure," Hutchings said, "any place in particular?"

"Not really,"

"Can't beat the Bell-Irving country," Hutchings said.

"The Bell-Irving?"

Hutchings laughed. "Yeah, that's the name of some explorer or politician or something."

"It's really wild country?"

"Unbelievable. But as far as you're concerned it's easy to get to." Hutchings grabbed a board, and with his carpenter's pencil drew a crude map. "Here's where we are," he said, scratching an X on the map. "You go around here, and up the Nass River to an Indian town called Aiyanch," he said, scratching another X on the map. "Got that?"

Johnny nodded.

"Okay, from there you follow the grease trail made by the natives to a telegraph line, and from there you go north."

"Grease trail? I don't get you."

"Indians along the coast pack fish oil inland, where they trade it to the tribes of the interior for furs and stuff."

Johnny nodded. "What's the story of the telegraph line?"

"That was built to run to the Yukon Territory during the gold rush. They got a trail all the way."

"Any possibility of missing it?"

"Nah, right before you reach it you go through a Tlingit town called Kuldo. Ask 'em," Hutchings advised.

Johnny patiently worked another three months accumulating a grubstake to purchase the supplies and gear he would need to go north. This included a twenty-two-foot skiff equipped with a twelve-horsepower outboard motor he purchased from another worker at the mine, and a Shetland pony that would pull the sled he was building. One day after work, Johnny asked Hutchings if he'd take a look at the sled. Hutchings accommodated him, then spoke: "Art, it's a fine job but too big for a dog."

"I'm not going to use a dog."

"You're not?"

"No, that's for a pony."

Hutchings shook his head. "I'm sorry, Art. I figured you were going to use dogs. The pony won't do up here."

"Why not?"

Hutchings turned around and pointed toward the mountains. "The snow-fall—it's too deep for a horse to browse. You need a meat eater like a dog. You can feed him game you shoot."

Johnny was still skeptical. "I can handle a horse better than I can a dog."

Hutchings nodded. "I agree, but in forty feet of snow you can't."

"I'll take my chances," Johnny said.

Hutchings realized that his friend was committed. There was no sense in trying to discourage him. "I suppose it's worth a try," he agreed.

Finally, in early September it came time for Johnny to leave. At the last minute he bought a .40–60 model 1876 Winchester from Hutchings for fifteen dollars. Hutchings helped him assemble his outfit and load it onto the skiff, including the pony. It was as odd looking a lash-up as Hutchings had ever seen, but he couldn't bring himself to joke about it with his serious friend. One last adjustment of the Seagull motor was made, and he was ready to leave. Hutchings held the lines for Johnny as he pulled the starting cord and the engine caught on the first pull. Hutchings threw the lines aboard and shouted his last piece of advice.

"Remember, when you get around the point, run into Kincolith for gas, then head up the Nass."

Johnny waved. "Okay," he said.

Hutchings waved good-bye. He was sad and a little envious. He had enjoyed talking with his quiet companion, and doubted he would ever see him again. That was the way it was in the camps, but now Hutchings had a wife and child living with him. His days of tramping the wilderness were over. He watched the skiff and the outline of the man and the pony until he could see it no more, then walked to his home at Anyox.

The trip down Alice Arm to Observatory Inlet was one of elation for Johnny. It was cold on the water, but he did not mind it. The exhilaration of being truly free blotted out any momentary physical inconvenience. The inlet was as smooth as glass and he had little to do but gaze at the magnificent scenery bordering the waterway. He vaguely recalled the fjords of Norway when he was a boy and he wondered why he had not thought about his home country more often. Though but six when he emigrated, it was not so young an age that he could not recall the stark beauty of Nordlands province. He thought of his mother and father and how their yearning for Norway almost overwhelmed them at times, especially when they gazed upon the monotonous plains of western North Dakota.

Johnny guided the little boat as it put-putted in a southerly direction toward Observatory Inlet. A drum seine fishing boat passed him. He saw a crewman run into the cabin and bring out another man. The two looked at him unbelievingly and then waved. Johnny did not wave back. He realized the reason for their behavior. It was not often that a fisherman saw a flat-bottomed riverboat with a pony and a sled aboard.

When he could, Johnny kept the boat near to shore. He did not want to get caught in the middle of the inlet if a storm came up. The tide was out and he could see gnarled driftwood among the cliffs. Ground swells surging against the gray walls flung white salt spray skyward like leaping ghosts. It was October and already the snow line was gradually creeping down the surrounding peaks and contrasted sharply with the dark green of spruce forests that loomed above the shoreline. Equally impressive was the verdant grass of the salt chucks browsed by deer. Overhead, billowy white clouds raced by like a herd of stampeding white mustangs, and closer, an endless procession of seagulls glided effortlessly above the water, only pausing to drop suddenly on unsuspecting fish.

"Pony," as Johnny called his little horse for want of a better name, did not seem to mind all this. Johnny at first worried that the horse would not take well to the confines of the small boat, but on the contrary the Shetland was not skittish. He tied the horse to a gunwale, but not so tightly that he could not be set free with one yank on the rope if the boat was threatened with any sort of a mishap.

A school of porpoises rose up ahead of the skiff and frolicked in the water around it like so many children. Then, as suddenly as they appeared, the porpoises submerged and were gone, and again Johnny, his pony, and the boat floated alone in the great fjord. They cruised steadily southwest, only stopping for Johnny to switch fuel tanks for his motor, and to take the pony ashore to stretch his legs.

They were nearing the junction of the Portland and Observatory inlets when Johnny spotted hundreds of round objects bobbing on the water. At first he thought they were the cork floats commonly used by fishermen in the area, but as he drew closer to them he realized they were seals. Hundreds of them were floating lazily with the tidal current. Johnny watched one dive and occupied himself by counting the minutes until it came up again. The curious seals seemed unconcerned as he steered the boat among them. The pony looked at these strange creatures as though he were trying to figure out what they were. His ears perked up when he heard their coarse croaks.

"Pony, I doubt if you've ever heard a seal before," Johnny said out loud. The horse's head bobbed as though he understood.

Johnny laughed at the little horse's antics and lay back with one elbow resting on the stern while the other flopped lazily over the steering arm of the outboard guiding the craft. Suddenly, a terrible commotion ensued twenty yards off the starboard. The water boiled, and at the same time, the forlorn cry of a seal in distress reached Johnny's ears as a thirty-foot killer whale rose up out of the sea with the mammal in its mouth and bit it in half. The head of the seal flopped convulsively and fell into the water with a sickening splash. The whale was so close that the blood spurting from the mortally wounded creature fell like rain on Johnny and the pony. The horse reared in fright as the boat rocked dangerously. Johnny quickly shut off the engine and leaped to the bow with a rag and quickly tied it over the pony's eyes and calmed him down.

"Take it easy, boy," Johnny said in a soothing tone, though he did not feel that way himself. He looked ahead and saw another seal disappear in a red swirl only to be hurled fifteen feet into the air with one flipper torn off. Even before the mutilated seal came down, the giant white and black marauder of the deep danced on its tail to snare the hapless mammal in midair like a trout rising to a fly. It was a spellbinding spectacle of the brutal power of nature at its rawest. The sea ran red with blood as the seals attempted to escape their attackers. Johnny saw a seal flop his way up to a ledge in an effort to avoid one of the huge predators, but the killer whale plucked him neatly from his perch and disappeared into the watery depths.

Johnny had stood absolutely still, his hand protectively over the pony during the massacre—which ended as quickly as it began. A few seals had climbed to safety, but many others had met as bloody a fate as anything Johnny had ever seen. He turned his head slowly, afraid the whales would come again, though he saw no evidence of them. Even the blood had quickly disappeared with the tidal drift. The scene was again utterly tranquil as though the whales' attack had been nothing but a bad dream. The only sound now was the persistent lapping of swells against the skiff.

Johnny patted the pony's head. "Take it easy, boy," he said, "it's all over." He returned to the stern of the boat, pulled the starting lanyard, and was on his way again.

The stark, bloodcurdling attack he had witnessed was difficult to forget, and only when Johnny reached Kincolith, a small native village sprawled along the banks of the Nass at its mouth, did he relax. He went ashore to refill fuel cans, and walked the pony to some grass. He let the animal graze for an hour and then set out again upriver to Aiyansh.

Johnny noticed the farther upriver he went, the lower the snow line. He was relieved to see enough snow to use his sled when he reached Aiyansh. He sold his boat and motor to a Tsimshian for fifty dollars, then hitched up the pony and set out over the grease trail for Kuldo. He reached it with little difficulty only to find the town deserted. As Hutchings had instructed, he ventured a few miles farther until the path hit the trail of the telegraph line. Then he turned left and followed it.

As Johnny and the pony plunged north into the heart of the mountains, the footpath wound through thick forests of hemlock and fir so high the way seemed in perpetual darkness. Occasionally Johnny and the pony had to veer off to avoid obstructions. One time Johnny had walked ahead of the horse, clearing the trail. He grabbed hold of the stem of a resilient plant with huge green leaves on its stalks, only to find his palms and fingers stuck full of hundreds of pinhead-sized thorns. He tried brushing them off, but only pushed them in deeper. Next, he attempted to pull out the microscopic needles, but it was a tedious job, and more often than not he was unsuccessful. His hands swelled up after a few days until they were half again larger than normal. Only then did he discover that he could remove the needles by squeezing the little pus sacks that encased them. The thorns would pop out with the substance that had surrounded them. Johnny's experience with this plant, devil's club, was not soon forgotten. Although pesky, it did not delay him.

Hutchings had told him cabins could be found along the trail about every twenty-five miles, explaining there were three types: quarter cabins, which were just shelters; halfway cabins equipped with stoves, utensils, and bunks; and full cabins with a telegrapher and a trail maintenance man and their equipment.

"There's no way you can die up there if you can hike twenty-five miles," Hutchings had said. "Just make sure when you camp it isn't in an avalanche area."

Snow was light at first and Johnny and the pony worked well together. It was near dark when he spotted a cabin and on his approach found that there was no door. He saw that the inside of the structure was ramshackle, obviously having been abandoned for a few years. Probably a quarter cabin, he figured, seeing that there was no bunk. But there was an old, rickety stove in good enough shape to hold a fire, and he'd rather have a stove than a bunk anytime. Johnny fed the pony, then moved his gear into the shack and lighted a candle for illumination. After taking care of those chores he built a fire in the stove, heated water, and drank tea, then ate some biscuits. This made him drowsy. He crawled into his sleeping bag, snuffed out the candle, and promptly went to sleep.

The squawk of a raven awakened Johnny in the morning. He opened his eyes to find that a porcupine was gnawing on a log with its deadly quill-laden tail right next to his face. Johnny's arms were inside his sleeping bag and could not be used to fend off the animal. The sweat poured off his brow as he waited for the "quill pig" to move away, but the critter seemed content where he was. Finally, the porcupine waddled a few feet and Johnny rolled quickly in the opposite direction. He stood up and herded the animal out of the cabin, and then stared after it, amazed that so gentle a creature could present such a danger.

Johnny repacked his gear, and hitching the pony to his sled, set out again. The little horse could still get grass, but as Johnny worked his way farther north and to a higher elevation the snow became deeper, too deep for the pony to graze, so he began feeding him the oats he had brought along. At one point along the way, a telegrapher had offered him hospitality, but Johnny declined. He pushed on through heavy snow, wearing snowshoes to break trail for the pony. Perspiration poured down his shoulders and sides in a virtual flood. Each time he brought up his snowshoes, snow rested on the webbing, causing that much more weight to be lifted with each step. He never realized how difficult snowshoeing could be.

Eventually, between the ninth and tenth cabins he climbed to an elevation where not even the most gallant pony could go. Johnny realized in the long run that Hutchings had been right. There was too much snow to allow the little horse to graze, and the oats he had packed along were now gone. He would have to destroy the animal. Normally, he could do this with nary a qualm. He had lived with horses all of his life and possessed no romantic illusions about them. Though he enjoyed working with the creatures, they were often stubborn, cantankerous, and not above literally biting the hand that fed them. Horses were a vehicle for man's use, and Johnny did not see them any other way, particularly as pets. But disposing of the little horse would be hard to do. He and the pony had shared and survived an ordeal that had brought them to the brink of death, and after a shared experience such as that, to kill the pony seemed unfair. The option, however, was even worse. If he released the animal to forage for himself he was bound to starve and in the process probably be torn apart by wolves, whose tracks were prevalent all along the trail.

Johnny unhooked the traces and pulled the sled around the horse. Reluctantly, he removed his rifle from under the tie ropes of the sled, then walked back to the little animal.

"Pony," he said pointing the rifle at him, "I have to do this. Understand? If I don't, the wolves will get you." He pulled the trigger and the rifle kicked hard against his shoulder. The forehead shot killed the animal immediately. There was no lingering death as he would have suffered from carnivorous wolves, or a passing cougar, or even a raging wolverine. His eyes watery, he stared at the pony for a long time. Finally he broke away, hitching himself up to the sled. He commenced pulling it, but found the sleigh too ponderous in the deepening snow, and abandoned it. From now on he would pack his supplies on his back and advance them in relays. Johnny had snowshoed before, but never under such adverse conditions as he now met. A chinook wind blew in and rising temperatures made snowshoeing a nightmare. The snow balled up under his heels, making it difficult to walk. He cut a stick and at every step whacked the webbing of the snowshoes in order to remove the snow. He tried tethering his feet to the cross braces to make the snow-laden shoes easier to lift. It worked for a while but was painful to his feet. Attempting another tactic, he fastened thongs to the tips of his snowshoes and literally hoisted them with each step. This helped some, but not enough to ease the agony of leg muscles unaccustomed to such an effort.

In the end, Johnny had no trouble surviving this journey. His supplies accounted for that, as well as the fact that the trail was relatively easy to follow because of the line's maintenance men. It was their job to clear away any windfall. He came across their tracks in the snow, but usually missed them except when he reached their "live-in" cabins. They were kindly and helpful, though he resisted the temptation to stay with them. This had more to do with the fact that he did not want to dip into their supplies when he knew that they themselves were running short. It was all part of the code of conduct prevalent in the North.

# Chapter 10

# WINTERING AT ECHO LAKE

Johnny had been on the trail three weeks, feeling himself getting stronger with each day's toil. Ultimately, in a storm, he holed up at a halfway cabin, which was better equipped than most. He collapsed on the shack's spruce pole bunk and fell into a deep sleep. He awoke in the morning with a man tugging at his shoulder. "Want some pancakes?" the man asked evenly. Johnny's shoulders ached, yet his legs were losing some of their earlier stiffness. It took him a while to shake the sleep out of his eyes. "Yeah, thanks," he said.

"I came in last night. Saw you sleepin' and let you be," the man said while putting a couple of tin plates on the hewn board table.

Johnny had come a long way and was not much for talking, but he did not have to be, as the newcomer carried on with little need for encouragement. The big, square-shouldered man, whom Johnny judged to be in his fifties, placed a pile of pancakes and a bottle of syrup on the plank table. He sat down opposite Johnny. "I'm fillin' in for Tom Hankin, the regular telegrapher at Echo Lake. He's been up here so long he's a little bushed."

Johnny nodded. "Just where am I?"

"This cabin is right at what we call the second crossing of the Bell-Irving River," the man said. "Hell of a nice spot in the summer. The area's got everything. Rainbows, access to lake trout and salmon. Bear, sheep, goats, deer, and moose. You name it."

"That's what a friend of mine told me," Johnny said, thinking of Hutchings's recommendation. He noticed the telegraph man was not inquisitive, and he liked him for it.

"You want a job?" the lineman asked.

Johnny wasn't prepared for that, and he had to smile. *People all over the country are looking for work, and here I stumble across a job in the middle of nowhere*, Johnny thought.

"Doing what?" he asked.

"All you have to do is keep the line clear from the north end of Echo Lake as far as the next quarter cabin," the man said eagerly.

"Any pay?" Johnny asked.

"Well, no," his companion replied, aware of the tight budget he was on.

"I'm planning to trap," Johnny said. "That's why I came up here."

The lineman pondered this for a minute, then the words came in a flood. "I'll tell you what. We all take skins up here. It boosts our income. You can trap to hell and gone, and I'll buy the furs. You won't get top price, but it will save you a whale of a lot of backpackin', and in a sense you'll be gettin' paid because you can run your trapline along the string of lakes that runs parallel to the trail."

Johnny pondered the proposal, and said, "I don't know."

The lineman had seen scores of men in different situations, and it came across plainly that the blond, Scandinavian-looking youth in front of him was a loner, and there was nothing more important to such a man than to be by himself. "If you're worrying about bein' crowded up here, you won't see more than five people all winter, I'll guarantee you that."

"Sounds okay," Johnny said.

"The trappin' ain't bad out of Echo," the lineman said. "I'll be runnin' Hankin's line this way. Is that a deal then?"

Johnny nodded and they shook hands.

"What's your name?" the lineman asked.

"Mine's Art Nelson, what's yours?"

"Bill Elder."

The lineman was a big help to Johnny, thanks to his dog team of five one-hundred-pound malamutes. He insisted on loading Johnny's supplies onto his freight sled.

"We got about twenty-five miles to go," he said, and added, "A good part of it is climbing Nigunsaw Pass."

"Won't it be tough on your dogs?" Johnny asked.

"These critters?" Elder said incredulously. "They can haul five hundred pounds easy. Your load and what little I got ain't half that. Besides, the trail's broken."

Johnny helped Elder walk the dogs into their soft leather collars, which he noted were not much different than those used on horses, and similarly, in tandem. The dog sled was about twelve feet long. The lineman put a tarp on it and packed Johnny's gear and his own aboard the sled. Then he wrapped the tarp around the bundles and lashed them down. He stuck his .30–30 Winchester and Johnny's .40–60 under the lash rope.

"Hop aboard," the lineman said. Johnny looked dubiously at the sled and the dogs.

Elder smiled. "Don't worry about them. They can pretty handily pull two hundred pounds each. That makes a total of a thousand. Even with you and me riding, it's way less."

Johnny climbed onto the sled and grabbed the lash ropes, and hung on. It beat walking.

They made a quick trip to the top of the pass, and stopped when they got a brief glimpse of the Nigunsaw River below. It dropped through a canyon that fortunately was wide enough for a trail.

"See those avalanche chutes," Elder said. "Well, in comin' here, I noticed a bunch of heavy cornices have built up at the top of them. You never know when they're gonna go, but you can reduce the odds of being hit by goin' past them in the morning."

Johnny's nod was enough for the lineman to expand on his theme.

The lineman pointed to the cornices. "It usually warms up a bit at mid-day, then when the sun goes down the temperature drops and refreezes the ground. This gives a nudge to the rocks, and they push out. One or two of 'em tumble and before you know it, you got an avalanche."

Johnny followed his gaze and there was no mistaking the chutes that had carved their way through huge stands of timber as if they had been sculpted with a knife. He counted at least six of them within a span of three or four miles.

"How about those cornices, what starts them?" Johnny asked.

"Wind builds them up and they get twenty, thirty feet high. They're top-heavy, and then they collapse and down they come," Elder said.

The two men set out with the dog team. The downhill run was quickly made, and they were soon following the trail as it twisted and turned along the river. One by one, they crossed the chutes. To Johnny, the slide crossings did not seem to be particularly dangerous. He figured that only a few avalanches might thunder down in an entire winter.

The two men finally broke out of the canyon and abruptly came to the telegrapher's camp. Staring down at it from a twenty-foot embankment that rose above, Johnny thought it looked like a den must look to a fox pup. Here was warmth and food and protection in the middle of the savage wilderness. The vast coastal range smothered the horizon on the west, while behind them several miles to the east, rose cliffs steep enough to chill the nerves of a mountain goat.

Johnny spent the night there, and then with the telegrapher's dog team he moved his gear to the northwestern end of Echo Lake.

Johnny built a temporary shelter using his tarp. He bent several trees that he tied his perishable food duffels to and then let the trees spring into the air. There the foodstuffs would be immune to the inroads of foxes, coyotes, and wolves. He did not want to build a permanent cache until he had ventured forth to study the area. It would be foolish to build a cache and then start laying traps and deadfalls and snares if there was no sign of game. One thing about winter, tracks did not lie. Even the craftiest of animals could not hide its footprints and he had seen plenty as he walked through the wilderness of northern British Columbia.

The next day he set out in a northwesterly direction, carefully examining the tracks and spoor of the animals as he went. They were all represented there—the various members of the canine species—with the tiny paws of the fox, the larger coyote, and the immense feet of the wolf. Johnny had large hands, which were about six inches from the palm to the tip of his fingers. One wolf's front paws spanned his hand.

A day's walk brought him through a string of little lakes extending in a northwest direction. He found the tracks of moose, the splayed feet of the caribou, and hoofprints of deer. There was visible evidence of the passage of weasel, marten, fisher, and the formidable wolverine, one of the great pirates and fighters of the animal world.

Ravens and blue jays set up a racket as he passed near them. Ptarmigan winged away from their hiding places at virtually every step he took. He had already gained a taste for this "chicken" of the northern forests.

The entire setup looked passable to him and he decided to build a cabin at the lake about a quarter of a mile from the telegrapher. It took him a month to do it, but he had nothing but time now that he was free. He learned one thing, and that was never to build a cabin in the snow season if it was possible to avoid it. The first time he cut a tree down it virtually disappeared in the ten-foot floor of snow. He eventually solved the problem of moving logs by borrowing the telegrapher's dog team.

That winter he trapped, spending most of his time on the move, checking his sets, which varied from steel traps to snares and deadfalls. Since the trapline ran parallel to the telegraph line it was easy to keep open. In trapping he had some success, taking fox, marten, lynx, weasel, and in the spring shooting a dozen muskrat. He did not expect anything other than rock-bottom prices, and that is what he got from Elder. However, he had to admit to himself, it beat toting the skins two hundred miles on his back to sell them.

One thing Johnny learned was that accumulating funds by trapping was a slow business. It was not that he needed a fortune, but for the amount of time involved, the funds he accrued were minimal. He was uneasy about it and he did not know why. He decided to try prospecting as a way of augmenting his income. He knew little about the subject, other than breaking quartz to look for indications of mineral content.

Spring came, followed by summer, and he backtracked part of the Nass River following a lead that Hutchings had mentioned to him. At the time he did not take the story very seriously because he was preoccupied with becoming a trapper, but now he looked at it from another perspective. If he was going to be in the wilderness anyway, why not be a prospector? He liked to walk and to camp and to fish and hunt, and he could do all those things while looking for ore samples. He wished he had thought more about it when he was at Anyox because there were plenty of books available on the subject of prospecting.

The one man who tipped him off on some of the guidelines of prospecting was Elder, who had apparently chased elusive metals for many years. Elder, though talkative enough, never mentioned where he was from or what he had done before he arrived in northern British Columbia. When a conversation veered in that direction, the friendly expression of Elder's face turned grim, and his eyes hardened. At such times, it was as if Elder were two individuals in one. Johnny wondered if he, too, had a past, but did not want to risk losing the man's confidence by asking him.

Backtracking the Nass, Johnny searched for a trapper's camp that was situated next to an Indian graveyard at the mouth of a creek flowing into the Nass.

The creek's canyon was supposedly so narrow at its upper reaches that a person could cross from one side of the canyon to another merely by felling a tree. Past that, and right at the timberline was supposed to be a ledge of quartz gold. Johnny had persisted in following the particulars of the story. However, he failed to put them all together at one creek. If the graveyard was there, the trapper's camp was not, and vice versa. Likewise, canyons were in evidence, but not one narrow enough to fell a tree across.

Johnny headed back to his cabin in September.

Hankin, the regular telegrapher, was now back at his post. He knew someone was approaching by the howling of the dogs.

"Shut up, you mangy curs," he spat at the dogs.

Seeing Johnny approach, he waved him in.

"Where's Bill?" Johnny asked.

"You know him, huh?" Hankin said.

"Yes," Johnny said. He figured the man must be the regular telegrapher in these parts.

"He's gone back to his mine."

Johnny scratched his head. "I didn't know he had one."

Hankin ignored his comment. "You must be the guy he mentioned."

"That's right," Johnny said. "I put up a cabin at the north end of Echo."

"Seen it," said Hankin. "Have a seat. You're just in time for baked beans and some of my sourdough biscuits."

Having heard that Hankin was bushed, Johnny was going to turn down the invitation but was starved for news. "Okay," he said, dumping his pack.

Elder, though friendly enough, had not been the sociable type. In fact, Johnny had never even been in the telegrapher's cabin but once and then at night. Now, he looked around. This shack was luxurious compared to his own place. The walls were lined with canned goods, books, magazines, papers, traps, skins, and a collection of guns that would make a gun dealer proud. There were two bunks, a homemade desk with the telegraph key on it, another table for eating, and two stoves, one a range to cook on, and the other a barrel stove for heating the premises. Hurricane oil lamps were used to light the cabin.

The telegrapher served up the beans.

"Where'd you winter?"

"North end of Echo," Johnny replied.

"Trap?"

"Yes."

"How'd you do?" Hankin asked.

"Okay, but it could have been better. A wolverine messed up my line."

"Ever trap before?"

"I did a little when I was a kid in North Dakota. Nothing big though."

"Wolverines can be pesky. Did you get him?"

"No."

Hankin poured two mugs of hot coffee and put one in front of his own plate and one in front of Johnny.

"Well, son, I'll tell you how. By the way, what's your name?"

"Art Nelson."

"Mine's Hankin, as you probably know."

"I figured," Johnny said.

"The secret to catchin' the wolverine is to play on his greed. All you gotta do is hang up a fox or a lynx carcass over a circle of traps and you'll get him."

"I thought they were smarter than that."

Hankin spooned some beans into his mouth before replying. "No, no he's just gotta grab that meat even though he knows there are traps under it." He paused to gulp some more beans and then continued. "He's like a card player who joins a game of poker he knows is crooked, but he enjoys the game so much he plays anyway. He just can't help himself."

The two men finished off the beans, and then Hankin took out his pocket watch and looked at it. "In a couple of minutes the line will be open for the six o'clock transmission."

The telegrapher got up and went to a cupboard and put some salmon-berry jam on the table with newly baked biscuits.

"I guess you'd call this dessert," he said, then looked under the table. "Okay, Willy, you can come out now," he said.

Johnny wondered if the man's vacation had done him any good. "Who's Willy?" he asked patronizingly.

"You'll see," said Hankin.

A weasel scampered up to the telegrapher's plate where Hankin had left a few scraps of meat from the baked beans. "He takes care of my mouse population," Hankin said as Willy cleaned up what was left on the plate.

Suddenly the telegraph key began to click.

"That's the six o'clock run. I gotta relay it," Hankin said and moved to the desk.

Johnny stretched his arm horizontally on the table and the weasel ran up it and perched on his shoulder.

"Willy, get off our guest," the telegrapher said.

Johnny took the weasel in his hands and placed him on the table. "Is there anything interesting on the line?" Johnny asked.

Hankin shook his head. "No," he said, "just a lot of requests for supplies from Telegraph Creek. They need 'em in the gold rush."

"What gold rush?" Johnny asked.

"By golly, you wouldn't know about that," Hankin said.

Johnny was amazed that the man could transcribe the signals yet still carry on a conversation.

"Last fall two men found gold on a stream they named Goldpan Creek. Now the rush is on."

Johnny had never been in on a gold rush, and really was not that enthusiastic, but the news of one he found fascinating. "Where's the creek?" he asked.

"The strike is east of the town of Telegraph Creek about seventy miles or so," the lineman said.

"Sounds interesting."

"You ever chased gold?"

"I've looked once but never found anything," Johnny said.

The telegraph key quit clicking and the weasel had disappeared.

"Run's over," Hankin said, and resumed his seat at the food table. "You know, gold sickness, once it gets ahold of some, it creeps into their bones, even their souls, and clutches their brains 'til they die. Have you ever seen raw gold?"

"You mean in a stream?"

"Yeah."

"No."

Johnny noticed a funny look come into Hankin's eyes, almost like he was hypnotizing himself.

"You get a good pan and all of a sudden you don't see gold. You see dancin' girls in Paris or a warm beach in Hawaii, or a huge hotel suite in Hong Kong . . . . It's all there for the takin' at the bottom of the pan."

"You sound like you've been bitten."

"I have, but not so as I'd sell my soul for it," he said.

Johnny noticed that the telegrapher's eyes seemed to lose focus as if he were in some kind of trance.

"You want to see some?" Hankin added.

"See what?"

"Gold, of course."

"Sure."

Hankin went out the door and in a minute came back to the table and placed a vial on it. A gleam came to his eyes as he tipped the contents onto the table.

"That's coarse gold my boy," he said and laughed oddly. "Find plenty and you're beholden to no one. A man with gold in his pocket can tell the whole world to go to hell."

Johnny stared at the gold. He'd never seen gold nuggets before. They ranged in size from mouse droppings to one large one that could pass for a cough drop. He did not see Paris or Hong Kong, just the gold, but then he thought if he owned the gold maybe he would see some of those places.

Johnny glanced at Hankin who seemed to be lost in thought. "Not beholden, huh?" he said. "I'd better be going."

Hankin continued to stare at the gold, oblivious to everything around him.

Johnny grabbed his pack and walked to the door and turned around to see Hankin mesmerized by the view of his own gold. Johnny cleared his throat.

"Mr. Hankin!" he exclaimed. The sound of Johnny's voice brought the telegrapher back to the present. "Thanks for the grub."

Hankin signaled him off with a wave of the arm. "Glad to oblige," he said.

Walking back to his cabin, Johnny thought about the gold. He was not bitten by any fantasies, but he did reason out the fact that he was not far from the place of the gold rush and that some day he would kick himself if he did not join it.

That day he packed his gear and headed north.

# Chapter 11

# STAMPEDE TO GOLDPAN CREEK

Johnny reached Telegraph Creek after spending ten days on the trail. The town was built on the banks of the Stikine River. That a gold rush was in progress was fairly evident to Johnny as he trudged through the streets. There were people everywhere, scurrying this way and that. After a few queries he headed for the Hudson's Bay Company trading post.

Johnny found the emporium was about the same as the old country store near his home in North Dakota, the difference being the presence of furs rather than dollars. In fact, at times, sundries for sale were priced in furs. Skins were everywhere: hanging from the ceiling, fastened to fur stretchers strung on the walls, and attached to parkas as trim for hoods. Furs were used as well for fringes on mukluks and moccasins deposited in the post by the Tahltan Indians. Strings of *babiche*, strips of rawhide used in making the webbing of snowshoes, were prevalent. Summer goods such as mosquito netting, rubber boots, work pants and shirts, gold pans, citronella, tents, and rain gear filled the store. Canned and dehydrated foodstuffs crowded the shelves. Hudson's Bay blankets—so coveted by Indians—were on display. Implements with considerable utility such as levels, pickaxes, shovels, and barrels of nails and screws were crammed into every nook and cranny of the trading post. Bottles of elixirs advertised to cure everything from the common cold to bunions were jammed onto shelves reserved for medical supplies.

Johnny noticed that there was a distinct absence of goods normally purchased by women. However, calico was one item that went against that general rule, there being rolls and rolls of it. Johnny learned that Tahltan women designed and made dresses out of such material.

Catching the eye of a clerk, Johnny asked him the obvious.

"Do you know anything about the gold rush hereabouts?"

The clerk laughed. "Do I know anything? We're supplying most of it."

"Where is it?"

"Goldpan Creek? It's about seventy miles north to Dease Lake, then another fifteen or twenty miles northeast from there."

Johnny pondered the options, then spoke. "I guess I'll give it a try. Anything special I'll need?"

The clerk shrugged. "The usual pick, pan, and shovel, and if you're a stranger, a British Columbia free miner's certificate."

"What's a guy do for identification?" Johnny asked, trying hard not to display any sign of emotion.

"You got money, you'll get the certificate. Want the stuff?"

Johnny nodded.

The clerk brought out the equipment and pushed it across the counter to Johnny. "Anything else?"

Johnny picked up his gear. Since he had to pass the mining recorder's office anyway, he took it with him. Just as the clerk had predicted, all they wanted was his signature and the fifteen-dollar fee.

The next day Johnny started out on foot up the crude dirt road to Dease Lake. He was loaded down with a tremendous pack and noted that every type of conveyance in existence seemed to be on the road. This included horses, tractor-drawn trains pulling wagons, and cars and trucks of every vintage from 1900 to 1923. The appearance of so much equipment in so obscure a part of the world was truly amazing.

A Reo truck pulled up next to him and stopped. The driver hollered to him and asked him if he wanted a lift.

Johnny hesitated briefly. He could probably navigate the seventy miles or so quicker than the truck as the road was hardly more than a trail, but he accepted the ride anyway. He wondered how they got the equipment to Telegraph and asked the driver about it.

"How did you get your truck here?" he asked.

The driver smiled. "By boat up the Stickine River from Alaska."

Numerous muskeg swamps slowed them down, but they finally made it to Dease Lake by the end of the day.

The next day he and the driver parted ways. Johnny joined a group of men climbing the long uphill trail across the pass to the gold diggings. It took him three days. Here he easily found space to stake a claim and made camp. He crafted a sluice box in short order, and commenced shoveling dirt and gravel from the creek bank into the box. Then he ran water through it. The box consisted of a series of riffles that caught the larger rocks and gravel, which he picked off and discarded. Johnny mined the host material for days on end without success. Two months went by. He was just about to give up on the whole operation in disgust, when he panned out some flakes of gold, and then a tiny nugget not much bigger than the head of a nail. It wasn't much, but it was enough to lure him into digging for more. Pickings were rare, but came up often enough to keep him at his work for another month. By then even what the prospectors referred to as "colors," or gold flakes, were not appearing. However, the damage had been done. Old Hankin was right. There was something about gold, particularly placer or loose gold, that enticed a person. Johnny wondered himself what it was, and decided it must be the simplicity of it. When you found placer gold you did not have to do anything to it. You did not have to crush it. You did not have to treat it chemically. You did not have to obtain trucks or horses or mules to carry it. You did not have any trouble selling it. Placer gold stood on its own merits.

Johnny finally broke camp, then asked a man he identified as a gold buyer if he would weigh his gold.

The buyer took out a small portable scale and set it up on a box. He took Johnny's gold poke and emptied its contents onto one of the cradles and placed tiny scale weights on the other until the two were in balance.

"Twenty pennyweight," he said.

"How much is that?" Johnny asked. He disliked showing his ignorance, but he knew he had to learn some way.

The mining man smiled, "A *chechako,* eh?"

Johnny recognized the Chinook term.

"Yeah, I guess I'm a newcomer."

"You got an ounce, son. There's twenty pennyweight to the ounce."

"What's the price?" Johnny asked.

"Thirty-two bucks an ounce," the mining man said. "But, of course, it ain't pure, so it'll be a little less than that. You want to sell it?"

"Sure," Johnny said, and asked, "What do you mean by less than pure?"

The buyer shook his head impatiently. "The *fines* explain it. Goldpan Creek is about seven hundred fines."

Johnny was really lost now, but was determined to pursue the point. "I—"

"You want to know what 'fines' are," the man interrupted.

Johnny nodded.

"It's easy to figure out," the man said. "Pure gold is one thousand fines. There ain't much of that around. Each creek has sort of an average. With Goldpan Creek it's around seven hundred, so you multiply that number times thirty-two—the gold price—which figures out to be roughly twenty-two dollars, but I'll round it off at twenty-five."

"Okay," Johnny said. He had enough arithmetic to understand the rudiments of the buyer's figures. He took the money and shouldered his pack. Then he climbed again back the way he had come—to the summit of the pass between Goldpan Creek and Dease Lake. It was a natural place for a man to take a breather. He spotted several other men on their way out from the gold diggings. They had a fire going and welcomed him with a wave. He walked over to their campfire but did not sit down. One of the men detached himself from the others and greeted Johnny. He was slight of build but with a certain wiry toughness about him that belied his frame.

The man extended his hand. "My name's Bill Hanna," he said.

Johnny reluctantly put his hand forward. "Art Nelson," he said.

"You want a coffee?" Hanna asked.

"No thanks."

"Where you headed?"

Johnny did not really know. He could go back to Echo Lake, but there were actually plenty of better spots to set up. He liked the mountains, but at Echo he had had too much of them. They were so high and his cabin so situated, that the winter sun was rarely seen.

"No place in particular," he answered.

Hanna looked back at the group. They were unconcerned and didn't pay much attention to what he and the stranger were talking about.

"We're tramping back to Thibert Creek," he said.

"Any luck here?" Johnny asked.

"We didn't even try. We just came up to take a look."

"You live around here?"

"Yeah, lower end of Dease Lake."

Johnny figured he might as well ask this man about wintering somewhere. "I'm looking for a good place to trap," he said hopefully.

"You wouldn't be from the old country, would you?" Hanna asked.

Johnny did not think his accent showed that much, but then his mother and father had never learned the English language. "Yes, Norway," he said.

"I caught a trace of a Norsk accent, not much, but it's there," he said, smiling. "There's another Scandahoovian like yerself who's got a trapline so long he can hardly cover it. He might cut you in."

"Who's that?" Johnny asked.

"We all call him Big Knute."

"He got a last name?"

"Yeah, but he doesn't mention it much. Something about jumping ship somewhere."

Johnny had nothing better to do. "Sounds good, I might try it," he said.

"You can join up with us if you want," Hanna offered.

Johnny figured he'd rather travel alone. "Thanks, but I have a couple of things to do."

Johnny shouldered his pack and descended the trail to where he had left it to head east to Goldpan Creek. Once there, he hiked north. This path took him to the lower end of Dease Lake, which he had heard was named for some ancient explorer. Thibert Creek flowed into Dease's west side several miles from its northern outlet. He could see buildings at the foot of the creek on the other side. A trail ran down from the ridge above the lake and he followed it to the water, where he found a dock. Johnny concluded that if there was a dock, sooner or later someone would come along with a boat. Maybe he could pay the owner to take him across the lake.

Johnny built a lean-to and made camp. He would wait as long as he could. The weather was turning chilly, but he was not inclined to hang around until the lake froze.

Two days later a couple of fishermen saw him wave, and fetched him across the lake. They would not take any money for the service, merely setting him onto dry land at the mouth of Thibert Creek.

Johnny walked ashore and saw a man painting a boat that was overturned and resting on two saw horses. The man was tall, probably three or four inches over six feet, and big of frame. He straightened up as Johnny approached.

"Does a man by the name of Knute live around here?" Johnny asked.

"You're looking at 'im," the big man said.

"You know Bill Hanna?"

The man named Knute nodded. "Some," he said noting the newcomer's accent.

"Bill mentioned your name. I'm looking for a place to trap."

"You're Norwegian?" the big man asked.

"Yes, came over as a kid from Bardu," Johnny said.

Knute knew where it was. "That's Sami country," he said.

Johnny nodded. He was surprised over meeting someone acquainted with the actual name for Lapps.

"I'm from Stockholm," Big Knute said. "Have you done any trapping?"

"A little last winter at Echo Lake," said Johnny. "I made a little over four hundred dollars."

"Why didn't you stay there?"

"Heard about the Goldpan rush and figured I'd keep on going."

"From what I hear Goldpan Creek could have better," the Swede commented.

"I got an ounce in two months." Big Knute shook his head. "Not much for all the work." He had logged and prospected in a region stretching from Wisconsin to Montana. Born in Sweden, he had sailed before the mast and finally "tossed anchor" at New Orleans. Eventually Knute had made his way to Dease Lake, where he met an attractive and intelligent native woman of the Tahltan tribe, who was now his wife. Knute was not a man to turn down the appeal of a fellow Scandinavian.

"So you want to trap?"

Johnny nodded.

"Okay. I can't see any hurt in you taking the upper end of my line, since I don't have time to cover it. Throw your gear in that shack over there, and I'll take you up tomorrow."

"Thanks," Johnny said.

The next day, Knute took Johnny to the corral, and rounded up a packhorse and two others. Johnny threw a diamond hitch neatly on the horse and boxes of gear. Big Knute realized immediately that the newcomer knew his way around pack animals. They saddled up. Johnny was as easy with the horse as if he had been born on it.

While they rode up the creek, Knute gave Johnny a rundown on the gold operations along its banks. They climbed steadily until they were high above Dease Lake. Snow covered the ground here while it had not been present on the lake shore.

About twenty miles up, the Swede reined in his horse next to a fast-flowing stream that dumped clear water into Thibert Creek. "Here's as good a place as you'll find. You got fresh water, plenty of wood, you'll get the morning sun, and you got neighbors. To the south you have Sam Scottee and Phil Hankin, whose brother runs the telegraph station at Echo Lake. They're on Vowel Creek. And to the north on Mosquito Creek you'll find George Adsit. The Mosquito Creek trail leads to Teslin Lake and then it's downhill all the way to the Bering Sea."

"It's a nice enough spot," Johnny said.

"You'll have two more neighbors. They're George Ball and George Finn on Deloire Creek. Most of 'em will be staying for the winter trapping, so if you're stuck for anything they can help you."

Johnny nodded.

The two men unloaded all of Johnny's gear. Then his host stayed with Johnny for a few days helping him cut logs, which they yarded to the site with Knute's horses. That chore completed, Knute decided to hike to a salt lick and show Johnny where he could get the occasional moose when he wanted a change in diet. The former seaman was walking ahead of Johnny when they came upon a glade of spruce trees bordering the creek. Unbeknownst to them a grizzly was in the same glade rooting around for food. The two parties saw each other at about the same time.

Big Knute, who was in front of Johnny, signaled a halt. "Let's wait him out," he said softly.

Johnny stood silently, his .40–60 Winchester in his right hand.

The bear started weaving his head back and forth.

"Bad sign," Knute whispered, bringing his .30–30 Winchester belt high.

Hair standing on end, and his teeth clicking, the grizzly suddenly charged, covering the fifty yard interval in three seconds. He was almost upon Knute when he fired from the hip. The gun failed to discharge as the bear bowled the big man over like a tenpin. In a split second Knute looked up at the bear and then at Johnny. The latter had leaped aside, and working his lever action with blinding speed, fired four shots into the bear's neck and head, any one of which could have killed the bear. One was a brain shot because the bear dropped as if he had been poleaxed. He fell across Knute's legs.

The Swede snaked his limbs out from under the bear and stood up. He'd seen a lot of men in the woods, but never one who could operate a lever action as fast as his companion just did.

"Thanks," Knute said. "It looks like I'm already paid back in full. Where'd you learn to operate a gun like that?"

The trace of a grin showed on Johnny's face. "Shootin' around the home farm," he said.

"Let's see what made Mister Bear so ornery," Knute said, bending over the dead animal. He carefully inspected the grizzly's teeth and feet, then his entire carcass, but could find no ills that would have inspired the charge. "Probably, just plain scared," Knute said.

"They're faster than I thought!" Johnny exclaimed.

Knute nodded in agreement. "I hear they can do one hundred yards in five seconds. Well, he's nice and fat. He was probably going to hibernate. I'll get the horses, skin him out, and take his hide and meat back to the landing."

"Never ate bear," Johnny commented.

"It isn't bad, but you got to cook it thoroughly. Sometimes they're loaded up with tapeworm," his host said.

Johnny built his cabin and cleared a trapline up to the farthest headwaters of Thibert Creek. Nobody was above him there. He built a small "overnight" shack at the end of his line. He passed the winter on the creek and did passably well. In the spring Johnny paid Knute a small percentage for his furs that Knute had not even asked for. Knute told him there would be plenty of jobs open that summer with an outfit planning to mine on Dease Creek, which flowed into Dease Lake about ten miles up the lake from Thibert Creek.

"They'll be looking for carpenters," was the last thing the Swede said to him in March.

Through the course of time, Johnny became acquainted with the men whom Knute had mentioned. Sam Scottee and Phil Hankin were both spinners of yarns as well as "walking history books" on the north.

George Adsit lived near Mosquito Creek, whose source was in the direction of Teslin Lake, gateway to the Yukon River, which in turn led down to the gold rush town of Dawson City in the Yukon Territory. In early May, Johnny snowshoed up the trail and in doing so came to Adsit's cabin. He had met the older man at Scottee's that winter when they all got together for a poker game.

"Headin' out?" Adsit asked once they had settled at the table with a cup of hot coffee.

Johnny shook his head. "No, just wanted to see what the trail looked like to Teslin."

"I see you got a pistol on."

Johnny had almost forgot he was toting a sidearm.

"Yes, a .38," Johnny said.

"You have any trouble with it?" Adsit asked.

Johnny nodded. "It's not very accurate over twenty yards."

Adsit walked to a rack where he removed a pistol belt with two holstered guns on it and laid the holster on the table. Taking the guns out, he asked: "How do you like 'em? They're matched ivory-handled .45s."

"Never seen anything to compare with them," Johnny said honestly.

Adsit smiled. "Look, I'm goin' huntin'. Gotta get a few grouse for the table. I'll tail along and show you the trail for a spell."

Ordinarily Johnny would have been a little leery of an offer like that, but there was something about Adsit that he liked. He sensed in him a kindred spirit. "Sounds good," he said.

Later that day, they forded a stream that was running fast. Adsit slipped and took a quick dunking. Johnny built a fire while Adsit took off his shirt and undershirt to dry out.

From years spent in various penitentiaries in the West, Johnny knew what a bullet scar looked like, and noted that Adsit had one that went across the wrist of his left hand. It reminded Johnny of a furrow back on the farm. Yet another scar was evident along his side. They seemed to confirm that Adsit was indeed a kindred spirit. One normally didn't acquire wounds like that merely from trapping and gold mining. They more likely came from war or from trouble with the law.

He was going to ask Adsit about it, but held back, not wanting to appear to be the prying type.

Johnny also met George Ball, who was in partnership with George Finn on Deloire Creek, another tributary of Thibert Creek. Johnny recalled a feud near the town of Saco, Montana, where a man named George Ball killed a cantankerous character called "Black Bill" Long. The Ball ranch, where the incident took place, straddled the Canadian–United States border. Johnny vaguely remembered that Ball had been sentenced to death, and that a lively legal wrangle resulted, which took the case to the higher courts. Johnny held his tongue but wondered if this Ball was tied in with the yarn.

# Chapter 12

# BILL HANNA'S ACCIDENT

Now Johnny found himself on an isolated frontier. He would not have to cringe at the sight of a lawman because there were none. He had missed Brown's Hole, the refuge for the men of the Butch Cassidy gang, but he had found Dease Lake, which was even more remote. Johnny suspected he had stumbled onto another hideout for lawbreakers such as himself. He liked his neighbors because they respected a man for what he was and did not ask prying questions.

Johnny prospected in the spring of 1925, then went to work as a laborer improving the road from Telegraph Creek to Dease Lake. Later on that summer, on July 13, his twenty-seventh birthday, he was offered a job as a carpenter by Dease Creek Mines under the management of J. B. Blick. The company had been incorporated in Seattle in 1923 and commenced an aggressive gold exploration program on Dease Creek in 1924. The need for planks to build flumes, cabins, and sheds resulted in the construction of a sawmill, which Johnny helped to build, at the mouth of Dease Creek. Johnny then went to work cutting planks for the mine. Later, he installed flumes, cabins, and sheds needed in the gold operation. Once the summer was over, he returned to his cabin on Thibert Creek.

Characteristically Johnny was not much of a talker, but he did like joining the occasional poker games held with the others camped along Thibert Creek.

Johnny was comparatively satisfied with his existence until the day of a poker game held at Scottee's cabin. The game terminated when Hanna won three hundred dollars.

"What do you figure on doing with your three hundred?" Big Knute queried half in jest.

Hanna smiled. Often the butt of jokes, he took it all in good humor. He had fled the east where he was supposed to have worked on a Montreal newspaper. Like every newcomer—he had only been in the Dease Lake area for three years—he was a tenderfoot. "That's easy," he said, nodding at old Scottee, "I'm gonna look for Sam's lost cabin mine."

Knute feigned anger. "Sam, you been holding out on us?"

Scottee laughed heartily. "No, no," he countered, then paused to light his pipe. "About twenty years ago I was at Fort McPherson in the Northwest Territories. A prospector named Cameron came out of the Richardson Mountains with twenty pounds of gold."

"What weight?" Hankin asked.

"What difference does it make at that weight?" Knute commented.

"Well, you know what I mean, regular pound weight, or gold pound weight?"

"Regular," Scottee, said "sixteen ounces to the pound, three hundred and twenty ounces."

"What was gold worth then?" Johnny asked.

Scottee looked at Johnny in surprise. "You got the bug, too, eh? At sixteen dollars an ounce, we figured it was worth about five grand, give or take a few hundred."

"Sam, that's a nice yarn, but it isn't exactly unusual," Hankin said.

"I ain't finished yet. Cameron never came back," Scottee said, pausing to puff on his pipe. "He did leave a clue, though. He said his diggin's were marked by a cabin."

"A lot good that will do. A cabin's a cabin," Knute said.

"This cabin was different. It's not square. It's three-sided."

"A triangle," Knute said. "That would be pretty unusual."

Johnny sat quietly, but Scottee was right, he had been bitten by the bug. "Did you look for it?" he asked.

"Yup, I did," said Scottee. "I went to the headwaters of the Bell River. Found colors too, but winter was closin' in fast. I had other things goin' so I left and never went back."

Hanna stood up. "You see. That's something to shoot for. I got to get back to camp."

Johnny collared Hanna as he headed out the door. "Are you serious about looking for that mine?"

"Sure am," said Hanna, "and the Lost McHenry as well."

Johnny scratched his head. "Where's that supposed to be?"

Hanna grinned. "It's a lot closer than the Lost Cabin. Actually, as far as we are concerned it's pretty close. You know the trail to Teslin Lake?"

Johnny nodded.

"Well, you take a trail from Teslin to the town of Ross River, then you head up the Ross to its headwaters, and that's where it is."

"You know where?" Johnny asked eagerly.

"No, no. That's the general location. Like the other one, it has never been found."

"What's the story behind that?" Johnny asked.

"This guy McHenry showed up here in Dease Lake with forty pounds of gold. He claimed the spot he found it is a creek bed, above which looms a huge snow cross that forms on the mountain in springtime."

"When did this happen?" Johnny asked.

"Way back in 1875," Hanna said. "He showed up here with the gold."

"Sounds interesting," Johnny said. "Need a partner?"

"Sure, but it's a heap of travel."

"I got no ties," Johnny said.

Johnny packed up his meager amount of gear and left a note telling Knute he and Hanna were leaving. The two men headed north that May. Travel could not have been better with the snow gone. The weather was warm in the day, yet the ground froze in the early hours of the rapidly shortening night. Above all, mosquitoes were not out in the pestering hordes that they would be later on.

Hanna, who hailed from Montreal, had tramped the Cassiar country for a couple of years, working the "city" out of his system. In the process, he had become a serious prospector. Hanna was inquisitive about Johnny's past, though more liberal in talking about his own. Johnny learned he had been a typographer on the *Montreal Star* before heading west. A sister of his lived in Boston, and Hanna was an army veteran, having inhaled a breath of chlorine gas during the war.

"I guess I didn't die because I was used to the air in Montreal," Bill said lightly, dismissing the horrors of the war while they sat around their campfire the second night after they had set out. He had headed west hoping to clear his lungs and now, after several years in the woods, they didn't bother him at all.

The two men were exact opposites in culture, upbringing, ethnic background, temperament, and lifestyle, but nevertheless they got along well. Since both were fleeing overcrowded conditions, they understood one another's appreciation for the freedom the wilderness provided.

They frequently stopped to rest, eat, hunt, or fish for grayling, which seemed to populate the streams of the country by the millions. During these breaks a peculiar habit of his partner's caught Johnny's eye. Hanna often leaned his rifle against his stomach when he took his pack off. This quirk made Johnny wince, and finally, one day when they stopped for lunch, he could no longer contain himself.

"You're taking a chance with that rifle, Bill," Johnny said.

Hanna chuckled. "Safety's on," he said. "I'm still here."

"Don't push your luck," Johnny said in resignation.

They finally reached the shores of lower Teslin Lake where they made camp. Hanna pointed out while cooking supper that night that they had crossed the border into the Yukon Territory.

"Doesn't feel any different," Johnny said.

"It is though," Hanna said. "It shows up in little things. Here, for example, you don't need a free miner's certificate."

Johnny learned from Hanna that the Royal Canadian Mounted Police virtually ran the Yukon Territory. They administered, among other statutes, those concerning customs, game and trapping, and law enforcement. Ordered to the Yukon while it was still a district of the Northwest Territories in 1895, the Mounties had been Yukon's only police force ever since. This was contrary to British Columbia, where provincial police had taken over their duties.

"They meddlesome?" Johnny asked.

"Not if a man keeps his nose clean," Hanna said.

"Do you need identification?"

"Yes. Why?"

Johnny said he had none.

"How come?"

"I'm an American."

"Any more to it?" Hanna queried.

"What do you mean?"

Hanna shifted uneasily. "You had law trouble?"

Johnny's eyes narrowed.

Hanna laughed. "Calm down. Dease Lake's full of guys on the run."

Johnny looked steadily at his partner. Hanna was so outgoing he did not take offense. "I rustled a few horses. I was paroled."

Hanna nodded. "You got a handgun with you?"

"No. I forgot. I left it hanging on a tree by my cabin."

"Good. You get caught with one and the Mounties will throw the book at you. Otherwise, they'll leave you alone."

The next morning Hanna and Johnny broke camp at dawn and went about adjusting their packsacks before putting them on. As he always did, Johnny carefully leaned his Winchester against a tree before putting his pack over his shoulders. Hanna, on the other hand, balanced the rifle against his belly. He put one shoulder into his pack strap, the pack slipped, and he grabbed for it. The muzzle of the gun shifted along his belly and the rifle went off with a loud crack. A surprised look came over Hanna's features, and he slumped to the ground. Johnny leaped to Hanna's prostrate form and turned him over. The color was draining out of his partner's features like snow melting in the summer sun. He unbuttoned Hanna's shirt to see a ghastly hole where there should have been a stomach. Johnny knew Hanna was a dying man.

Though weak from shock and the loss of blood that was rapidly draining out of his belly wound, Hanna still managed to summon enough vitality to speak. "Get a pencil," he said.

Johnny looked perplexed. "I don't have one," he said.

"Okay, a bullet then," Hanna said, his voice now barely a whisper.

Johnny took a bullet from his pocket and handed it to the wounded man.

"Paper," Bill said faintly. "Gotta write, to say it was an accident."

Johnny quickly grabbed a map from his pack and folded it. He held it so Hanna could write on the blank side. Hanna tried valiantly, but was too weak.

"Don't worry about it," Johnny said.

"They'll never believe you . . . Johnny?"

Johnny leaned close so he could hear better but it was no use. A rush of air emanated from Hanna's lungs, and he was dead. Johnny wrestled with the idea of notifying authorities, but Hanna's last words hung in his mind. They might not believe the story and pry into his past with predictable results. He decided it would be prudent not to mention Hanna's death. He went through his friend's pockets and removed the poker winnings, which he stared at for a while, then shrugged and put the money into his pocket. Johnny buried his companion by using an army entrenching tool. He carefully contrived a cross to mark the grave, then threw it away. Instead, he cut a blaze in a nearby tree, for no other reason than he felt there should be at least some mark indicating the final resting place of one of the few friends of his life.

Johnny trudged north to the shores of Teslin Lake. He could hear machinery working somewhere and, as the path was heading in the same general direction, he kept to it. An hour or so later, the footpath veered past the sound and left it behind. All told, including his days with Hanna, he had been on the trail for over a month when he reached the shores of an arm of the lake across which lay the community of Teslin. He built a smudge fire in hopes that someone might see it. Signaling by smudge was the only practical way of seeking help for crossing bodies of water too distant for a rifle shot to be heard. In a short time, he saw a man come down to the shore, shove off with a boat, and head in his direction.

Andy Bride, trading post manager for Taylor & Drury, had seen the signal and was quite used to picking up people. Usually some business would fall his way as a result of the favor. He noticed this fellow was carrying a huge pack with two bearskins for sleeping robes. Other than that the newcomer could have been any one of a handful of prospectors who had walked the Teslin trail.

Johnny gave Bride a dollar in recognition of the assistance accorded to him, and then walked along the beach as he had before. He saw a sawed-off stump that was so alluring he sat down on it and debated what he should do next. He was deep in thought and, consequently, surprised when an Indian lad seemingly arrived from nowhere.

"Need any help?" the young fellow asked.

"Not that I know," Johnny said.

"We got tea all the time," the lad replied. "We live up there," he said and pointed toward the west.

Johnny looked and saw a small cabin perched on a shelf of land ten feet above the beach. "Thanks," he said, "I'll join you after I get camp set up. What's your name?"

"Tom Smith."

Later, he joined Smith and his family, and found them to be kindly. He asked them about the machinery he had heard, and they explained that it was a mining operation run by a man named Albert Huston on Wolf Creek. He deliberated going there to see if there was any work, and then decided against it. If he was going to search for the Lost McHenry mine, he had best make tracks for Ross River, which he would have to go up to make camp before winter set in. He thanked Tom Smith, then returned to his camp next to the stump.

The next morning he was up and on his way at dawn, having learned from Hanna that the route from Teslin to Ross River lay along the Nisutlin and Lapie rivers. The path was in fairly good condition and his progress was tolerable. Occasionally he stopped to fish, easily gathering in grayling with a hand-hewn willow pole, a bare hook, and worms as bait. He crossed the Big Salmon Range and descended the Lapie River. He had been several days on the Lapie when he rounded a bend in the footpath to suddenly find himself in the midst of an Indian camp that straddled the trail. The encounter was so sudden, Johnny was immediately on his guard. Having been raised in the heartland of the warlike Sioux, he could never bring himself to believe that an Indian was not bent on his destruction. He made up his mind to be on the alert for any hostile move.

Equally leery, but for different reasons was Frank Slim, leader of the group. A strongly featured, ramrod-straight man of thirty summers, he had contracted to stake claims for old man Puckett, a trader in Whitehorse. He had just completed the job, and on seeing the stranger come into camp he figured the hiker was going to "tie on" to the claims just staked. There was nothing illegal about this, but it was irritating that the word got out so fast. He addressed the fair-haired man, "You here to stake?"

Johnny, surrounded by these unfamiliar faces, felt uncomfortable, but not in danger. Obviously, the natives had been staking claims. "No, I'm heading for Ross River," he said.

Slim was relieved. "Sit down and have some supper with us," he said.

The death of Hanna remained fixed in Johnny's mind and every move he made was with the thought that somehow the law would find out about it and hold him responsible. He intended to decline the invitation for yet another reason. In toting Hanna's winnings and his own cash, he realized he was fair game if anyone wanted to relieve him of it. However, the tasty odor of broiling moose steaks was overwhelming. He unshouldered his pack and was given a tin plate covered with steak. He sat down with his back to a big tree while keeping a sharp lookout to his right and left.

Slim's normal occupation was on the bridge of a trading post boat that plied the Yukon River and its tributaries. Having learned the vocation through a long apprenticeship that saw him rise from deckhand to pilot, Slim was used to meeting people. The visitor appeared to be extremely nervous, but that, too, was nothing new. Some white men were always that way when they were outnumbered by Indians.

"We came out from Ross River," Slim said looking at Johnny. "Trail's okay, but when you get to Ross fire off your rifle, so you can get across the Pelly River."

A man always welcomed news about the trail, and Johnny was no different. "Is there anyone around who'll take me across?" he asked.

"Yeah, old man Buttle operates the Taylor & Drury trading post there. He'll pick you up," Slim replied.

The possible presence of a lawman ate at Johnny's mind. "I suppose there's a Mountie at Ross," Johnny said as casually as possible.

Slim nodded. "There is most of the time, but right now, no. The policeman is away on a long patrol. He won't be back for a month."

Immensely relieved by the news, Johnny finished his meal and thanked Slim and his partners for the food. He shouldered his pack and strode northward along the trail to Ross. The ever irksome scourge of mosquitoes had eased off to be replaced by blackflies, irritating cousins of the former, which gnawed rather than pierced one's pores with a needle. If it was not one thing, it was another. It seemed no matter where a man went there was some insect like that to torment him.

Pausing occasionally to swat flies clustered on his neck, Johnny went about making camp along the Lapie. He cut down a small spruce sapling, and lopped off its limbs with an ax and weaved them into a ground mat. On this he laid two bearskins for blankets. He rigged up a mosquito bar as a refuge, and extended a tarp lean-to to cover his gear. He searched out a dead tree that he cut up and split, and trimmed off the knots to use for kindling, and in a short time had a roaring fire going. This was more than he needed for cooking, but he had seen grizzly sign and wanted to discourage the bears from venturing too close.

The perfume scent of newly cut spruce boughs and the crackling of the friendly fire soon lulled him to sleep. The next morning he again rose at daybreak and resumed his northern trek.

# Chapter 13

# BUILDING A BOAT AT ROSS RIVER

Johnny descended the trail to the Pelly River, some sixteen miles from where he had met the claim stakers. This brought him out directly across the river from what appeared to be the trading post Slim had mentioned. The store was one of a handful of log cabins scattered among spruce trees bordering the clear waters of the river. He was surprised at the number of wall tents lining his side of the river, noticing their occupants were native. It was like a scene out of the past.

Johnny spotted a heavyset, bespectacled man puttering around what looked to be a supply building for the trading post, and noticed a small riverboat with an outboard attached to it tied to the bank. He unshouldered his rifle, racked a shell into the breech, and pointing the gun skyward, pulled the trigger. The crack of the rifle resounded off the surface of the river and the individual on the far bank turned around. He waved to Johnny, untied the boat, and started the outboard and made his way across. It seemed as if he had done this many times before. Johnny cleared his rifle, slung it over his shoulder, and fingered the money in his pocket that would pay for the ride. The man beached the boat in front of Johnny.

"No charge," the man said. "Throw your gear in and hop aboard."

"You must be Mr. Buttle," Johnny said when they were about halfway across. "An Indian staking claims along the Lapie told me about you."

Buttle nodded. "That would be Frank Slim."

"My name's Art Nelson," Johnny said without additional comment.

When the craft bumped ashore in front of the trading post, Johnny vaulted out of the boat and shouldered his pack. "I want to buy some stuff, so I'll be back after I make camp." he said.

"We have a spare cabin here if you want to use it," Buttle advised.

Johnny figured he'd be more comfortable by not accepting the offer and declined.

Buttle's gaze followed the fair-haired newcomer as he strode away. Although quieter than most, the stranger was just one of many drifters roaming the woods trapping and prospecting. The potential mineral strike was their form of chasing the pot at the end of the proverbial rainbow, and it was up to Buttle to see that they could get the proper supplies. He helped them when he could. It was good for business. One never knew when a man would strike it rich.

Johnny bivouacked that night a short way from the community. He mused over the primitiveness of the natives whose moose-hide moccasins with porcupine quillwork were an odd contrast to their twentieth-century caps, shirts, pants, and calico dresses.

Johnny returned to the trading post in the morning.

Buttle was up and greeted him. "You're an early riser. Just about every man that has come through here of late has been a Scandinavian."

"Tough times in the old country," Johnny commented.

"Are you from there?" Buttle asked.

"Yeah," Johnny replied. "Norway."

"You speak good English."

"I should. I was raised in North Dakota."

"What can I do for you?" Buttle asked.

"I'm heading to the MacMillan country."

"Easiest way is to follow the Ross to its headwaters."

"I'll need a lot of supplies," Johnny said. "Maybe I should build a boat."

"We've got the wood. You could build it right here."

"Okay, I'll give it a try," Johnny said.

The trader offered to help him, but Johnny declined the assistance.

Johnny was a pretty good carpenter, but that did not necessarily make him a boatbuilder. He realized he would need help and after a few days asked Buttle to join him. With the trader's skills, the two men completed the craft in nine days. He offered to pay the trader for his help, but Buttle said it was all part and parcel of operating a trading post.

Buttle was first and last a salesman and did not miss an opportunity to sell Johnny some goods. Noticing the heavy bearskins Johnny carried around, Buttle suggested that packing five pounds of an eiderdown sleeping bag was better than thirty pounds of hide.

Johnny fingered the bag inside the store. "We never used these on the range," Johnny said. "Just a bedroll made up of a couple of blankets. But we didn't have to pack 'em either. How much is it?"

"Twenty dollars," Buttle said.

"Okay, I'll take it."

"How about a stove?"

"Well, I don't know," Johnny said.

"You gotta have one come winter," Buttle advised.

Johnny bought the stove and a load of supplies as well.

The next day he stowed these and the gear from his camp aboard his boat.

"Join me for a cup of tea tonight and I'll tell you about the country," Buttle said. "It might help you."

"All right," Johnny said.

That evening Buttle brewed a strong tea that he poured into a couple of mugs when Johnny showed up.

Motioning Johnny to a chair, Buttle did not bother with preliminaries, having correctly assumed that his guest tended to be on the impatient side when it came to long-winded conversations.

"About eighty miles up the Ross Trail you'll come to Sheldon Lake and there you'll find an abandoned cabin that's in good shape. Move into that, and you can save yourself a lot of the energy that you could use cutting firewood."

Johnny was slightly confused by the old trader's directions. "I take it the trail follows the river," he said.

Buttle nodded. "Not much difference, but it can be confusing. The river's better, because that way there's no chance of missin' the cabin. You just keep going up the Ross until you run into a lake about seventy miles up. You cross that and enter another lake and cross that to its north end. That's where you will see the shack. The Ross flows in near it."

Having scanned more than his share of maps, it was easy for Johnny to visualize the trader's verbal picture. He knew that poling, paddling, and lining his boat up the Ross would not be an easy trip.

"Is there much of a current through the lakes?" Johnny asked.

"No, hardly noticeable," Buttle said, appreciating the fact that Johnny was a good listener. "The first lake you come to is called Lewis Lake and the second is Sheldon Lake. They got kind of an interesting history. There's a high mountain that towers over the farthest north lake which two trappers called Kipling Mountain, after the writer. Naturally, they called the lake Rudyard."

Buttle took a long sip of his tea before continuing.

"Seven or eight years later, a naturalist named Charles Sheldon from the Chicago Museum of Natural History collected several specimens of stone sheep in the area. As a result, Joseph Keele, of the Geological Survey of Canada, who came through there at about the same time, renamed the mountain and lake after the collector."

"Kipling lost out," Johnny said.

"Yeah, he sure did," Buttle said, figuring his companion would certainly register interest over what he was going to say. "Keele's guide was Charles Wilson, a man with a murky past, though, of course, Keele did not know that. He named a mountain that you'll see thirty miles to the northeast of the lake after him."

Johnny was beginning to lose the trader's verbal trail. He felt like he was being slowly drowned in a sea of names cast forth by the old-timer. He supposed the trader was trying to make a point, but he had difficulty figuring out what it was.

The trader got up and walked over to a trunk and opened it and lifted out a bulky object that he brought back and deposited on the table between the two men. In the dim light of the oil lamp it took a moment for Johnny's eyes to focus on exactly what it was, then he was riveted. In front of him was the most beautiful chunk of gold-laden rose quartz he had ever seen. Johnny was a novice as a rock hound, but there was no mistaking the value of the quartz.

"Where'd that come from?" Johnny asked automatically.

Buttle smiled. "If I knew, I wouldn't be here. That's where Wilson comes in. It was his. He was looking for the Lost McHenry mine."

Johnny stared at Buttle. He couldn't possibly know that Johnny was looking for the same mine. But then any man as shrewd as the trader could easily put two and two together.

"I heard about it at Dease Lake," Johnny said.

"I kind of figured you may have," Buttle said. "Wilson moved into the upper Ross about 1903 and had been searching for the mine for three years when Keele came through with his survey crew."

Johnny scanned the chunk of quartz under the light of the oil lamp. Veins and strings of gold laced the host rock.

If a man could find a bed of that, he'd be free forever. He turned to Buttle. "I'd gather the place where this came from is still unknown."

Buttle nodded, and then got up and paced up and down in front of the table. "Yes, that's the sad part about it."

"Wilson must have known where this was from," Johnny said, shaking the rock. "How'd you get it?"

"Cece Poli got it from Wilson."

Johnny's brain was already whirling with prospectors' names, and now there was another. "Who was Poli?" Johnny asked.

Buttle ceased pacing up and down and took to his chair again. "Another prospector. I swapped him a rifle for the rock about five years ago."

"What did he say?"

"Said Wilson played coy. Wouldn't tell him."

"Poli look for it?"

"Yeah, but gave up. He's scratching a living on a claim near Dawson City."

"Sort of a dead end," Johnny commented.

"Not wholly. Wilson may have found it, but cold winters and heavy snows have kept the vein covered ever since," Buttle said.

Johnny recalled Hanna talking about the clue to finding the McHenry. "You talking about the snow cross?" he asked.

Buttle nodded. "My guess is we'll need a really hot spring after a winter sparse of snow before the cross will appear again."

"I'll stick with trapping," Johnny said, though he was not altogether certain he meant it.

"One thing more," Buttle said, "the only people you're liable to see up there are some Indians who hunt beaver in the spring, so make sure you don't forget anything." Johnny rose to leave, and Buttle handed him a tiny bottle.

"What's this?" Johnny asked.

"A painkiller for a toothache; the last guy I outfitted lost a filling and went crazy out there."

The next day Johnny launched himself and his boat up the Ross. He fastened a tracking line with a fifty-foot loop to both ends of the canoe. He also threw a paddle and a pole into the boat. He paddled through calm water as far as he could, and when he reached deep, fast stretches he pulled the boat upstream with the tracking rope. This was attached so it resembled a giant bowstring and could be used to veer the craft around boulders, tree stumps, and other flotsam in the water that blocked the path of the craft.

Johnny slowly, patiently worked his way up the Ross, lining the boat through Prevost Canyon and Skookum Rapids. Ultimately he broke through to Lewis Lake and knew the worst part of the trek was over. He camped there several days, taking time to straighten out his gear and enjoy a magnificent view of the lake and the distant spire that he assumed was Mount Sheldon. One morning the wind was right, and rigging a sail out of his lean-to tarp, he set forth on the lake. The wind pushed him north into Sheldon Lake and in half a day he had reached the cabin described so well by the trader.

Johnny figured even if he hurried things up, there was no way he could squeeze in a prospecting trip that fall. First, he cut and stacked eight cords of wood for the Sheldon Lake cabin. Next, he hiked to the Macmillan River and built a cabin of seven by nine feet on the shore. When he completed it, Johnny put up a high cache to store his food supplies in, and then spent a week cutting and splitting firewood. Next he concentrated on brushing out a circular trapline trail between the Macmillan and Ross rivers, the two cabins being halfway points.

Back at Sheldon Lake he shot a moose, which he dressed out, then he stowed the meat in the cache behind the cabin.

When the first snow came he set out his trapline. He possessed only six steel traps, as any more would have been too heavy to backpack. He depended, therefore, on his skills in setting deadfalls and snares in order to obtain the principal fur bearers he was after: mainly marten. These were relatively small, not difficult to catch, and brought a good price.

Johnny enjoyed the solitude of trapping. He traveled endlessly on his homemade snowshoes, tending the line. Lean-tos supplied with wood were placed at convenient places in case he was weathered in. During the long winter nights, comfortably warm in his eiderdown, he could look up and see the stars twinkling in an untarnished sky. This was a welcome change from those years where he stared dumbly at bleak cell walls. No longer did he have to listen to the slide of iron doors grating on the cell block as they slammed shut behind him. No longer must he listen to screams of men gone mad from confinement. No longer did the air around him resound with the tread of hundreds of convicts marching to a prison guard's command.

The only sounds were the occasional hoot of an owl, the flutter of a ptarmigan's wings, the howl of a restless wolf, and the crunch of his own snowshoes in the frigid snow. Each night his mind flooded with an awareness of his freedom—freedom that he had previously pawned for little in the way of prospective gain.

Not unpredictably, his sense of social propriety had gone askew, and all that remained was a lasting bitterness toward those who had rebuked and punished him for his transgressions of the law. Police, therefore were suspect, and like a lynx nimbly dodging the clutches of a grizzly, Johnny went to great lengths to avoid them and the society they represented.

Bitterly cold weather that winter resulted in a poor harvest, but he did manage to take a wolf, three wolverines, and ten marten, the pelts of which he put on fur stretchers he had carved for the purpose.

Early one day in March, when he returned to his cabin at Sheldon Lake, he came upon a newly broken trail with five sets of snowshoe tracks that he recognized as belonging to Ross River natives. He recalled Arthur John, a lad in Ross River Buttle had introduced him to, saying he hoped to go beaver hunting at the headwaters of the Ross in the spring. He followed the trail made by the visitors and then returned to his cabin. Johnny deduced they would probably return as soon as the ice went out in the spring.

The ice began to break up the first week of May. Johnny waited for a number of days until he saw no more ice floes running, and finally launched his boat at a cabin he had built about ten miles up the Ross from the lake. He tied the boat to a willow and loaded his furs and gear prior to shoving off downstream.

Unknown to Johnny, half a mile above his accessory cabin, a log floating in the swirling current had been flung up against a tree trunk, jamming itself between the tree and a boulder, thus spanning the creek. The flotsam of branches, more logs, and ice blocks washed up against the obstruction, causing the river to back up and deepen. More debris and ice floated into the pool to stack up against the jam. This, in turn, resulted in the water level rising ever higher until a substantial pond was formed. Finally, the tremendous weight of water against the jam caused the log to crack, then break, and the dam gave way with a roar.

A wall of water and ice let loose, descending on Johnny's little camp like a tidal wave. He fled for his life, just barely making it to higher ground. The torrent flooded his cabin, chest high. Then, as suddenly as the water had risen, it fell. In a matter of minutes he was able to return to assess the damage. His boat was gone and the furs and rifle along with it, the exception being a handful of pelts on fur stretchers hanging from the beam of the cabin.

Several weeks later six Ross River natives showed up floating in a moose-skin boat they had sewn together at the headwaters of the Ross. Johnny was not really surprised to see them, having spotted their tracks earlier. He offered them some tea. The hunters accepted the invitation and congregated outside his cabin to sip the hot brew. Arthur John, whom Johnny figured to be about fourteen or fifteen, seemed to be the spokesman for the group. Probably, Johnny judged, because he spoke the best English. "Our hunt was good," said the lad. "We got plenty of beaver."

"You have flood," one of the older natives said, and pointed to grass and debris hanging on the cabin.

"Yeah," Johnny said. "I lost most of my furs and my boat. I even lost my rifle."

The oldest of the Indians spoke rapidly to Arthur John, who then translated it for Johnny.

"He says you can travel with us in the skin boat,"

Johnny was leery of traveling with anyone, but that was not the only reason he declined the invitation. He was fairly certain the supply boat would not be in for at least another month, and he simply did not want to hang around Ross River waiting for it.

A man could be without many things in the wilderness, but a rifle was not one of them. Johnny knew that he would have to make the long journey to Ross River no matter what. Luckily, he still had his ax. A month later, he built a raft and floated downriver until he reached Skookum Rapids, then walked the rest of the way. The trip took four days.

Arriving at the Ross River post in mid-June, he found to his disgust that the trading boat *Thistle* was not expected until the middle of July, meaning he would have to remain in the vicinity for a month. He purchased more supplies from Buttle, and set out on a short trip up the Pelly River, panning sandbars for gold as he went. Near Hoole Canyon he put up a tent and made a semi-permanent camp. He tested the ground there and found colors. He rigged up a sluice box, notching riffles to catch the heavier particles of the yellow metal, and spent the days shoveling gravel into the box. He earned roughly a dollar a day at the task, and before the *Thistle* arrived, had panned enough gold to supplement his funds.

Johnny was against mingling with people, but as the date for the expected arrival of the supply boat drew near, he broke camp and moved in closer to the trading post. He wanted to buy a rifle and get out quickly. A Mountie was stationed there and he had no desire to meet him. The arrival of the boat with all of its supplies, particularly sweets and fresh fruit, was a magnet that drew native and white trappers for miles around. As distasteful as mixing was to him, he put up with it by maintaining a rigid silence. The day the boat arrived he was on hand waiting for it. He saw that the pilot was the same man he had met on the trail a year before. Frank Slim waved to him and he acknowledged him with a nod. As soon as the craft was unloaded, he entered the trading post.

Trader Buttle, puffing on a pipe that seemed never to leave his mouth, was busy unpacking supplies and sorting out bales of fur to be loaded. If the trader was lucky, the boat would make one more trip before freeze-up. Buttle looked up from his work and greeted Johnny with a wave.

Johnny buttonholed him for a rifle. The trader broke one out of the packing case—a .30–30 featherweight, takedown Savage. Johnny examined the rifle closely, testing the takedown screw, which separated the stock from the barrel of the piece. It was just what he needed—a compact weapon he could backpack. He purchased the gun, five boxes of shells, and additional supplies.

Buttle was obviously busy, and could not take time to talk, which was all right with Johnny. He paid for the rifle and other goods, and dropped them into his pack. Then he returned to camp. Early the next morning he departed without a farewell. He had not seen the Mountie at Ross River, and as far as he was concerned, the less anyone knew about his route the better.

Johnny always carried enough warm clothes with him. He knew no month in the subarctic was free of snowfall. And he was well aware that the blistering heat of summer could change to shivering cold by nothing more than sudden cloud cover. He was never without his ax, rifle, and mosquito net. These were fundamental items a man could not live without in summer.

After leaving the Ross River post, Johnny trudged back to his cabin at Sheldon Lake, taking ten days to get there. The long wait at Ross had thrown a crimp into his plans. He delayed his search for the McHenry mine in favor of journeying to Mayo on the Stewart River, where he hoped he would receive a better price for his furs. Grabbing seven marten skins—all that remained of his fur catch—he traveled northward. He crossed the south fork of the Macmillan River and tramped toward the upper reaches of the Hess River.

# Chapter 14

# PROSPECTORS OFFER ADVICE

Johnny reached the Hess and walked along it searching for a place to cross. Finding only deep water as he walked downstream, he sought out a spot where the river was narrow, felled a tree to span it, and continued on his way down the opposite side. Camping at night on the bars of the Hess, Johnny panned the sands for gold. He found colors but nothing worth following up.

Johnny had been on the trail for over a week when one morning he came upon a gold camp operated by three men who were having breakfast. One of the prospectors shook hands with him, saying his name was Oscar Erickson, and introduced his partners, Norman Niddery and Ole Johnson. Johnny, harking back to the alias he had been using, said his name was Arthur Nelson. He slid the heavy pack off his back and sat down on top of it. One of the men handed him a cup and poured tea from a billycan hanging from a stick propped over their campfire—which also served as a smudge to fend off mosquitoes. The smoke was thick as a Missouri River fog, but it was effective. He saw flat bread cooking in their large frying pan, its tasty odor wafting over the camp. Glancing about, he noticed more smoke emanating from a hole twenty yards away. This indicated they were burning their way through permafrost to get to bedrock.

Buttle had mentioned permafrost to him. At this latitude (over 62 degrees north), only eighteen inches below the surface rested a layer of ice that encrusted the earth in its gelid grip. To get through it, where the gold was, logs had to be dropped into the hole, set on fire, and covered with some heat-resistant surface such as corrugated roofing. When the cover was removed, the thawed dirt was shoveled out. It was a slow way to excavate a hole, as the depth with each burn only averaged about six to eight inches. Pieces of equipment were scattered around the hole. He noticed a makeshift ladder made by hacking steps in a spruce log, a pick and a shovel, an ax driven into a stump, two gold pans, and a bucket with a rope attached to its handle. Going by the amount of dirt hauled out, Johnny estimated they were down six or seven feet. It was a tedious job.

The men seemed friendly enough.

"Where you headed?" Erickson asked. He was an open man, and considering the time and place his question was not to be taken as prying.

"Mayo," Johnny answered. "I figured I might get a better price for my furs."

"Have you been there before?"

"No."

"It's quite a ways; there're a few obstacles. Five miles downstream from here, you'll come to Twin Falls. There's a trail around it. Once you get past the falls, you can build a raft and float to the Stewart River. Save you a lotta work," Erickson said.

"How about the other falls?" the man named Niddery chimed in.

Erickson nodded. "Yeah, when you reach the Stewart, you go down that 'til you hear a roar. That will be Frazer Falls. You pole down the left side 'til you see a trail. Beach the raft and start walkin'. You'll come into Bob Levac's trading post below the falls."

"How's he on fur prices?" Johnny asked.

"Not bad, considerin'," Erickson said.

"I'm not so sure of that," Niddery chipped in.

"Why?" Erickson asked, puzzled.

"You gotta watch 'im," Niddery said. "If you let him get outta yer sight he'll switch furs on you."

"Whatever," Erickson said. "If he gives you an estimate, make sure you know your own furs."

Johnny felt at ease with the three outdoorsmen. They were about the same age as he. "Any trapping areas open in this part of the country?" Johnny asked.

"Sure," Erickson said. "Just watch for lopsticks—small trees with branches slashed off leaving only the crown. These mark a man's trapline."

Johnson, who had been silent, spoke up. "You ignore them at your own risk. Usually, if you search the guy out, you can make a deal with him. A trapper can only hold his ground by prior use."

"How's the government on licenses?" Johnny asked.

All three chuckled over his query. "For one, trapping and hunting are on the same ticket. But mainly, it depends on where you sell your furs. If you deal with all the outlying posts like Zimmerlee on the Macmillan, or Levac's, or old

Mervyn at Lansing on the upper Stewart, you'll never have to go to town at all, and you'd likely never see the Mountie enforcers. Otherwise, they'll surely ask to see your license sooner or later."

Johnny's associates were friendly enough, and he could see they were not overly partial to lawmen. They were individuals of his generation who lived off the land as he was doing, and were, in effect, living examples of the free trappers of the old West. It was not hard to imagine them with the names of Carson, Sublette, and Glass. Johnny wished that it was in his nature to team up with men like them, rather than to suffer the loneliness that occasionally affected him. He'd walked the lonely trail so long he knew no other, and was past the point where he could reconcile himself to the cooperation needed for getting along with any partners—Hanna being the exception.

Johnny thanked his hosts for the information, drained his tea, and stood up. "I'll try Levac," he said. Nodding to the others, he hoisted his heavy pack onto his back and departed.

Johnny heard the falls long before he reached them. Actually they were more rapids than they were falls. The Hess was compressed into a canyon where it hollered its objections as its waters were squeezed by the walls of the gut. As he walked along the precipice above the racing water, he stopped to look down. He dropped a large stick, and found out the depth of the canyon was much more than it looked at first glance. It was deceiving, and in his mind he thanked the three prospectors he had just met for telling him to walk around the falls. From above, the rapids did not look as threatening as they really were. Anyone unlucky enough to be swept into that maelstrom would be hard put to survive. At the end of the portage he proceeded to build a raft of four twelve-foot logs. He cut a long pole to guide, put his pack on the raft, and shoved off into the current.

Not particularly in a hurry, he spent a week drifting the length of the Hess River. At its junction with the Stewart, he angled the raft ashore at the site suggested by Erickson on the left bank where he pitched camp and built a fire. It was near midnight, but still twilight by the time he hunkered down to rest in front of the campfire. The hypnotic effect of the blaze mesmerized him. The flames darted and danced and crackled and sizzled as the spruce logs were devoured. Another kind of movement caught his eye. A column of ants erupted from an aperture in a log. Panic stricken, they scurried in all directions, reminding him of so many humans fleeing a hotel fire. He broke his stare to gaze across the top of the flames at the Stewart River. Never in his wildest dreams had he expected that one day he'd be camped on its banks enjoying his freedom. Ed Morrell, an ex-con from Folsom who had befriended the crooks of the Santag gang, was a legend in the prison. He was the guy who, with his writer friend, Jack London, rid Folsom of the horrors of the "jacket" merely by writing a book. Just about every convict there knew it by heart. London had written the story, but Morrell had smuggled the information out to him. The jacket was no ordinary straitjacket. It warped a man's body until it was a twisted knot of flesh capable of nothing else but groaning. The jacket was gone by the time Johnny got there, but the lack of it hardly made the hell of Folsom any easier to bear. Thanks to Morrell, London had got it right.

The book had brought changes, which included importing reading material. One such work was a dog story by Jack London, which Johnny had read, that ended with the huge animal trekking to the headwaters of the Stewart, where his master found gold. The dog reverted to the wilds after his owner was killed by Indians. The account was so realistic, Johnny half expected to see the beast emerge from the gloom of the surrounding forest.

A loon's cry pealed from across the river. This was echoed by a great snowy owl hooting softly from the top of a nearby spruce tree. The sweet scent of sage came to him on the night breeze. Memories of Folsom faded and he crawled into his sleeping bag and went to sleep.

Johnny set out walking the trail the next morning. It took him right to a complex, which included a long, white building that he guessed was Levac's trading post. Next to it was a cabin. He entered the store part of the building and saw a solidly built, austere-looking individual whom he assumed was Levac.

"Mr. Levac?" Johnny asked.

"That's right," the man said.

Levac was perplexed by the sudden appearance of a man he had never seen before or even been made aware of. Normally, moccasin telegraph brought word to him of anyone approaching, but not this time. Few people ever went by his place whom he had not met. The reason for this was that the easiest access to his part of the world was by the water artery at his back door. If a man did not travel by that route, he had a nasty trip on his hands. He'd have to come clear across from the Mackenzie River in the Northwest Territories, or down the Hess, which in itself could only be reached by an inordinate amount of toil.

"I have to tidy up some of my gear. Could I rent your spare cabin for the night?"

Rationalizing that he might be able to do some business with the stranger, Levac obliged him.

The next morning Johnny walked into the store and laid seven marten skins on the counter. "I'd like to sell these," he said.

The visitor puzzled Levac. Normally a man would come into his place and have coffee or tea, and gab with him, but the visitor had done none of that. He picked up the newcomer's skins and looked them over. He blew on the pelts to lift the guard hairs so he could see the quality of the underfur.

"Hold on a minute while I take 'em in the back and check 'em more closely. The light's better there," he said.

Johnny had been warned about the trader switching pelts on him. He placed a hand down firmly on top of the furs.

"No, no," Johnny countered. "Either look them over here, or not at all."

Levac figured he could barter with the stranger—one of the few pleasures he experienced in the course of his work. He carefully eyed them over again.

"I'll give you two hundred for the lot," he said.

Johnny's face flushed. The price was thievery. "They're worth double that," he said.

Levac presented his side of the argument. "Sure they are, but I'm way out in the woods. It costs me a small fortune just to be here."

"Forget it," Johnny snapped, sweeping the pelts off the counter. "I'll sell them in Mayo," he said, and stomped out the door.

The trapper's quick exit caught Levac by surprise. He went out with nary a good-bye. Whoever he was, he had a short fuse. Levac shook his head in disgust. The skins were prime. He should have upped the ante, and would have, if the jousting had gone as he had planned.

Johnny found that his quick exit inconvenienced him. Whereas he might have garnered some information in hopes of getting a ride downriver to Mayo, he now found it necessary to build another raft.

Floating downstream and loafing along the way, he reached Mayo after three days. He spotted the town from far enough away to beach the raft upstream near a clearing, which he judged was an airstrip. He felt that here, he would be far enough from the town to avoid prying eyes and his gear would be more secure. He walked into Mayo and quickly found the Taylor & Drury trading store on Front Street. He repeated the process with his marten skins, placing them on the counter.

One look at the clerk's reaction was enough for him to realize they would bring a good price.

The clerk examined the furs carefully and said he would give Johnny forty dollars a piece for six and thirty for the last.

"Why thirty?" Johnny asked. The clerk took the pelt and motioned for Johnny to follow him to the window. He held the pelt up to the light and pointed out a number of bluish spots.

"See those?" He said.

"Yeah, sure."

"On prime fur the hide has to be white," the clerk said. He added. "Besides, your other six are matched. The neck collar on this one is too large, too light."

Johnny realized he could not gripe at the offer. "Okay, take them," he said.

The clerk wrote out a voucher and handed it to John. "You can cash that at the bank."

Johnny eyed him distrustfully. "Never mind the note," he said, "just give me the money." He did not want to fool around with a lot of rigmarole, not when he did not have a trapper's license to begin with.

The clerk threw up his hands. "We don't carry that much in our till," he said.

Johnny hesitated then grudgingly picked up the voucher and took it to the bank. There they cashed the voucher with no problems. He stuffed the cash in his pocket and walked to the store, purchased some supplies, then returned to where he had beached the raft.

Johnny remained in Mayo for several weeks. During this time he occasionally talked with a prospector named Jack Alverson, who had spotted his camp and would drop by to say hello.

Alverson was a veteran sourdough. He had traversed most of the drainage of the upper Stewart River on foot. He had plenty of experience. As a boy he had bar-mined on the Rogue River in Oregon. He joined the stampede to the Yukon in 1899, and since then had lived most of his life on the upper Stewart. His knowledge of prospecting was extensive.

After Johnny's first week in Mayo, a trader arrived in town named James Mervyn, who had established his post at Lansing, located far up the Stewart River above Levac. Mervyn was a solidly built man in his fifties. He met Alverson and mentioned he was looking for someone to run one of his traplines.

"I know just the man," Alverson had said, "his name's Art Nelson, and he's been living near the air strip."

Mervyn stopped by Johnny's camp. He noted the stranger was oiling a new .30–30 Savage rifle by his campfire.

"Savage makes a good gun," Mervyn commented to break the ice.

Johnny, though surprised and a bit wary, relaxed when he saw the older man was only making small talk. "It works," he said laconically and motioned for Mervyn to sit down.

Mervyn accepted the invitation while he scanned the visitor's outfit and camp. Adequate wood was chopped and piled neatly near a small fire backed with stones. The ground around the camp had been swept clean with a spruce bough used for a broom. A wash basin rested evenly on three poles driven into the ground for the purpose. Cooking gear was clean and sorted for easy access. A pot of water was placed on hot coals culled from the fire, providing a steady source of warm water. Green forked sticks held another pot from a rod stretched between them spanning the low fire. His sleeping bag was rolled up and placed on a bed of fresh moss, which appeared to have been changed every day like linen. Mervyn noted Johnny was clean shaven and his clothes, though ruffled, were freshly washed. He'd do as a trapper.

"I'm looking for somebody to run one of my traplines," Mervyn stated going right to the point. "Jack Alverson said you might be interested. The line's got a base cabin about fifteen miles above Levac's, and several outshacks farther up the Stewart, and they're stocked with traps."

Johnny cogitated on the offer. Being skeptical of traders in general, he wondered what sort of gimmick his visitor had in mind. He looked at Mervyn. "Why would you want to hire me when you don't know anything about me?" he asked.

Mervyn returned Johnny's gaze. He was a forthright man. "For the money," he said. "One third of the take will be mine and you'll get the rest."

Johnny had to smile. "You'd trust me not to set aside a few and sell them somewhere else?"

Mervyn shrugged. "A man takes chances in everything he does."

Johnny was at loose ends and knew such opportunities did not come along every day. It was almost fall. "Sounds okay," he said, "I'll take it."

Mervyn stood up. "I'm headin' upriver in two days. I'll pick you up right here. I got a couple of dogs, if you want any."

"I'll take the job but not the dogs. Too much trouble," Johnny said.

"Suit yourself," Mervyn said, and turned and walked off.

Johnny went back to doctoring his rifle. He lingered over it as a mother hen does a newborn chick. He expertly disassembled the gun, carefully oiling and wiping clean the various parts before putting it back together. When he had finished the job he poured himself a cup of coffee and sipping it, listened to the sound of the river as its ripples caressed the shoreline by his camp.

Johnny passed the winter up along the Stewart. He saw only one person during that time, Alverson, who stayed with him one night while mushing down the river. Johnny was not free with conversation, especially when Alverson inquired about his past. What was the use of going into such talk when all it led to was more questions about something he did not want to disclose? He had nothing against Alverson, yet he did not go out of his way to ask the man to linger.

Johnny was most content when he was traveling through the limitless expanse of the country around him. The surroundings invited comparison with his confinement at Folsom, whose cold walls were as stifling to him as a man buried alive in an avalanche. Prison was like a bad dream in which he tried to run yet couldn't move, and hollered for help but no one heard. The fear of returning to such a living hell was akin to a dull toothache that could only be obliterated by removing the cause. He could check his status relative to his parole, but it could mean more time in prison. He could not go back. The mental wounds incurred by his imprisonment, which at first rankled like festering blisters, were slowly subsiding, as if freedom itself was a poultice salving his hurt. However, the very conditions under which he assumed this rebirth snared him.

He was constantly moving and he no sooner reached one place than he felt compelled to go somewhere else.

Later that month Johnny found one of Mervyn's dogs caught in a trap along his line. He doctored the canine's foot with spruce sap, but first wrote a note that he attached to the dog's harness explaining what happened. He respected Mervyn, and that was his way of showing it.

In April, as previously agreed, Johnny delivered his furs to Mervyn, then returned to the cabin he had occupied that winter near the junction of the Hess and Stewart. While waiting for the ice to go out, he counted up his funds, which now amounted to more than three thousand dollars that he had saved from working for wages, trapping, and prospecting over the last nine years.

Not trusting banks, he packed the money with him, but he wondered if he should not do something with it. Any mishap, and he could expect to lose all or a part of the money.

Shortly afterward the ice went out, so he placed his pack on his back and rafted back to Mayo where he boarded a riverboat and traveled to Stewart Island on the Yukon River. Then he took another riverboat to Fort Selkirk and from there boarded yet another boat that took him up the Pelly and Macmillan to the town of Ross River. He hiked from there to his cabin at Sheldon Lake, arriving in June. Now back in his old haunts, he intended to make an extended effort to look for the Lost McHenry. After performing camp chores such as cutting wood and cleaning up, he set out on foot and ascended to the headwaters of the Ross looking for the telltale cross that would supposedly point out the lost mine. He climbed above the timberline and scanned the surrounding peaks, but saw nothing encouraging. Then it dawned on him if he circled to the north side of the range where the snow lasted longer he might see something of interest. Surprisingly, once he was on the weather side of the peaks, he saw not one snow cross, but many. However, one of perfect symmetry stood out above all the others. It was formed by snow that had obviously piled deep in two intersecting fissures. Even more interesting was the fact that a huge avalanche had broken off and filled the fissures as it passed over them. Very possibly, it had taken forty or more years for the snowfields that caused the avalanche to build up, meaning that Wilson may have never seen this snow cross. Ironically, it was on the mountain that bore Wilson's name.

Johnny lined himself up with the cross and walked toward it, ultimately finding a stream that emanated from a cut below the avalanche. Following its course, he panned out a few colors. Deciding to do more work on it, he returned to his cabin on the Macmillan, retrieved a pick and shovel, and hiked back to the creek. Johnny dug and burned his way to bedrock, finding it relatively shallow at less than four feet. He brought up gravel, which he panned with no success. He tried another hole farther down the creek, eagerly digging it out and washing its contents. There were a few colors—just enough to give him cause to try again—but the next hole was worse than the last. He decided the creek was a bust and not worthy of further work.

Johnny realized he was probably wasting his time looking for the legendary McHenry mine, yet continued his wanderings among the peaks. This took him to the headwaters of the South Nahanni and Flat rivers, but his search was unrewarding and, with the coming of autumn, he ceased prospecting.

Fall comes early in the subarctic. The temperature drops and the ground hardens. Mosquitoes flutter, fly awkwardly, fall, and die. In the mornings, traces of ice cover firewood like glazing on a cake. The sun begins to droop in the sky and the moon becomes perkier as if knowing in a short time the long nights will provide its turn at glory.

The land is splashed with color for a brief period. The leaves of poplar, aspen, birch, and willow take on a tinge of amber similar to the eyes of a wolf reflecting the light of a campfire. Buck brush assumes the rosette tint of spawning dog salmon, creating an organdy mantle enveloping the slopes above the timberline. This overlying hue is enhanced by the golden glow of cottonwood trees in the river bottoms where the water is now low and clear. The air tingles and nips, but it is not uncomfortable. The animals, free from the insect scourge, move again. The bellow of the rutting bull moose echoes among the spruce trees announcing his defiance of those daring to challenge him. Migrating caribou soon swarm through the forests—the smack of the horns of the milling, fighting bulls permeating their world. Overhead, millions of wings beat a whirring tattoo over the rivers as geese and ducks make their way southward. At this time the sheep rams, lords and masters of the peaks, duel and smash their heads together with such jarring force as to startle even the mighty grizzly that is now plump and slightly lethargic from toting the body fat that will last him while he hibernates in his den through the winter.

The effect of the seasonal change likewise surged through Johnny's veins, and he returned to his cabin to hunt and stow meat for a season's trapping. And that winter he had moderate success. Johnny relished the life, but in February his forest void was pierced by strangers.

One night he was returning from his trapline under the light of a full moon when he heard dogs barking. He listened intently, surmising that the owners of the dogs had made camp. Unslinging his rifle, he set out in the direction of the newcomers to assure himself that the visitors were not going to post themselves permanently on his line. Making a wide circle through the forest, he eventually worked his way to a point directly across the frozen river from the camp. The dogs sent up a howl, but he stood motionless, and they finally quieted down. He heard two men chatting and judged they were probably Ross River people. From the temporary nature of the camp it looked like the two were on their way downriver and would not be raiding his trapline. He retraced his steps and went to his cabin.

The next spring the impulse to drift welled up in him again. This time he headed for Russell Creek and the trading post located there. Situated a few miles from the confluence of the north and south forks of the Macmillan, Russell Creek was one of the few streams in that immediate vicinity that produced much gold.

Arthur Zimmerlie had built this post twenty years earlier to accommodate trappers who drifted into the upper Macmillan area to take advantage of rising fur prices. This included supplying Indians who lived around there. A gold stampede had occurred in 1927, but only a handful of men reached the creek, and they did not find much to sing praises about. Johnny sold his furs to Zimmerlie and then remained camped outside Russell Creek for several weeks. He became acquainted with several men there, including two Swedes by the names of Pete Frederickson and Pete Linder.

One day, while he was brewing tea over a small fire in his camp, Linder came to visit him. Johnny motioned for the visitor to sit down. "Have a cup," Johnny said, handing one to his guest. Linder obliged and helped himself to the billycan, pouring the hot fluid into the cup. While Linder sipped the tea, Johnny's rifle caught his eye. He put the tea down and strode to the weapon, picked it up, and hefted it in his hands.

"Good piece you have here, Art," Linder commented.

Johnny, for once, was caught flat-footed. He had not expected Linder would make such a move, and it aroused his suspicions. If Linder was bent on foul play or happened to be a lawman, Johnny could be in deep trouble. Johnny damned himself for not having a pistol on him. There was only one thing he could do and that was to run a bluff. He put his right hand across his chest and under his coat. His eyes were glued to Linder's back. Any fast move and his only alternative would be to dive across the fire and tackle Linder.

Linder fingered the rifle, and at the same time spoke out. "Nice weapon, light, and you can take it down. Wouldn't mind having it myself," he said and not having heard any comment from his companion, he turned around to see the newcomer with his hand tucked in under his armpit where one might normally find a shoulder holster. Linder carefully put the gun back down. Johnny lowered his hand, and the incident was ignored, but not forgotten.

Johnny remained silent, judging the other man was probably only being neighborly, but when it came to a stranger picking up his rifle, he had too long been on the other side of the law not to take precautions.

A few minutes later the two men were joined by two more prospectors, one of whom, Frederickson, had sold Johnny a canoe a few days earlier. Now the breakup of the ice had come and Johnny planned on leaving.

"Hello, Art," Frederickson said, joining them. "I wish you luck."

"Thanks," Johnny said, answering automatically to his alias.

Another trapper and prospector named Anton Leland joined them and they jawed while Johnny went about packing his gear. Finally, everything was assembled and placed in his canoe, with the exception of three oranges Johnny had purchased from Zimmerlie. He gave the oranges to the men visiting him and then stepped into his canoe and shoved off. He heard Linder yell his thanks, but Johnny did not bother to look back.

# Chapter 15

# WRONG TURN

Johnny made up his mind to search for the Lost Cabin mine originally mentioned to him by the old prospector at Thibert Creek. This meant he would have to make his way to the Bell and the Porcupine rivers. He figured he could do this by going to the town of Keno, the jump-off point for trails to the Arctic, and situated about forty miles north of Mayo.

Ten years had gone by since Johnny was paroled and he had learned to live with the idea that his status would always be questionable. On an impulse he decided to write to Magnor and see if his brother could clear him completely with the parole board. He placed the letter in an envelope addressed to his mother, asking her to forward it to Magnor. In it, Johnny asked his brother to send information to him—giving his name as Albert Johnson, care of general delivery in Fort McPherson, Northwest Territories. Johnny mailed the letter from Mayo, Yukon Territory.

Johnny reached Keno in the latter part of April 1931. The town was a loose collection of cabins nestled together at the timberline on the approaches to the formidable Wernecke Mountains that towered on the northern horizon. Here, he became acquainted with another Norwegian, Ole Ostenstad, who lived in a small cabin at the base of the hill below the tiny hamlet. Ostenstad was easygoing. In fact, Johnny actually enjoyed his company, but other than telling him that he, too, was a Norwegian—which was obvious to Ostenstad—Johnny remained reticent.

Johnny managed to find a tiny abandoned cabin just up the creek from Ostenstad's place, and after discovering that his Norwegian friend was not liable to gab much, asked him if he could point out the trail to the Porcupine River.

"I'm not the guy to ask," Ostenstad said. "Instead, try Hardrock McDonald. He's hiked from here to the Arctic Ocean."

Johnny found McDonald, who, using a stick, drew a map in the dirt for him. "Just follow the trail to Beaver City. North of there, head up Police Creek to its headwaters and cross over to the Hart. You can raft from there to the Peel.

There you bear west with your compass and hike straight across the height of land to the Whitestone River, which you can float down until it reaches the Bell. That's the beginning of the Porcupine River."

Johnny had a pretty good memory for maps, but also realized reading a map and actually following it were two different things altogether and said as much.

"I'll tell you," said McDonald. "A partner of mine named Sullivan is going partway along the trail out of here tomorrow. You go with him and at least you will be headed in the right direction." He pointed out Sullivan's cabin.

"Tell him I sent you."

Johnny joined up with Sullivan and his partner on May 6 and set out on the trail to Beaver City. Johnny, who was in tremendous physical shape from his perpetual walking, found that the others were too slow for him. He elected to camp separately that night, and long before the others arose, he set out on the snow-covered trail by himself. This took him across a wide flat of grass hummocks to the south branch of the McQuesten River, which he reached near midday. An angler was fishing for grayling by the little bridge that crossed the creek. He acknowledged Johnny's presence with a wave, and Johnny waved back, continuing on without stopping. The snow grew deeper as he climbed up the trail that crossed the Potato Hills separating the south branch of the McQuesten from the north branch. It made for tough walking. He knew sooner or later that he would have to put on his snowshoes, but delayed as long as he could.

Johnny was about halfway up the long hill when he heard the crack of a dog whip. Observing that the dog driver had not seen him, he darted off into the forest. He saw a man stop and tie his team to a tree and walk slowly through the deep snow carefully checking Johnny's trail. As the man approached, Johnny could see that he was a Mountie, and wondered why the policeman would be so concerned about the path of a man he did not even know. Then Johnny wondered if it had something to do with him personally. If so, how could the cop have learned his route when, in fact, he did not know it himself? There had to be another reason. Johnny wracked his brains trying to figure it out as he drew a bead on the man from his hiding place behind the fork of a tree. His finger tightened on his .30–30 Savage. The policeman stopped, looked around, then retraced his tracks. Johnny breathed a sigh of relief, put away his rifle, and continued north.

Royal Canadian Mounted Police Corporal Tom Coleman was mushing back from a visit to the Beaver City and several small mining operations north while taking the Canadian census of 1931. Suddenly, he came across the path of a man departing from the main trail. The tracks in the snow were so fresh he wondered if the man may have deliberately fled in order to avoid him. He followed the impressions in the snow and ultimately ascertained that he could ill afford the time it would take to check him out. He returned to his team and mushed down to the south fork of the McQuesten where he saw John Kinman, a prospector of some repute, angling for grayling. "You see anyone go by here, John?" Coleman asked.

"Yeah, a guy toting a huge pack with a .250–3000 rifle in his hand," Kinman responded.

"Did he say anything?" Coleman asked.

"Nah. Just waved and walked on by."

Coleman never forgot the date because it was May 7, his birthday.

The wet snow slowed Johnny's regular pace from five miles an hour to three as he cut back to the trail from where the officer had come. Johnny continued his northern trek in the direction of Police Creek, gateway to the Hart River.

Years spent walking, trotting, running, and wandering through the endless wilderness had given him a tremendous physical capability. He could walk so far that he would actually get sleepy before he became tired. However, he had been too long in the bush not to know his limitations. When he dueled with a swamp or muskeg or wet snow, or the irritable *têtes-de-femmes* (grass hummocks), he would have to slow down his pace. No man could hurry through such obstacles without tiring. He also understood that when he came to firm ground he could increase his cadence and make up for lost time. He thought about this as he once again gained the trail north. The trampled snow was not much easier to walk through than the snow off the trail. The May sun beat down, turning the path into a gluelike mass. He knew better than to tire himself this way. He would make camp early and then hike during the hours of dawn when the snow was frozen like a plank boardwalk. There was no other way to travel in the spring.

Johnny continued up the trail until he reached an abandoned cabin. He removed his pack and built a fire in the cabin's small stove. He ate a dinner of boiled rice and dry meat. When he finished, he curled up on the spruce pole bunk and went to sleep.

That next morning, Johnny tramped resolutely northward, paralleling the north fork of the McQuesten River. He was well aware of the area's history as told to him by local residents of Keno. Indians, prospectors, and trappers had drifted through the Keno area at scattered intervals during the narrow stretch of time that was Yukon history. The path he followed was only eight years old, having been built as a road the year after silver was discovered in close proximity to Braine Pass. The stampede with regard to the silver strike soon died and with it the road, which had deteriorated from nonuse.

Johnny reached what he thought was Police Creek and followed it to its source. Once over the divide he would be on the Hart River. However, he had climbed into winter and the whole route was choked with snow and ice. Two glacier-encrusted slopes defied passage as he gingerly picked his way across them. He accepted these hazards with the instinctive reaction of an animal, conquering such obstacles with his physical stamina and coordination, and a patient tolerance born of years in the wilderness. Like a willow in a gale, he had learned to bend with the elements. Johnny did not confront them, he waited them out. The patient man lived—an old axiom, but a true one. He saw examples of these extremes virtually every day. The prints of a rabbit ending suddenly at those of a fox, moose bones scattered among the tracks of a wolf pack, a few feathers left of what once was a ptarmigan—the predator waited and the impatient and unwary victim perished.

Successfully traversing the pass, Johnny headed down the creek on the other side, picking his way through giant snow tunnels formed by water running under the huge slides that engulfed the stream during the winter. He emerged where the creek widened into a river, but the larger body of water was still frozen. Johnny had errantly reached the Wind River, not the Hart. He followed it for forty miles, until he reached a tributary stream that flowed into yet another river. He gauged that the water at this point would be deep enough to float a raft when the ice went out. He made camp there and lived off the land, hunting caribou, moose, ptarmigan, and snaring rabbits. He built a raft by hacking inverted V-shaped apertures into logs felled for the purpose. Lining these up, he drove cross-braces through them. They would swell up when wet, holding the logs together.

The warm weather of spring finally descended and melted the river ice, and Johnny launched the raft, guiding it with the current of the river. At likely looking spots, he poled the raft ashore to prospect for gold. During many of these side trips he plodded through muskeg typical of the north. The wet moss surface was matted with grass hummocks and unfrozen for only a few inches. From this sparse strata grew forests of black spruce. As the snow melted, water remained trapped on underlying permafrost. Stagnant pools and ponds resulted in ideal breeding grounds for mosquitoes that rose in clouds to harass him. He was thankful he possessed a head net for protection. He discovered nothing to be enthusiastic about in the way of prospecting, but he did come across engaging traces of those who had gone before him.

One day Johnny spotted the ruins of an old camp on the left bank of the river. He pulled ashore and climbed the fifty-foot incline, then poked among the ruins looking for items that could be of some use to him. A dilapidated carved board inside a broken-down cabin revealed the name of the settlement—Wind City. His guess that the community was probably a relic of the gold rush was confirmed when he found an envelope dated 1898 stuffed into a crack in a log. He found nothing of use to him that he could physically carry away, but he did discover something that was of interest. This was a furnace made out of willow saplings set on end and banked with clay. He studied it carefully before moving on.

Johnny retrieved his pack and made camp on the bank, first putting up his mosquito bar as a refuge he crawled under when the insects became too numerous. He built a fire and threw wet moss on it to create a cloud of smoke for added protection against the irritating swarms of the critters.

Almost simultaneously, he was surprised to see a caribou that obviously had sought relief in the cool river water to escape the same menace. Picking up his rifle, Johnny worked his way around to a spot downwind of the animal and brought it down with one shot. Years spent hunting made his rifle so much a part of him that to point it at something was the same as aiming his finger. He rarely missed. He cut the meat of the animal into strips and smoked them, taking a week to finish the chore.

Johnny took to the river again and floated down to its junction with a surprisingly large watercourse that flowed in from the west. He was puzzled. He had been told that after reaching the Peel he would have a short portage to the

Whitestone River that he would float down until he reached the Bell, the confluence of the two rivers forming the Porcupine. From there he would go up the Bell looking for the Lost Cabin mine. He cached his gear and followed blazes along a faint trail on a small creek that flowed down from the north.

Johnny traveled most of the day before coming up against a seemingly endless range of mountains stretching to the north of him. There was absolutely no landmark to indicate the Whitestone River.

Johnny camped that night by an abandoned cabin—it seemed as if no matter where a man went men had been there before—and the next day he retraced his steps to his cache on the larger river. Distant canyons made the watercourse look forbidding from the standpoint of a man with a raft, but he decided to chance running it anyway. He shoved off into the current and within a short time found his raft in a millrace of water that bucked and slammed his crude craft against boulders and canyon walls as he fought to keep his heading downstream. Occasionally, in some stretches, he was able to glance at the walls above him and saw smoke spiraling up from what were probably lignite beds, which once afire never went out.

The most dangerous part of his passage was a whirlpool that reached out like some giant monster to gather Johnny and his raft into its vortex. Only with a great heave and a shove with his pole was he able to avoid this treacherous hole in the water. Caroming off boulders and cliffs, hitting snags, dropping violently over step-down cataracts, twisting and turning among rapids of the river, he rode through the turbulence. He was alone and there was no room for mistakes. Finally, he reached the mouth of another large tributary where the water was calm and placid, and poled ashore. He put up his tent, made camp, and remained there for several days trying to figure out where he was—but to no avail.

Taking to the river again, standing up as usual on his long, narrow raft with his hefty pack and rifle, he floated downstream past several cabins, their presence confusing him. He was now in the land where the sun never set at the height of summer, nor rose in the depths of winter. Flies and mosquitoes swarmed in clouds along the spruce-endowed banks of the river. After hours of drifting, he spotted a sandy patch, poled ashore, and made camp. Not long afterward, he saw two Gwitchin Indians paddling upstream. He quickly hoisted his mosquito bar and hailed the two men. They paddled over to him and pulled up along the shore, not leaving their canoe.

"Hello," one of the Gwitchin said.

"Is this the Porcupine?" Johnny asked.

The natives laughed. "No," said the first one, "this is the Peel. The Porcupine is five days that way." He pointed to the west.

"You are near Fort McPherson," the other said.

"Damn," Johnny said, and yanked down the mosquito net so hard he almost tore it off. He'd obviously missed a trail somewhere. He was disgusted that he had made such a mistake. He had not figured on going to Fort McPherson until after he had searched the upper Bell for the Lost Cabin mine. Now he would have to reverse the process. However, since he was here earlier than planned, he might as well check the mail to see if his brother had written. Then he would buy a canoe and try to get to the Bell and build a cabin.

The next day he floated downriver until he saw some cabins and made camp again on shore about a half mile above McPherson. Climbing the fifty-foot bank behind him the next morning, he easily spotted a path along its rim and followed that into the community, his pockets bulging with his three thousand dollars.

He scanned the surroundings as he walked among the cabins of the hamlet. The Hudson's Bay Company's store, which was built with alabaster, was in marked contrast to the plain, primitive cabins scattered around it. Equally prominent was the log church of the Anglicans. One thing that was a bit odd, but not so odd when he thought about it, was the vast number of newly dug graves in the cemetery. Johnny figured they arose from a flu epidemic that ravaged the north country two years earlier. Obviously, it had devastated this community.

Behind the town the country was flat with a number of small lakes and muskeg swamps and scrubby spruce trees in abundance among them. Heat waves produced by the incessant broiling arctic sun shimmered above the swamp. Mosquitoes unfolded their wings in the torrid atmosphere and rose up in vaporous clouds that rolled over Fort McPherson like a mist from the sea. The constant near hum of the insects fastened the community in a soniclike grip, and was a relentless annoyance. Occasionally a breeze brought relief from the pesky marauders, but it was only temporary, and the drone always returned and the persistence of it all was depressing.

Johnny noted there was another store beside Hudson's Bay, that being Northern Traders. A number of Indian children were playing among the buildings and several adults sat idly on benches in front of the stores.

He elected to visit the Northern Traders post first because such "independents" often gave a man a better deal than a larger company, just so they could stay in business.

Johnny roamed the store, casually checking its contents and prices. The goods were a colorful mixture of everything needed in the north country from snowshoes to mukluks.

An Iver Johnson single-barrel, 16-gauge shotgun located in a rack behind the counter caught his eye. It would be an excellent weapon for bringing down ducks, geese, and swans in spring and late summer. He also spotted a .22-caliber Winchester rifle in another rack. This would take care of his ptarmigan hunting.

Johnny pointed the guns out to the proprietor, who laid them on the counter. Automatically, he grabbed a box of shells that fit each weapon and put them next to the guns.

"Anything else?" he asked.

Johnny nodded. "Three more boxes of ammo for each should do," he said.

The storekeeper added them to the pile.

Johnny then went around the door picking out staples such as flour, sugar, and tea that he would need for a year.

The trader then tallied the bill. "That will be nine hundred and sixty-eight dollars," he said.

Johnny extracted the cash from a number of pockets, counted it, and handed it to the proprietor.

"Thanks," the proprietor said. "By the way, you ever heard of a man by the name of Bill Hanna?" Johnny was startled by the question. "No, why?" he lied, recalling his friend who had the accident with the gun.

"A letter was sent here asking if anyone had run into him. It said he disappeared after leaving Dease Lake."

"I am looking for a letter for Albert Johnson," Johnny said.

"Is that you?"

"Yeah."

"You'll have to go to the Hudson's Bay store for that."

Johnny nodded. "All right," he said to the storekeeper, "Put all this stuff in burlap sacks and I'll be back for it later."

The storekeeper nodded. "Okay."

"One more thing," Johnny said. "Here's an extra buck to buy the kids I've seen outside some candy."

"I'll take care of that right now," the Northern Traders man said. "You going to trap around here?"

"I don't know. I might go to the Yukon," Johnny said.

Johnny walked out of the Northern Traders store and into the Hudson's Bay post. He asked the clerk if there was any mail for Albert Johnson, and again, the answer was no.

"However," the clerk added, "a boat's due for one more trip before freeze-up if you want to wait."

"How long is that?"

"A couple of weeks," the clerk said.

Johnny really wanted to hear from Magnor. A letter from him might cushion his worries. "Thanks," he said, "I might."

When Johnny walked out of the Northern Traders post, a cleric wearing a collar passed him going in. He was Bishop Geddes, who gave Johnny the once-over as he walked by him. The Anglican Bishop had been in the north many years and, as a result, was inclined to be patronizing toward his flock, and possibly overly protective.

"What can I do for you, Reverend?" the storekeeper asked.

"I'd like a few knickknacks, Mr. Douglas. That would be some coffee, tea, and a pound of sugar."

"Fine," said Douglas, and gathered up the items and placed them on the counter.

Bishop Geddes nodded toward the door. "A new man?"

"Yes, Reverend, I believe he is."

"A hard-looking man."

"Why do you say that?" Douglas asked.

"His eyes. I can often tell a man by his eyes. Looks like he has a chip on his shoulder a mile wide."

"Aren't you being a little quick to pass judgment?"

"Contrariness shows on some people"

"He wasn't any trouble for me. He bought almost a thousand dollars' worth of goods and paid cash. And it looked like he had plenty more."

Geddes shook his head in disagreement. "That's a lot for a man to have up here."

"Some trappers make big money," Douglas retorted.

"Tell me, Bill, do you have one man who is not in debt to you?"

"Well, no, but—"

"How did he get here?" Geddes asked, cutting off the storekeeper.

"Indians say he came down the Peel on a raft."

"On a raft?"

"Yes, on a raft."

"What time does the postal boat leave for Aklavik?"

"Same as usual, tomorrow."

"Let me have an envelope and writing paper."

Douglas looked at Geddes curiously, then handed him the material.

"The Mounties should be advised of this man's presence."

"Okay, Reverend, but aren't you being a little hasty? The stranger didn't do any—"

Bishop Geddes interrupted Douglas by putting up his hand. "You understand, Mr. Douglas, that I have to protect my flock." Geddes began scribbling a note, and then looked up. "Do you know his name?"

"Yeah, he told me it was Albert Johnson."

"A likely story," the Bishop said suspiciously as he was completing the note and stuffing it into an envelope given to him by Douglas.

"Have it your way," Douglas mumbled with a shrug of his shoulders.

Bishop Geddes handed the envelope to Douglas. "Would you see that this gets sent? I have some calls to make upriver."

"Sure."

As Bishop Geddes walked out of the store a flock of Indian children with the usual pennies in their hands pushed their way in.

"You're in luck today," Douglas said, reaching into a bowl filled with sweets and grabbing a handful. "The candy is free."

Two days later the bishop's letter was delivered to the police post in Aklavik.

"This all?" asked Corporal Dick Wild.

"That's it," the mailman replied and left.

Wild was a slim man of moderate height who sported a pencil-thin mustache. He walked to his desk and sat down.

Hanging from nails in the wall were several sets of crossed snowshoes. To his side was a gun rack that held a half dozen Enfield rifles. Most of his work was routine, which made for a fairly boring existence. He opened and scanned the letter and then brought it into the inner office of Inspector Alexander N. Eames, his boss.

Eames was a big man, over two hundred pounds and six feet tall. His slightly balding head betrayed his age, which was over forty. Behind his desk was the flag of the Dominion of Canada, and the British Union Jack on his left. Centered between the two was a large photo of King George V.

Eames looked up.

"Well, what is it, Corporal?" Eames said impatiently.

"A letter from Bishop Geddes," Wild said, handing it to the inspector.

"So?"

"He doesn't like the looks of a drifter named Johnson who showed up at McPherson."

Eames glanced at the letter.

"The good reverend is playing policeman again," Wild commented.

Eames looked at Wild sternly. "Bishop Geddes is not only a good friend of mine, but he is extremely keen of observation."

Wild knew better than to argue with his superior. "Yes, sir," he said.

Eames read the letter, initialed it, then handed it back to Corporal Wild. "Tell Constable Millen to check this man out on his next patrol to McPherson."

# Chapter 16

# GOLD STRIKE!

The Hudson's Bay mail boat distributor finally arrived two weeks later, but there was no mail for Johnny. While he was waiting for it, he became acquainted with a native, Abe Francis, who had set up a fish camp directly across from him on the Peel. He appeared to be about the same age as Johnny who would turn thirty-four on July 13. He and members of his family would canoe across the river and land near Johnny's camp before proceeding to town.

Having noticed that Francis had at least three canoes beached across the river, Johnny figured he might be able to buy one from him. "You sell me canoe?" he asked one day, pointing to the boat.

Francis looked at the canoe and then at Johnny. He was surprised by the offer, and had to think about it.

"Sell you canoe?" he asked.

"Yes," Johnny said. "I want to go to the Bell River."

"He's in good shape. I will sell," Francis finally said.

Johnny noticed that these natives, most all of whom spoke some English because of Anglican missionary work in the area, often referred to objects as "he" rather than "it."

"How much?" Johnny asked.

"Thirty dollar," Francis said.

"Okay," Johnny said with little deliberation. He took ten dollars out of one pocket and twenty dollars out of another pocket and handed the bills to Francis.

"How would I get to the Bell?" Johnny asked.

Abe Francis pointed down the Peel River. "Half day to Blake's post. Then ask him."

Johnny thanked Francis. Later that day, Francis delivered the boat to Johnny who loaded it up with his gear and broke camp. He made one last stop at the settlement to pick up additional supplies.

Meanwhile, Geddes's letter was forwarded to Corporal Edgar "Spike" Millen who commanded the Mountie detachment at Arctic Red River, located on the Mackenzie River where it was joined by the Arctic Red about forty miles east of Fort McPherson. A tall, gaunt-looking man whose exterior belied a friendly personality, Millen was, like Johnny, an immigrant from Europe. He was born in Belfast, Ireland, in 1901, and emigrated to the New World with his parents at a tender age. He joined the Royal Northwest Mounted Police at the age of nineteen. True to an adventurous spirit, he volunteered for northern service and was posted first to Aklavik in 1920. Later, he was promoted and transferred to Arctic Red River.

Millen set out on his normal patrol toward the end of July, taking the Mounties' skiff down the Mackenzie to the mouth of the Peel, then up that river to Fort McPherson.

Johnny had paddled his canoe to Fort McPherson and was packing supplies down the steep bank to the landing when he encountered a policeman. The Mountie had just tied up his skiff. Other than a casual glance, he had said nothing as he walked by, and Johnny went on with his packing.

Constable Millen went to the Northern Traders store and walked in. He was immediately greeted by Douglas.

"His majesty's finest. Hello, Spike," Douglas said.

Millen walked to the counter with a slightly preoccupied look. "Good morning, Mr. Douglas, how are you?"

"I'll pass in a crowd if I walk right along."

Millen eyed the interior of the trading post. "It's quiet around here. Where are the kids today?"

Douglas smiled. "When the word gets out that you're here, they'll be around," he replied, adding, "What's up?"

Millen shrugged. "Nothing in particular. Usual patrol."

Douglas wondered if his visit might have had something to do with Bishop Geddes's letter. "Usual call, eh?"

Millen pushed his Stetson back on his head. "Well, Bill," he said, "not quite. I've been ordered to—"

"Check out a strange white man," Douglas interrupted.

Millen grimaced and nodded slowly indicating he was nonplussed. "The Bishop's seeing goblins again?"

"You should be a detective," Douglas responded with a grin.

"No, you should," Millen said. "Where can I find this guy?"

"He's stocky and blond and as inconspicuous here as a duck on land."

Millen spotted the candy jar that was always full on the counter and took a few. "You didn't answer my question."

"No wonder, you're eating all my candy," Douglas replied. "You must have walked right by him when you came up. Try the landing."

"Thanks," Millen said and turned to leave the store. At that moment the door opened and a flock of native children barged in. Millen picked up a little girl and hoisted her onto his shoulder. Her name was Mary and she was as cute as a button.

"What's your name?" Millen asked knowing it all along.

Mary chewed her thumb and was so shy she did not answer.

"She doesn't know her name," he said, winking at Douglas. "Everybody gets free candy, but Mary. Now, what's your name?"

The temptation was too much for the little girl. "Mary," she said quickly.

Constable Millen put her down on the floor again and reached into his pocket, taking out a dollar. "This is for the candy," he said and winked at the storekeeper.

Harried by the mob of little hands extended toward him, Douglas waved off the Mountie. "Thanks," he said and then focused his attention on the moppets in front of him.

"You're all getting spoiled," he said to them.


Johnny had just finished loading a flour sack into the canoe when he straightened up and found himself face-to-face with the Mountie who had previously walked past him.

Millen, a veteran policeman, carefully studied the man in front of him. He was immediately struck by the man's eyes. They were like a Siberian husky's, icy blue and just as unfathomable. The pupil of one eye, the left, was dilated, possibly from some sort of injury. It gave off an effect of permanent hostility. The face was grim and unsmiling.

"My name's Millen," the Mountie said.

Johnny, at a loss for words and dreading what the policeman might have on his mind, only nodded.

"Nice day," Millen said pleasantly. "You planning on staying on in the country?"

"Why do you want to know?" Johnny asked as wild fears raced through his head and he tried to suppress his anxiety.

Millen was reasonable, and felt he should give the blond man an answer. "Routine. It saves us a lot of time and expense if a man gets hurt. What's your name?"

Johnny relaxed a little. "Albert Johnson," he said.

"Are you going to trap?"

Johnny was irritated. "Do you ask everyone that?" he said.

"You don't have to answer," Millen said. It was not unusual for trappers and prospectors to be evasive about their prospects and trapping intentions. They were well aware the Mounties were allowed to supplement their income by pursuing both avocations in their spare time.

"Yes, maybe," Johnny said.

"Any idea where?"

Johnny turned and pointed to the Richardson Mountains.

"Up the Rat, maybe in the Yukon."

"Where are you from?" Millen asked.

"The prairies," Johnny replied. "I spent the winter there." Johnny always possessed the feeling that if the police traced his past he would be returned to Folsom Prison. He just did not know what his status was and he was afraid to ask. That was one of the reasons he had written to his brother who had either let him down or never received the letter.

Millen figured he had anticipated about everything without actually putting the stranger under arrest. "Look," he said, "if you are going to trap in the Northwest Territories, you can get a license from me right now. It will save you a trip later on."

Johnny saw the logic in it, but the fact that he was being pressured grated on his mind. "No," he said, "not now." Johnny turned away from the cop and nervously sorted some of his gear.

Millen never liked to leave anyone on a sour note. "That was just a suggestion," he said.

Johnny took it the wrong way. He turned around and glared at the policeman. "Am I bothering anybody?" he asked.

Millen figured he'd given Johnny every courtesy. "That's not the point," he said.

Johnny turned his back on Millen and tended to his boat. He stepped into it, and pushed off from shore. He, too, had calmed down. "So long, Constable," he said respectfully. Then the Peel River swept Johnny and his canoe downstream.

Millen returned to the Northern Traders store and joined the trader, Douglas, for a cup of tea. It was lunch hour and no one was around.

"Bill, was Johnson any trouble around here?"

The trader placed a cup of boiling tea on the counter. "On the contrary. He camped out of town. He was never a problem. Why?"

Millen sipped the tea and set the cup back down. "He was pretty close-mouthed. A stubborn guy. When I suggested he buy a trapping license, it was like I insulted him."

Douglas frowned. "Spike, for God's sake, is that unusual?"

"No. You're right. I'm getting as bad as the bishop." He sipped the tea. "I've got to be going."

"You wouldn't be planning a stop at Cardinal's fish camp, would you?"

"I might. Why?"

"Here's some mail for them. Not that you need an excuse."

Traveling in the opposite direction of the blond stranger, Millen headed south up the Peel about ten miles until he saw a fishing camp on the right and beached the skiff. A striking young woman emerged from the recesses of the camp and took the bowline when he tossed it ashore.

Lydia Ladoucer was a tall, willowy, half-breed stepdaughter of a former special constable of the Royal Northwest Mounted Police. Educated in a mission school, she spoke fluent English. She wore a caribou-skin dress decorated with artful designs of beadwork.

Lydia extended a hand to the Mountie when he jumped ashore.

"Here's your mail," Millen said impatiently.

"Spike, aren't you going to stay with us for a while?" Lydia asked, her eyes searching Millen's.

Constable Millen shook his head. "No, Lydia. I would if I could. The inspector wants a report. I have to run down to Aklavik." Spike grabbed her hands and held them, then kissed her.

"When's the season over?" he asked.

"In a couple of weeks," she replied.

"That long? I'm getting awfully lonely."

Lydia's eyes lit up with humor. "Constable, spawning fish can't wait, but you can."

Millen smiled, and pushed the boat off. Lydia threw the bowline to him.

"Say hello to the old one for me," Millen said as the Peel's current took him back past Fort McPherson to the Husky River where he steered the skiff downriver to Aklavik.

Constable Millen stood at attention in front of Inspector Eames, who was intentionally slow in ordering Millen at rest.

"You didn't find out where Johnson came from. You didn't find out where he was going. You have no idea why he came here," the inspector said, and paused before continuing. "Why did you bother talking to him at all?"

"Do I have liberty in speaking out?"

"Go ahead."

"I told you, sir, Johnson said he came up from the prairies, and was going to trap, possibly on the Rat or over in the Yukon. That's all I could get out of him."

"At rest, Constable," the inspector ordered, obviously trying to hold his temper in check. "Maybe I wasn't explicit enough, but you know as well as I, you can invoke section twenty-four of the game regulations to find out what a man's doing. You can even search his outfit if you have to."

Constable Millen had enough years of volunteer service in the Arctic to speak his mind even if he did not have permission.

"I thought this was a free country!" he exclaimed.

"Not when it comes to people's lives it isn't," Inspector Eames retorted.

"Since when does a man have to answer my questions if he doesn't want to?"

Eames knew his men in the Arctic were a testy bunch. They were all volunteers. The inspector relished a good argument once in a while, especially when he knew he was right. "If he's got nothing to hide, why wouldn't he want to?" he said and paused for effect. "No, Millen, you let this man off too easy."

"I disagree—"

"You've had your say," Eames interrupted, and held up a balance sheet. "I have a budget to think of. A few pointed questions now can save long, expensive patrols later."

"Yes, sir," Millen said.

"By the way, say hello to old man Cardinal for me," he said softly, turning away from Millen to focus his attention on budget documents.

Johnny, after packing the equipment he had purchased in the canoe, paddled down the Peel past Fort McPherson to Blake's post.

Blake was a former Mountie who had cast his lot with a native wife and raised a family there at his trading post on the river.

Johnny paddled ashore and asked the older man how he could get to the Bell River.

Blake was used to strangers, and though they were few and far between there always seemed to be someone looking for something, whether it was gold or a good place to trap or hunt. "Easy to find if you go the long way, down the Husky to the mouth of the Rat, then up that to the lake that separates the Bell from the Rat," he said, and then paused briefly before continuing. "You can take a shorter route right back of my place," he said, pointing in that general direction, "but it involves a mess of portages."

"Thanks," Johnny said. "You got any dry meat for sale?"

"All you want," Blake said.

"I'll take a couple of pounds."

Grateful for the sale, Blake called one of his sons and sent him after the meat.

In a short time, Johnny had the dry meat packed aboard the canoe and, taking the second more difficult route, paddled up the Rat River as far as he could go. Then he rigged up a tracking line and pulled the boat until he found a nice place to make camp right where the Rat burst out of the mountains, making an L-shaped turn to the north. He liked the spot so much he decided to build a cabin on a promontory in the right angle of the L. This gave him a good view of the river both upstream and down.

Johnny was satisfied that this was a promising place for trapping, and a good base to search for the lost mine, but first he had to get his camp ready for the winter. One of the spot's most important advantages was its accessibility to plenty of spruce trees large enough to provide logs for the cabin. The structure he built measured eight by ten feet. It was just right for one man in that it did not take much in the way of firewood to keep it warm, but was large enough for him to move around in. He countersunk the floor of the cabin by digging two feet down, then piled soil from the hole around the sides of the shack. He also pitched dirt onto the log pole roof of the cabin. He built a bunk made of spruce logs, and he carved up logs to make shelves and a crude chair. He covered the cabin's one window with a couple layers of cellophane. Johnny shaped a door latch and rigged the portal so he could bar it from the inside with a stout log.

Preparing for winter, Johnny fished for arctic char with a gill net he had devised for the purpose, stripped the fish, and smoked them.

Johnny roamed the sparsely treed Richardson Mountains hunting caribou, completely in awe of the incredibly green tundra grass that stretched as far as a man could see.

After he made a kill he would transport the carcass to a hunting camp set up for the purpose of dressing the caribou. He then relayed the meat and hides to his cabin where he stowed the cuts in a hole dug and shored up in the permafrost. He soaked the hides, scraped the hair off, and hung them up. Later he sliced the skins into strips known as *babiche*, which he used for webbing in a stout pair of snowshoes. He fashioned moccasins and shirts out of caribou skins, and mukluks from the hide of a moose he killed. When temperatures hit extreme lows, he stuffed his mukluks with grass for extra warmth. He also packed meat to other caches he built in trees far up the Rat and Barrier rivers in anticipation of the winter's trapping.

Frost was already heavy on the tundra when he completed these basic chores. Finally, he was able to take the time to look for the Lost Cabin mine. Recalling that a triangular cabin marked the location, he set out on his search. Following Scottee's suggestion he tramped up the Rat to its source, then followed the headlands into the jumble of hills from which the Bell and Big Fish rivers drained. Once there, he began tracing every tributary stream flowing through that part of the country.

Looking for such diggings was at best a dubious quest, yet for Johnny the search tended to give his compulsion to roam and to drift a sense of purpose. Consequently, failure was no deterrent to his trying again.

Moving at a snail's pace, he worked his way from stream to stream and pup to pup. No artery of water was too small for him to follow, nor too inconsequential for him to check. From years of experience in the bush, he knew where to look for cabins. They were not just put up at random. An experienced bush dweller looked for many factors that spelled the difference between a good location and a bad one. Necessities such as a southern exposure to obtain the maximum amount of winter sunlight, the close proximity of water for easy hauling, the presence of timber both for building the cabin and supplying firewood, and locating the structure so that it was above the flood line—all were taken into consideration. If a man built in the fall when the ground was frozen, he had to make sure the cabin was not set on potentially soft ground or he would find his shack sunk in a swamp come spring.

Johnny thought long and hard about a cabin that was only three-sided. The most practical reason he could think of to create this kind of structure would be a scarcity of logs. That would mean such a cabin would more than likely be found at higher locations. That is why he stuck to the headlands during his initial search.

Though keeping his eye out for cabins, Johnny was not remiss in testing gravels of the creeks for gold. Fine gold washed up in flakes and appeared in his pan, but coarse gold was what he wanted. It was composed of chunks that could range in size from a head of a pin to that of a thumbnail and, on occasion, larger. This was the lure that drove men to the ends of the earth seeking it.

Johnny traveled in a northwesterly direction crossing one headland after another until he was not sure if he was on a tributary of the Bell, or possibly had dropped into the upper reaches of the Driftwood River. Johnny realized if there was a grain of truth to the story, the gold would be of the coarse variety, and the presence of volcanic rocks would be a bellwether of potential mineralization in the area. These igneous rocks burst from the bowels of the earth via a natural pipe, and often gold was found among them.

One day he descended to the timberline and made camp on a bank carpeted with spruce needles at the confluence of the main stream and a tributary that tumbled down from the surrounding peaks. He put up a tarp and cut wood and stacked it next to a rock fireplace he had hastily thrown together. After completing those chores he walked up the side creek with his 16-gauge shotgun—which he had sawed off for convenience in packing—in search of ptarmigan. He heard a cluck farther back in the bush and headed toward it, his mind on nothing more than obtaining grouse for supper. He went into the clump of spruce and stumbled head-on into a clearing where he discerned a cabin at the far end. From his angle it appeared to be a normal cabin with four sides. Only when he walked around it did he realize—it only had three sides. The roof had caved in. He peered over the east wall of the cabin and saw the rotted frame of a sluice box. He vaulted over the wall and examined the box more closely. It was withered but easily identifiable, indicating that someone had mined in the vicinity.

Johnny was too accustomed to setbacks to become overly excited about the find. Trappers often placed items on the roof to store them, and the fact that a sluice box was there, though encouraging, was not proof that gold would be. He continued his hunt, bagging two ptarmigan with one shot of his shotgun, which was sawed off so far the barrel was only two inches long. He returned to camp, plucked the feathers from the birds, and then boiled the meat.

Johnny's thoughts went to the cabin and to the sluice box. He had noticed a number of satellites of igneous rock in the vicinity, and though not necessarily guaranteeing the presence of gold, there was a possibility. Johnny sank his teeth into the ptarmigan and chewed the meat slowly, savoring the delicious flavor.

He judged that if gold was found in a large quantity, it might not be located in the immediate area of the cabin. A miner who espied a pay streak in that far-off country would be extremely wary of putting up a cabin right next to it. Not being able to stake the claim without making a two-month journey to the nearest mining recorder's office, a man would probably stay and work it, amassing all he could in a one-shot effort prior to carrying the gold out with him. A miner would tend to be secretive about the location for fear that someone might stumble across the workings and rush to record it before him. On the other hand, this area was so remote, Johnny surmised that the builder of the cabin, pressed for time, possibly neglected normal precautions in favor of speed. If he was without dogs he would want to make his way out by floating downriver with his precious cargo, and in order to do this he would have to depart before the rivers froze up.

Johnny did not suffer from buck fever pertaining to his find. He made some tea, sipped it, and then crawled into his sleeping bag. Tomorrow would be soon enough. That night, the sky was afire with the multicolored swirls of the ghostly aurora borealis as it flitted in curtained curves from horizon to horizon. In conjunction with the convulsions of light, great verdant streamers tipped with pink would pierce the darkness and just as suddenly retreat like dying rockets, only to flare off in another direction. It was as if two behemoths were tossing hot coals back and forth in the heavens. The Samis thought it was their ancestors up there.

Johnny did not consider himself a superstitious individual, though some things that arose in nature could tempt a man to become that way. And now, overhead, he witnessed a strange manifestation of the northern lights that he had never seen before, and he had been in the north country now for almost ten years. Glancing upward at the night sky he saw that an aurora spiral had formed right above him. Startled, he realized he was looking at a whirlwind of color enclosing him at its base like the bottom of a shaft dug to bedrock. This circular mass of light ascended into the heavens in dimensions unknown and all but impossible to measure. He supposed that human eyes had seen it before, but not often, he judged. No one had ever mentioned such a spiral to him or had he ever read about it. The walls of light did not descend to the ground, but they did appear to dust the surrounding peaks with their celestial rays. This lasted only a few minutes and then fused into curtains the likes of which he had not seen before.

Naturally enough, he wondered if the cylindrical splash of light was a forecast of success in his search for gold, and he went to sleep thinking about it.

The next morning Johnny ascended the tributary stream off what could have been the north fork of the Bell; he was not sure. He filled his gold pan with the gravel and sand he had scraped from the downstream side of a boulder in the bed of the creek. Here the stream was virtually on bedrock. Then, squatting by a pool and holding the pan in both hands, he dipped it into the pool, washing away the lighter material. He sloshed water in the pan, and each time he did, soil was washed out. Small rocks surfaced, and he picked these out and cast them aside. In such a way, he patiently worked the pan until the first touch of black sand appeared. This substance, iron pyrite, was often found with gold. He moved the pan a little slower now, gently wafting the water back and forth. Some more of the pyrites slipped out of the pan, this time revealing brilliant specks of yellow of about the size of mouse droppings. It was gold, coarse gold. He washed all of the black sand from the pan and counted at least half a pennyweight of the yellow mineral. He took a vial out of his pocket and carefully poured the tiny nuggets into it, then filled another pan from the same spot and was just as successful. One pennyweight in two pans was an average he had never before encountered in all of the years he had prospected for gold. Gold was worth thirty-two dollars an ounce. Twenty pennyweights made up an ounce, which meant he was making eighty cents to the pan—an incredible find if it held up. Johnny had been disappointed too many times to get overly exultant. He knew gold could pinch out from one spot in a stream to the next within only a few feet. More testing had to be done. He wandered up the creek loading his gold pan to the brimful with gravel and then washing it. He panned leisurely, stopping to eat lunch and to figure out various places to test. A dry streambed caught his eye. He dug into the soil and washed material from that and found more gold among the roots of the overburden, but the average was about the same. He worked forty pans and accumulated thirteen pennyweights or, allowing for three hundred fines off for impurities, about ten dollars' worth of gold before he quit.

That night, absentmindedly tossing and catching the vial filled with gold as he stared into the campfire, Johnny calculated it took about six hours using a pan to wash out the nuggets. But, it was all surface stuff, which ran about twenty yards along the creek. Once that was cleaned up, farther on he would have to burn through the permafrost to get to bedrock, which he guessed was not very deep. The area where he found gold covered about two hundred yards in length and—including the dry streambed—blanketed an area ten yards wide. Even calculating just the minimum quantities, he knew he was rich!

Johnny went to bed that night a happy man. While he slept, the mercury plummeted to twenty below zero. The cold forced Johnny to get out of his sleeping bag and toss more logs onto the fire. To his dismay, when he awoke the next morning he found that the ground that had yielded so easily for panning the night before was now frozen solid. Johnny realized this was a harbinger of things to come. He could not stay around and do much in the way of placer mining. He was realistic about the gold. It would still be there in the summer of 1932. Taking out a pencil and a packing label, he carefully sketched a peak on the back of the label and marked the Porcupine and its tributary, the Bell River. He depicted a triangle on this feeder stream of the Bell and tucked the paper into the vial.

Back at his cabin, the cold set in and Johnny prepared for winter.

# FACE-OFF

William Nerysoo had trapped in the vicinity of the Rat River for years, as had
his father and his father's father. Therefore, one day while hunting ptarmigan,
the sight of a newly built cabin on a bend of the Rat came as a complete surprise to him. Returning to his hunting camp he reported this to his wife, who was
busy tanning a moose hide. "*Unchit* (white man) move in upriver. *Neezyqua* (no
good)," he said.

The Mounties of the Arctic Red River detachment were often bored and found
that a good way to alleviate their malaise was to schedule target practice.

Constable Alfred King, a square-jawed man with dark, wavy hair and blue
eyes; Corporal Millen, the tall and angular commander of the detachment; and
Constable Melville were shooting one day in December of 1931 behind the
detachment cabins. Millen's rifle was a bolt-action .303 Enfield. Melville and
King were carrying lever-action Winchesters. The men were firing at stones set
on stumps. Millen took careful aim with his Enfield, pulled the trigger, and a
stone flew off a stump.

"Not bad shooting, Spike, but I still think you ought to use a lever-action.
Speed is what counts, especially for a grizzly," King commented.

"The same with people," Melville said, and paused, "Bolt isn't much good
if you're up against a man with a lever-action."

Millen laughed. "What people? When would we ever be shooting at anyone up here?"

"You never know," Melville said.

"Yeah, it's so quiet here the dogs don't bark, they whisper," King chimed in.

King then levered off six shots in half the time it took Millen with the bolt-
action. Rocks flew. "Let's see you do that with your Enfield, Spike," King said.

The snow was deep at Johnny's cabin and the river was frozen. The long darkness was on the land. In the grim light of a sunless sky Johnny finished chopping wood and carried an armful inside his new home. Johnny had cleared the land behind the cabin so he could see anyone approaching on the river behind him. The same applied to the front, which he had cleared. There was no window in the back of the cabin, but if he had to, he could easily peruse the back area by knocking out the chinking between the logs.

About twenty yards in front of the cabin was a bank about four feet high. This had been formed by water swirling around the end of the peninsula and cutting into the bank. Johnny had an excellent field of vision from the front with the exception of the bank. Spruce and cottonwoods grew on the right and left sides of the cabin, but were not so dense that they obscured a sight line of at least twenty yards. Johnny put down the wood and lit a candle, which gave off an eerie glow revealing the interior of the countersunk cabin. The floor was about two feet below the surface of the ground. A spruce pole bunk covered with boughs and a caribou hide thrown over them was situated lengthwise along the right wall of the cabin. To the right of the door, which faced south toward the river, was the structure's one window, made up of strips of cellophane and framed by a burlap curtain. The rectangular-shaped Yukon stove whose stovepipe extended through a pipe guard to the roof, was in the left back corner. His three guns—a Savage .30–30, a sawed-off 16-gauge, and a .22, also with the stock sawed off—rested on nails driven into the log wall by the door. Firewood was piled four feet high by the shack's left wall. Mukluks, socks, and a shirt hung from a rawhide thong that was stretched across the cabin. Shelving filled out the open spaces. Johnny put a number of wire snares and several traps into his backpack, then shouldered it and headed out the door.

William Nerysoo, mushing his dog team, went up the Rat River setting traps as he went. Making sure he did not interfere with the lines of Jacob Drymeat and William Vittrekwa, Nerysoo finished the task in three days and returned to his camp.

Tracks don't lie and it did not take Johnny long to figure out that he had moved to an area already being trapped by two or three other men. Therefore, he set his traps in areas the others neglected. Only in one place did his tracks cross that of another man. Seeing a trap set there, he tripped it and then hung it on a tree branch easily viewed from the trail. Johnny knew his trap was set there first.

William Nerysoo found the sprung trap. Knowing his line had been established long before the new trapper had come into the country, he saw this as an infringement that was against the law. Right then and there he decided to file a complaint with the Mounties. The area was crowded enough without another man added to share the fur crop. Nerysoo returned to his camp and told his wife about it, vowing to report the incident when he returned to Fort McPherson at Christmas. And so he and his wife mushed into town for the holidays. The Indian trapper then took his complaint to Millen at Arctic Red River.

"You say a white man is springing your traps?" Millen asked incredulously.
William nodded.
"You know who he is?"
William nodded again. "Abe Francis sell him canoe."
"Johnson! I should have known," Millen blurted out. "Where's his cabin?"
"You know Longstick River?"
"Sure, runs into the Rat at Destruction City."
"He one hour by dog team up Rat from there."
Millen did some quick figuring. "Eight miles?"
Nerysoo nodded.
The Mountie stood up. "Okay, William, we'll check it out."
After the Indian trapper had left, Millen called in Constable King who was a veteran of five years' service with the Mounties in the north. He had joined the force in 1926 and volunteered for a northern posting. Previous stations included the isolated detachment at Old Crow on the Porcupine River one hundred and fifty miles west and across the Richardson Mountains from Arctic Red River. King also served in Dawson City, and had participated in dog and horse patrols throughout the famous Klondike region.

"You wanted to see me?" he said.
"Yes, sit down, Alf. That stranger who came in last summer—"
"Johnson?" King interrupted.
Millen nodded. "The same. He's messing around with an Indian's trapline."

"Robbing it?"

"No, not that bad, but springing William's traps," he said and paused before continuing. "Inspector Eames will hit the roof when he hears this."

"Hell, Spike, a bird can spring a trap."

"Yeah, but he can't hang it on a tree branch."

"I see," said King.

Corporal Millen stood up and walked over to a huge wall map of the country. King followed him and the two stood before it.

"Here's what I want you to do," said Millen pointing to the map. "Johnson's cabin is here. Find out his side of the story, and I stress *his*. Who knows, maybe William was trapping before the season started. And while you are at it, find out if Johnson's trapping. I know he didn't buy a license."

"You don't want me to leave today, I hope."

Millen smiled. "Christmas? No. Tomorrow's okay."

"Should I tell Bernard?"

"Yes, take along Special Constable Bernard. He knows the whole country like the back of his hand. If you have any problems, don't come back here. Head for Aklavik. Inspector Eames can spare more men than I can."

"You think there will be trouble?" King asked.

"I don't know what to think. Both Bishop Geddes and Eames have a sixth sense about Johnson."

"Some guys," said King, "give 'em off like a skunk does a stink!"

Millen rubbed his chin reflectively. "Yes, but most of the time skunks don't throw off an odor without a reason."

The day after Christmas, King and his guide, Special Constable Joe Bernard, set out for the Rat River. The weather was extremely cold with a biting wind nipping at them as they mushed westward to Fort McPherson, where they spent the night.

Christmas had come and gone, but Johnny brooded about it as he marked off the twenty-eighth day of December. It was midday, yet too dark to see much in the recesses of the cabin with just the light from a candle flickering off the walls. A fire, stoked with spruce wood, crackled cheerfully in the stove, providing adequate heat in his makeshift home. Johnny noticed the frost line inside the cabin climbed higher as the temperature plummeted. Outside the thermometer read thirty-eight below zero. Dim memories of holidays in Norway as a little boy flooded his mind and served to magnify his loneliness and irritability. He had, in a sense, returned to the land of his birth, though he was halfway around the world from it. He wondered if the lure of gold had brought him to the Rat River, or if it was really some sort of homing instinct that had drawn him north to again cross the Arctic Circle and live at the same latitude where his life had taken root thirty-three years earlier. His accumulation of personal belongings was small. Other than a handful of pearls purchased earlier, and twenty-four hundred dollars in cash, and the gold he had recently panned, he owned nothing that was not essential to survival.

He recalled Thora, his girlfriend when he was a teenager. He reminisced over Christmases spent with her in North Dakota before he chose the outlaw trail. He recalled his mother, and of the days on the farm with his sisters. He recollected the antics of his drunken father, long dead, and wondered who now owned the farm where he and his family had toiled so long for so little.

Mushing down the Peel after a night spent at the Hudson's Bay Company with trader Firth, Constable King was well rested and felt good. Firth had invited both him and Bernard to a New Year's Eve party he planned to hold. Firth was famous for such dos and a man could feel lucky to be invited to one of them.

Bernard estimated the Longstick River was about two sleeps from Fort McPherson by dog team. That meant they could easily make it back to Firth's over a beaten trail by New Year's Eve.

They pushed hard that day and managed to reach the junction of the Rat and Longstick that night where they made camp, and were up early the next morning for the eight-mile run up the Rat to Johnny's cabin. King found himself musing more about the New Year's Eve party than about Johnny, and strove mightily to focus on the events at hand as he drove his team upriver. Since King had never seen Albert Johnson there was little for him to go on other than the say-so of Constable Millen.

Millen had mentioned the intuitions of Geddes and of Eames, but they were feelings about a man that Geddes had but passed on the street, and Eames had never met at all. How in hell could they come to any conclusions at all on such sparse information? But then they were fifteen or more years older than he was and had fought in the Great War, so it would not hurt to honor their worries. There was no sense in being reckless. King would do what he had to do.

King and Bernard mushed the eight miles quickly. Sure enough, right near the bend of the Rat where it ushers out of the mountains to curve north before it drained into the Husky River, King could see smoke issuing from the tiny cabin's stovepipe. He could approach the cabin from behind, but that might cause more problems than it would solve. King knew trappers and prospectors living alone in the woods often did not take kindly to being victims of a sneak attack. They expected a loud greeting. King and Bernard mushed around the bend of the creek, halting by the bank in front of the cabin. Constable King's experienced eyes took in the setting of the cabin at a glance. He saw the loner's crude but ruggedly crafted snowshoes leaning against the cabin. Bernard had spotted their peculiar markings in the trail about a mile downriver, and immediately deduced they could only have been made by a white man. Indian's shoes of that area were lighter in weight and of a much finer construction than these blunt snowshoes. The constable saw that the trapper had provided himself with an ample woodpile to last through the winter. He observed that the smoke that rose from the stovepipe of the cabin hovered over it, indicating the temperature must be at least forty below zero. King's eyes narrowed when he noted no evidence of a rifle, which trappers often left outside when the mercury bottomed out. Bringing a cold rifle into a warm atmosphere tended to make it sweat then freeze up when taken out again into the cold, thus rendering it inoperable. The constable wondered about the rifle, and then shrugged off his anxiety realizing there could be any number of reasons the gun had not been left outside. But it made him wary just the same. He turned to Bernard. "Stay here, Joe, and I'll check him out."

King climbed the bank and walked toward the cabin, then stopped. "Anybody home?" he bellowed.

The shout battered the brittle arctic silence and caught Johnny completely by surprise. Jolted out of his reverie by the startling interruption, he snuffed out the candle, grabbed his Savage, and leaped to the window. Fear and anxiety gripped his guts, and without taking his eyes from the window, he quietly levered a shell into the breech of his rifle. Whoever it was out there, Johnny was taking no chances.

Not getting an answer King walked to the door and knocked. "Mr. Johnson, are you there?" he said loudly, knowing on occasion some men he had visited were partially deaf and only felt the vibrations of his pounding on the door. No answer was forthcoming. Puzzled by the trapper's silence, King glanced toward the twelve-inch square window to the right of the door and found himself face to face with Johnny peering out at him. The way Johnny was working his shoulders indicated to King he may have been loading his rifle. A hand flicked down the sack curtain and the face disappeared. King saw the image, but there was no way of identifying the man because of the frost on the window. He turned again to the door. "Johnson," he shouted, "I'm a Mountie and want to ask you a few questions about a trapline complaint."

Johnny backed away from the aperture and turned toward the door, his rifle at the ready. He quickly guessed the Mounties were after him for trapping illegally. If they took him in they would probably uncover the fact that he was an ex-con with a prison sentence hanging over his head, then it would be back to jail. If he hadn't stubbornly refused to purchase a license, he thought, he would never have left himself open for this. He lowered a log bar across the door and waited silently, his mind working like a trip hammer as the Mountie paused for a response. At least he was safe for a while, as the lawman could not enter his cabin without a warrant, and to get one he would have to backtrack to his place of origin, wherever that was. By that time, Johnny could dispose of the furs he had already taken, and the law would be none the wiser. He could flee, but to where? With no place to go, he decided to remain and to bluff or battle his way out of his predicament. He had shot it out with the police once before to escape after the bank holdup. The two other times, when he meekly surrendered, he was railroaded into jail by the courts and in both cases felt that he had gotten a raw deal.

King stood out in the cold, and felt more like an idiot than he did a policeman doing his job. He could not force in the door because it was against regulations, and if this guy did not talk with him, he'd have to mush three score miles to Aklavik, and in all likelihood miss Firth's party.

"Johnson!" he shouted, "If you won't talk with me I'll have to get a warrant." All King was met with was the squawk of a raven from somewhere behind the shack. If he could not roust out the loner he was faced with a 120-mile round-trip. He walked around the cabin repeatedly seeking some sort of retort from the man inside. King's thoughts went to Inspector Eames and Bishop

Geddes. By god, they'd been right. For a man to ignore a knock on the door, or a greeting, when he lived in such a degree of isolation was weird and unnatural. King also knew that some people, though honest and law abiding, did just not like cops, so he tried again.

"Mr. Johnson, I'm leaving now to get a search warrant, "if that's the way you want it." King shook his head in disgust, and turning away from the cabin rejoined his partner.

"It looks like we got a hard case, Joe," he said.

"Didn't even ask you for tea?" Joe asked.

"Not even tea," King said. "How would you like a trip to Aklavik?"

"What about the party?" Bernard said.

King noted that he was not the only one thinking of New Year's Eve. "I don't know. We still might make it. We got four days counting today to get down there and back. If we hightail it we might make it."

"I got an uncle in Aklavik."

"You got uncles everywhere," King retorted.

They turned their teams around and mushed down the Rat to the Husky River and then steered left, taking the trail north to Aklavik.


Johnny remained stationary in his cabin for a long time before he edged out of it to see if the Mounties had left. He followed the trail of the lawmen for two miles to make sure they had truly departed. Then he returned to his cabin where he carefully packed his furs and hid them back in the forest. After that he hurried around his line collecting his traps, which he also secreted in the bush. Once he had completed those tasks, he returned again to his cabin and pondered the fix he was now in. Possibly he should talk with the Mounties. Maybe, after all, they were only curious about the hassle with his neighbor.

Johnny lay on his bunk. For a while he felt secure in his cabin. He had plenty of time to think, and the nagging doubts about the real cause of the Mounties' visit returned. They must have suspected something about him or they would not have been so nosey at McPherson.

Johnny thought of prison, and his mind went back to his first day in the Wyoming jail in Kemmerer. It had been a completely dehumanizing experience. All for stealing two flea-bitten nags.

Eight months in Wyoming jails and eighteen more months at hard labor in the Montana State Prison toughened not only his physical endurance but his emotional stamina as well. During that time he talked little and backed down to no one. He purposely kept his silence. When the other convicts found out that he had not only robbed a bank but had also shot his way through a posse to make his escape, he was placed on a plane of admiration above the average run-of-the-mill prisoner.

No matter what, however, the years in prison were more than just years. They were one regimented day after another, day in and day out until three years had gone by. When other lads were completing high school or working on the farm, chasing girls, going to church suppers, and growing into manhood in freedom, he grew to maturity among the dregs of society. For an outdoor man such as Johnny, prison was a particular torture, and its confinement weighed greater on him than all of the inconveniences of prison life. Not to be able to go where he wanted when he wanted affected his thinking far beyond that of others more able to accept and adjust to conditions of imprisonment.

Not only was Johnny unwilling to accept the life of a convict, he could never accept limitations imposed on him after he got out, and this brought him more trouble. In California when he needed a horse, he helped himself to one, and had been sentenced to seven and one-half years in Folsom Prison for the offense even though he had turned the horse loose. And now, faced with a return to that prison where he knew his mind would decay, he decided to fight it out. Maybe he would get lucky and get away, like he did after the Medicine Lake bank holdup.

Johnny's thoughts stirred him into action. He rose from his bunk and brought firewood inside, stacking it high enough to ensure plenty fuel to keep him warm through a siege if the need arose. He loosened the chinking between the lower rungs of logs, so at a minute's notice he could clear them to provide a field of fire around the cabin. He brought in dry meat and water and laid out his three guns, the .22 with the stock sawed off, his 16-gauge sawed off to a two-inch barrel, and his .30–30 Savage. He loaded them and stacked the ammunition around the cabin so it was easily accessible.

Johnny hummed and sang a western ditty as he made these preparations. Things were less complicated now that he had made his mind up. He was almost happy about it. If it came to a battle he would do the best he could.

# Chapter 18

# CONSTABLE KING SHOT

Lawmen welcome excitement and danger or they would not be in the business. North of Sixty in the western Arctic was a volunteer posting. The Arctic was a lonely place to be, and it soon weeded out the unfit. A sense of humor was almost a prerequisite for those who were stationed there. Constable R. G. "Mac" McDowell fit into that category. On the night of December 29, 1932, he was on duty. He was a lean, hard, brown-haired man over six feet tall, with enough service in the Arctic to be called a veteran. Nurse Elizabeth Brown, a pert, attractive woman of twenty-three, stationed at All Saints Hospital in Aklavik often dropped by to visit him to pass the time, but now she was mad.

"Mac, this is the last time I make a date with you."

"Calm down, Lizzie," McDowell responded.

"Do you realize how much work it is to press a dress?" she asked.

"If you're wearing it for me, it's worth it."

Liz frowned. "You big ape, you stood me up at the Christmas party."

"How was I to know I'd be sent on the Herschel Island patrol?" McDowell said, then paused before continuing. "Besides, it didn't cramp your style any."

"You mean those Signals lads?" she asked, knowing full well he knew that she knew who he was talking about.

"Who else?"

"They are gentlemen."

McDowell ignored her comment. "Just think, Liz, on New Year's Eve you'll have wine, songs, and me."

Liz wrinkled her nose. "You Mounties are all alike in thinking we have scarlet fever."

McDowell smiled and said: "Maybe just a little temperature."

"You conceited—"

McDowell raised his index finger to interrupt. "Ah, ah—"

The door was suddenly flung open and Constable King burst into the room. Startled, McDowell and Liz leaped to their feet and automatically sized him up. He was obviously tired, and was encrusted with frost from hours on the trail.

McDowell feigned disgust. "Leave it to Alf King to come between me and my girl."

"Since when am I your girl?" Liz complained.

Constable King exaggeratedly cleared his throat. "Do you mind if I interrupt you two?"

"It seems to me you already have," McDowell said as he stepped forward to shake King's hand. "What could be important enough to bring you here from Arctic Red River?"

King took off his parka before replying. "Some nut down on the Rat. Where's Corporal Wild?"

"He's having holiday cheers with the inspector and Doc."

"I'd better see them first. I'll tell you about it later."

King went out the door, not bothering to put his parka back on even though it was forty below zero.

Liz frowned. "I smell a rat!"

"Yeah," said McDowell, who could never miss a pun, "Rat River."

Liz grimaced. "Right now there is no one here but you and the corporal. If Alf needs help the inspector will send you."

"So?"

"You idiot, you won't be here New Year's Eve."

McDowell bowed deeply. "I knew you cared."

Liz shook her head in disgust. "Can't you ever be just a little bit serious?"

King did not bother to knock on the door at Inspector Eames's residence. He figured there would be little in the way of objections to his informality considering the news he was conveying. In one glance he spotted not only Inspector Eames, but also Doc Urquhart, who ran the hospital and was the Department of Northern Affairs representative in Aklavik, and Corporal Wild.

"Constable King!" Inspector Eames exclaimed on seeing him. "My god, you look beat. Have a chair."

Eames had his favorites like everyone else. Constable King was one of them. Eames liked his demeanor. He was a big, tough, no-nonsense Mountie who never botched an assignment. The law was the law, and it was to be enforced. Eames could depend on King to get the job done no matter how "touchy" it might be. To Eames, Constable King in some ways mirrored his youth. The inspector was aware of a rumored affair King had had when he was in Dawson City. Whether a rumor or not, King was single, and nobody was hurt by that. The inspector could hardly blame one of his men when all of them had to become virtual monks during the first eight years of service because of the force's outdated rule that prohibited marriage. They'd lost a lot of good men because of it.

King took the chair.

"What brings you here?" Eames asked.

"It's that stranger who came into McPherson last summer."

"Johnson?"

King nodded. "Nerysoo complained he's interfering with his traps."

"Fits the image," Eames said.

"I went to his cabin, but he wouldn't talk."

"How do you know he was there?"

"I spotted him looking at me through the window."

Inspector Eames got up and started pacing the floor. Every once in a while he would stop and say something.

"Johnson is trouble. It sticks out all over him. He's got a past."

Doctor J. A. Urquhart not only headed up the hospital in Aklavik, but was also the coroner and Indian agent. He was thin of hair and big of frame like Inspector Eames, but less likely to rush into judgments.

"I have one question, Inspector," Doc Urquhart said.

"What's that?"

"Would he bother fooling with another man's trapline if he was trying to hide something?"

Eames who had recommenced his pacing, stopped again, and looked at the doctor. "Doc, some men just can't think ahead. If they did, they'd never be in trouble in the first place."

He turned to Corporal Wild, who was deep in thought while sipping his holiday libation. "Corporal, who do we have available?"

"Only McDowell," he said turning his hands outward in the universal sign of frustration. "We're always short of men."

Eames turned to King. "Get a night's rest. You might need a backup. Take McDowell and a special back with you.

"Yes, sir," King said and got up to leave.

"And, King,"

"Yes, sir."

"I expect results."

"I'll do my best," King said and walked out into the cold. Relaying the news of this assignment to McDowell would be good for a few laughs at McDowell's expense.

Corporal Wild followed him out the door. "Hold up, Alf," he called. "Get Lazarus Edwards for McDowell's guide. Good man. Mac will tell you where he lives."

"Thanks, Corporal," he called after Wild.

The four men left early the next day, witnessed by nurse Liz Brown. Almost unidentifiable in her parka, Liz walked up to Constable McDowell and saluted him.

"You big oaf! Why didn't you talk your way out of it?"

The big Mountie smiled. "Don't fret, my dear. I'll be back for New Year's Eve. I swear it."

"No you won't. The party's tomorrow night. Even I know it's at least forty miles to the mouth of the Rat River."

"No problem, Liz."

"Oh, heck, be careful, Mac," she said.

The Mounties and specials left early for one reason, they were all thinking about New Year's Eve. They hoped to take care of the Johnson matter as quickly as possible, then King and Bernard would go on to Fort McPherson for Firth's party, and McDowell and Edwards would head back to Aklavik in time for the celebrations there.

McDowell figured he could easily make it back in time if the trail held up. They would have to push it, but it was not impossible.

They made camp that night on a cutoff that ran diagonally between the Husky and Rat rivers, thus bypassing the junction of the two.

That night they slept under the stars because to take down a tent takes time, which they did not want to waste when they broke camp the next morning.

"Let's skip the grub," King suggested when they awoke.

"Yeah," McDowell agreed. "Tea's good enough for me. How about you, Lazarus?"

"*Unchit*, no eat?"

"No, just tea," said Mac.

"New Year Party tonight. White man have no time to eat," the other Special Constable, Bernard, added.

Lazarus laughed. "All time drink."

King and McDowell joined in the good-natured laughter.

Lazarus continued. "Constable Mac chase nurse like fox after rabbit."

"No, no Lazarus, you got it all wrong," said McDowell. "She chase me."

King stood up. "If we don't get going, we'll miss that party."


Normally a cabin in the bush would have been sought as an oasis of warmth, but on this day Johnny's shack loomed in front of the men as a deadly parapet representing the obstinacy of one individual. Smoke curled lazily from the chimney—the loner was still there! The four dog teams pulled up in front of the cabin and halted under the bank.

The men gathered around King and then squatted as he drew lines in the snow.

"I'm going to knock on the door," he said. "Mac, you climb the bank and cover me."

"You think he's that bad, eh?"

"In a way, no, but I'm not going to beat on that door and stand in front of it!"

"Joe, you make sure the dogs stay in one place," he said and paused, then added, "Laz, you cover me from upstream."

King motioned to McDowell who proceeded to post himself where he could cover King anywhere he ventured in front of the cabin. Edwards moved around to the side of the cabin. Bernard remained on the river with the dog teams.

King was taking precautions, but he really did not think there would be serious complications. There could have been any number of reasons for the trapper not to have been cooperative. For one, Johnny might not believe King was a policeman. A man with the kind of money Johnny reportedly had on him would be reticent about welcoming strangers into his home.

King figured he would announce himself first and knock immediately afterward, but then decided it would be more circumspect to announce his presence before he reached the door. Johnny would certainly know they were there. Two dog teams were not exactly noiseless.

Only the rasp of King's snowshoes was heard as he strode through the snow toward the door. Then he stopped and shouted.

"Mr. Johnson, are you there?" The sound of his voice broke the great silence like something profane in an inherently pure world.

The man inside the cabin remained mute like the pristine world of cold and forest and animals and snow and ice around him. King waited but there was no answer.

King stood his ground. A dog yelped and Bernard quieted it. McDowell fidgeted expectantly. The sole movement was the smoke from the cabin's stovepipe forcing its way into the gelid atmosphere. The sudden squawk of a raven almost tripped off a reaction on King's part. Until then he did not realize how tightly wound up he really was. Even approaching Johnny's cabin diagonally from the left side took a tremendous effort of will on his part. Each crunch of his snowshoes seemed like an eternity. He noticed his own breathing, the puffs of his vaporized breath hanging in the forty-five-below-zero air like clouds of smoke emanating from a fire.

Johnny had heard the approach of the dog teams and suspected it was the Mounties coming for him. He cleared the chinking from between the logs and posted himself well back from the opening, but not so far that the area in front of the cabin was not in view. He saw four men standing on the bank; they conversed briefly, then separated and disappeared from his line of sight. He dared not stir from his position for fear the sound of his own movement would obliterate the noise of theirs. He waited. Finally, his acute hearing picked up the rasp of the Mountie's snowshoes. The lawman was approaching the cabin in such a way that Johnny could not see him.

Then a voice reached his sensitive ears, and was obviously the same policeman back again. He identified himself as a Mountie. Here again was the law at his door. And again the problem with the trapping license came to mind. He could have purchased one easily enough the previous summer. The burden of having done time always seemed to gnaw at the edges of his mind. Some men he knew threw off the yoke and went on with their lives as if nothing had ever happened and the busybodies be damned, but he was sensitive about it and went to great lengths to avoid the subject of his past. That's one of the reasons he was where he was. In this country he thought he'd be free of that, but as much as he ran from it, the past was always there in the form of the law he thought was ready to ask him about it.

A scratching sound suddenly jolted his ears. He looked into the corner of the cabin and saw his pal the squirrel. "You back again?" he said softly.

The squirrel sat on his haunches waiting for the inevitable handout.

Johnny turned back to the open space and continued talking to the squirrel. "You've never been in a cage," he said, then grabbed a scrap of bannock and threw it to the little animal, not taking his eyes off the opening where he had removed the moss chinking of the cabin. Johnny pointed his rifle toward the door. "Well, you wouldn't like it," he added, as the squirrel scampered down a hole he had burrowed somewhere under Johnny's bunk.

Constable King turned briefly to see if his comrades were covering him, then turned again to the cabin.

"Come on, Johnson!" he shouted. "We want to talk."

King really did not expect an answer and did not get one. He shuffled to the left, and he extended his left arm and knocked on the door with the back of his left hand. He waited. Now he had maneuvered so he was facing toward the river, and could view his companions, McDowell, Bernard, and Edwards. He could see that they were concerned. All were in a firing position at the riverbank. His mind drifted and he had to shake his head at the incongruity of it all. Here he was bracing some nut in the frozen wild—not like his old horse patrols in and around Dawson City where cabin dwellers often fell all over themselves for the privilege of giving him coffee and finding out the latest news. He thought of some of his old pals, Nipper Carcoux, Jimmie Miller, and Tom Coleman. They were Mounties he had bunked and gone to parties and pulled duty with. Now they, too, were scattered to the four winds. He was tense at first, but now, his train of thought relaxed him, and he became almost indifferent to what was going on. Once he got this chore out of the way, he and Bernard would bolt for Fort McPherson. By god, they might make that New Year's party at Firth's after all.

He shouted again but in a more formal tone, "Johnson. In the name of the king open the door."

Johnny heard the creak of snowshoes as the Mountie approached the door, then his words loud and clear. He resolved to shoot his way out with a simple sound shot, and brought his Savage to bear on the cop's voice. He had already racked a shell into the chamber of the rifle so there was no noise from the lever action. Slowly, coolly, he squeezed the trigger of his takedown weapon and felt it buck in his hands as the gun went off. The slug ripped through the door at an angle, and Johnny heard a grunt as the slug walloped the Mountie in the chest, bowling him over. Johnny was as impassive over the shooting as a wolf hamstringing a moose. He did not bother to analyze his reasons. To him, his antagonist was nothing more than an obstacle that had to be removed. Instinctively, he dropped to the floor of his pit cabin just in time to avoid counterfire from the guns of the men along the riverbank. After the first volley, he gambled a quick look and saw the wounded Mountie pick himself up and stumble to the safety of the riverbank. Then, as suddenly as it had started, the first flurry of shots came to an end. Johnny waited tense and unyielding. The die was cast. There would be no turning back now.

"Keep firing!" McDowell shouted to Bernard and Edwards, then rushed to King who lay gasping in the snow. "Alf, you hit?" he asked, knowing he probably was but hoping for the best.

"Yeah, in the chest," King groaned.

"Bad?"

"I think so."

"Before we poke around, we gotta get you out of here."

McDowell turned his head, shouting to Bernard. "Joe. Quick! Mush your team over here. As soon as we get King onto the sled, we'll take off."

Bernard brought the team over and they put the wounded man on it.

"We'll go about a quarter of a mile, and then take a look at King," McDowell said. "Laz, as soon as we get down the trail, fire a couple more shots, and join us. We'll see you then."

Edwards nodded.

McDowell yelled "Mush" and he was off following the trail, which took them east and then north. McDowell sweated out the area they must pass to the rear of Johnny's cabin that was within gun range. Thoughtfully, however, his Indian guide kept up covering fire until McDowell and Bernard passed the exposed section. One hundred yards farther on, they halted the team and attended to King.

"Alf, you awake?" McDowell asked.

"Yeah."

"We got to take a look at you."

"Okay," the wounded man said weakly.

"Joe, prop him up so I can take off his parka."

Bernard moved King, which brought a groan.

"It won't work, it's a pullover," Bernard ventured.

"Jesus, you're right. We'll have to cut it off him. Dig out our sleeping bags."

McDowell unsheathed a hunting knife and quickly cut through the parka, then through the layers of clothes under it. McDowell could see plenty of blood but to his amazement could not find the wound. "Alf," he said as evenly as he could under the circumstances, where the hell are you hit?"

"Under the arm, the armpit," King whispered.

Edwards showed up, out of breath.

"He follow you?" McDowell asked.

Edwards shook his head. "No. He stay home."

"Laz, grab the medicine kit in our pack."

Edwards retrieved it and handed it to McDowell.

"Help me here, you guys."

As gently as possible under the circumstances the three men rolled King onto his right side.

McDowell gently lifted King's left arm. "Can you handle it?" he asked King. King nodded.

"Wow, you got it all right," he said, and plugged the wound, which was already congealing because of the cold. He stuffed bandages over the hole, and let King's arm down, automatically sealing the bullet hole.

"Alf?"

"What?"

"We're going to have to move you again. We got to find out if the damned thing came out."

"Sure."

"Gently boys," McDowell uttered, as they rolled King face down on top of the dogsled. Pushing the clothes aside he found another hole, much larger than the entry wound. "You're in luck Alf," he exclaimed as he watched steam rise from the contact of the warm blood of the wound and the gelid atmosphere at fifty below zero. "The bullet went right through. And the cold is sure doing a job," he said while putting on the bandage.

They turned King over and wrapped him in what remained of his clothes. Taking two sleeping bags, they slipped them over the wounded man.

King was still conscious.

McDowell figured he should say something. "It looks good, old man. The wound isn't bleeding too badly. I figure you'll make it okay."

They strapped King into the cariole, and headed northward.

King's thoughts were not even on his wound. He was preoccupied with the New Year's party at Fort McPherson he knew he was now going to miss.

Rivers, by and large, seek their way by the laws of gravity. The Husky River was no different. Consequently, there was the usual frequency of twists and turns in the watercourse as it sought lower ground.

The trail to Aklavik was like the river it paralleled. Where there was a bend in the river, the trail often cut straight across it, and though quicker, it often entailed climbing and descending high banks. These were to prove difficult when handling a wounded man.

A wind had sprung up with drifting snow filling up their back trail. That meant they had to perform the excruciating task of breaking trail all over again.

McDowell cursed the wind-driven snow with the vehemence of a drill sergeant addressing a stumbling recruit. The combination of wind and cold turned King's features into a white mantle of frost that grew into an icy rime with each labored breath as he lay on the sled. Fluid froze in his nostrils, and a film of ice collected on his eyelids. His cheeks and eyes had to be constantly rubbed and warmed, which took up precious minutes. In only a few hours darkness enveloped the trail as they plunged northward toward Aklavik.

The winding trail continuously rose and fell over steep banks and impeded their progress. Mile after mile, hour after hour, they diligently lowered and hoisted King over steep inclines. This necessitated frequent rotations of the dog teams. The strain on the men began to overtax their strength and will, and precipitated an accident that was to slow them even more.

Each time they climbed a bank and then descended it, the men would have to make sure that King's sled did not turn over. At one particularly sharp incline, the sled got away from McDowell and commenced sliding down sideways. He leaped in front of the sled to break its progress and it sideswiped his legs, pulling a ligament in his right knee. The adrenalin was pumping so hard through the Mountie's veins for fear of King being hurt that he hardly felt it, but from then on he limped badly.

Ultimately, after twelve hours of pushing snow, they spotted the amber lights shining through the window of Jim Koe's cabin. McDowell figured he had never seen anything more welcoming in his life than that single beacon along the trail.

Koe was awake and threw open the door when they arrived.

"Mac, you guys are travelin' late," he said and went forward to help with their dogs. "We'll get the dogs bedded down and fed in a jiffy and then—"

"Sorry, Jim," McDowell said hastily, "we haven't got that much time."

"You're limping pretty bad," Koe commented, figuring the Mountie's injury might have something to do with it.

"It isn't me," the Mountie replied. "It's Alf King, he's been shot."

"I'll be damned," Koe swore, "get him inside. I got tea on. Jesus, he looks like a snowman."

"Thanks," McDowell said, preoccupied. "We got to warm him up. How's the trail from here on in?

"Good," said Koe, "just broke by my nephew. Two to two-and-a-half hours to Aklavik at the most."

McDowell turned to King's Special Constable Bernard.

"Joe. Get some tea and grub, and then highball it for headquarters."

"I got some char softened up," Joe offered. "I'll feed your dogs."

The three men unloaded King, and toted him into the cabin and put him on one of the bunks.

"Can you drink anything?" McDowell asked King as Koe's wife toweled the ice and rime off the wounded man's face.

King nodded.

"It's all downhill now'" McDowell said, trying to buck up the wounded man. "You made it this far, you'll make it all the way."

King drained a cup of tea, and his color improved almost immediately.

"He's a tough bugger," Koe said, pointing at King after returning to the cabin.

"Ha," McDowell exclaimed, relaxing a little. "His nickname is 'Buns.' He could throw every Mountie in Dawson, and that's a big detachment."

"You ready, Joe?" McDowell asked.

"Yes."

"When you get there, find the doc. Since it is New Year's Eve, he'll probably be with the inspector."

"Where will they be?" Bernard asked.

"I forgot that you aren't from Aklavik. They will be at Moccasin Square Gardens. That's the dance hall."

"Are you sure they'll be up? I probably won't get there until two or three in the morning."

"You are forgetting it is New Year's Eve. You'll be celebrating it on the trail. Nineteen thirty-two."

"Me and the wolves and dogs will howl," Joe said and smiled.

"Tell 'em King's got a chest wound. Must have missed the heart or he'd be dead by now. Tell 'em he lost a lot of blood, but he's pretty strong just the same."

"Okay, I'm on my way."

"We'll follow along in an hour."

# Chapter 19

# THE NEW YEAR'S EVE BALL——1932

The New Year's Eve ball was in full swing in Aklavik's dance hall. It was, indeed, a strange mixture of peoples of various cultures. There were Gwitchin men dressed in blue suits, white shirts, and ties, and Inuit and white men who were similarly attired; all wore mukluks on their feet. Then there were the men of the Royal Canadian Mounted Police and the Royal Canadian Corps of Signals soldiers in full dress uniforms and polished boots and shoes.

The women were also varied in their dress. The native women wore gingham and calico dresses, while the nurses wore formal gowns. Liz Brown was stunning in her gown, as was her friend Jean McKay, a raven-haired beauty who worked with Liz as a nurse. They had been sitting at a table with Corporal Wild, Inspector Eames and his wife, Dr. Urquhart and his spouse, and Sergeant Hersey of the Royal Canadian Signals.

The music was provided by several fiddles, guitars, and an accordion. Every kind of dance had been tried, from square dancing to the Charleston.

Corporal Wild had asked Liz to dance, and while so engaged, Liz spoke, "Will you tell me something, Dick?"

"Certainly, Lizzie," he responded, wondering what was on her mind. "What is it?"

"How did this place get its name?"

"You mean Moccasin Square Gardens?"

"Yes."

"I take it you aren't a sports fan?"

"Yes, I'm not."

Corporal Wild nodded with a twinkle in his eye. "No, you aren't," he said.

"Yes, I *aren't*." Liz replied, not letting the Mountie put one over on her.

Wild laughed. "You should be a comedian."

"But Dick," she replied, "you still have not answered my question."

"This," he said pointing to the various sides of the building, "is it. It's named after the famous sports arena in New York City, Madison Square Garden."

Liz nodded, then frowned. "I still don't get the connection."

Wild shook his head in feigned disgust. "I don't know about you, Liz. The one in New York has prizefights and wrestling matches."

"So?"

"Well my dear girl, as the night goes on you'll see the connection."

"Oh, I see. Not to change the subject or anything like that, but . . ."

"Yes, Liz?"

"Do you think Mac will make it back for the dance?"

"I guess that depends on the guy he's checking out."

"You mean that man Johnson?"

"Yes."

Just then a soldier approached.

"Pardon me, you two. Mind if I cut in?" asked Sergeant Earl Hersey, a rugged man of medium height and sandy hair.

"Earl, we just got started," Corporal Wild whined.

"Yeah, yeah, I've heard that before. You've been on the floor for half an hour."

Corporal Wild went back to his table.

Sergeant Hersey took Liz in his arms, and proceeded to whirl her around as a waltz played.

"Sergeant, I understand that you have been a marathon runner."

"What's this 'Sergeant' stuff? Call me Earl. Yes, an Olympic runner."

"Are you fast?" Liz asked merrily.

Hersey quickly caught the gist of the conversation. "Sometimes," he said and smiled.

"Sometimes?"

"Yes, it depends on what the goal is."

"What goal?"

"You guess," Hersey replied.

"Do you think Mac will be back in time for a dance with me?" Liz asked, changing the subject.

"Of course not," Hersey replied. "I told him I'd take care of you."

The tiny orchestra started playing a Charleston number.

"Earl, I'm beat. Let's us sit down."

"Okay, Liz."

The two sat down, but not without noticing Sergeant Frank Riddell, Hersey's pal in the Signals who was standing next to Jean McKay, who was sitting next to Dick Wild.

Riddell was a man of medium height, wiry, and knowledgeable about radios and any sort of mechanical equipment. In addition, he was an expert at living in the bush.

"Well, Jean, how about a dance?" Riddell asked.

Wild looked up. "Frank, what is this, a raid? Signals is already monopolizing one nurse."

Jean ignored the remark and rose from her chair. "I'd love to, Frank," she said.

"Cry, yellow legs, cry," Riddell said with a friendly glance at the Mountie corporal, and escorted the nurse out onto the dance floor.

"Nice-looking couple," Dr. Urquhart commented to Inspector Eames.

"Yes, they all are at that age," Eames said.

Urquhart laughed. "I guess you're right," he said and paused. "Inspector, I hear you've got a haywire somewhere out in the wilderness?"

"Probably cabin fever," Eames replied.

The doctor nodded. "That ailment isn't only limited to trappers in the bush. If I spend much longer here I'll be joining him."

Inspector Eames thought of the long days and nights with nothing to do but show up at the detachment office. "I know what you mean," he said laconically.

Urquhart smiled, "Nearest thing to excitement I've had was that breech birth I delivered last month."

"Well, Doc, that's more than we've had."

"Except the haywire," Urquhart offered.

Eames nodded. "Yes, except the haywire."

"I'm no kid trying to build a practice, but a surgeon without patients, pardon the analogy, is like a cop without crooks," said Urquhart.

"Doctor, may I interrupt?"

"Surely, Mrs. Eames," the doctor answered. The inspector's wife was a likable woman and very attractive with jet-black hair, a pert figure, and a winning smile.

"It seems to me," said Mrs. Eames, "we can hardly wish for crime and poor health for our community."

"Of course not, but . . ."

"My turn to interrupt," said the doctor's wife. "It's the inactivity."

Inspector Eames figured he had better get in his two cents. "I've had one arrest in six months, but we have other duties."

"Well you know what I mean," Doc said, adding, "not to overstate the case for cabin fever. What's with the guy out in the bush?"

Inspector Eames normally did not comment on such matters, it was really not the policeman's way, but it was New Year's Eve, and he'd had a couple of drinks to loosen him up and felt expansive. "This guy's a loner, and none too cooperative."

"That's nothing new up here," the doctor commented.

"Let me finish. I sent one of our lads out there, and this guy looked at him through the window and wouldn't even invite him in for tea."

"That is a bit of a downer," Urquhart responded.

"It's not normal, that's for sure," said the inspector.

Urquhart was an incisive individual or he would not have been a doctor. "Why did you send your man out there?"

"Really a very minor complaint," said Eames. "An Indian reported this man was interfering with his traps."

Urquhart frowned. "Not much of a reason for not offering tea."

"That's what I thought," Eames said. "The cabin's sixty miles or so from McPherson."

"This character, whose name is ostensibly Albert Johnson, would not even talk, so our man told Johnson he'd come back with a warrant."

"Did that stir him?" the doctor asked.

"Believe it or not, no, it didn't."

"What now?"

"I sent Constable King back with another constable and two specials with a warrant."

"You think you're overreacting?"

"What else could I do?"

"I don't know," Urquhart mused, "ignore the guy. He's not bothering anyone."

"Doc, you forget, the reason I authorized sending a man out there in the first place was to answer a complaint."

"Is King back?"

"No, and I don't expect him. I authorized McDowell to execute the thing, and told King he and Bernard could return to Arctic Red River. As you know that's in the other direction."

"It's twelve o'clock!" Mrs. Eames broke in. "No time for heavy talk now. Happy New Year!"

Special Constable Bernard and his team were alone on the trail. He judged it was near midnight and he'd be reaching Aklavik in an hour. There was nothing worse than being the bearer of bad news. Someone had to do it and he was selected. It was his job to get the way prepared for King. By alerting Inspector Eames and Doctor Urquhart, the job would be done. They were the prime movers. Though he did not live there he knew that the doc was also the chief of the Department of Indian Affairs for that part of the north, and Inspector Eames ran the law end of it. Bernard knew they did not always see eye to eye on things, but they would be together tonight. They'd be at the party and that meant he should head for the dance hall. The dogs, having been fed and watered, were now in pretty good shape to make the trip. He figured he'd get in there at about one in the morning. Since he was about an hour ahead of King and McDowell and Edwards, it would give him plenty of time to do what he had to do. One thing for certain, he would never forget this New Year's Eve.

"Hey, you dogs!" he shouted. "Step it up!"

The dance was still in full swing. It was at least an hour past midnight, and Liz, now sitting with Corporal Wild and the others, was getting anxious.

"It's getting late, Dick," she said.

"Ah, don't worry, Liz. Mac will make it for sure."

"He'd better," she quipped. "Who's that?"

"Who's what?"

"The man in the parka who just came in."

"I don't see anyone."

"Well, he's right behind you talking with the inspector and Dr. Urquhart."

Corporal Wild turned around and looked down the table. "I'll be damned. Constable Bernard!"

Eames and Urquhart had risen, and Eames called Wild who joined them briefly and walked back to Liz.

Liz saw that he was deadly serious. "We're going to need you and Jean."

"Both of us? Why?"

"A man has been shot."

"Oh no . . . Who was hit?" Liz gasped.

"King," Wild answered and walked to the band's platform.

Liz summoned Jean and the two left the hall.

The band stopped playing as Wild approached. He held his hand up for silence, which under the circumstances was a wasted gesture.

"There's no need to stop the party," he said, "but I would like all Signals and hospital personnel to step outside for a minute. One of our men from Arctic Red River, King, has been shot. Though serious, we think he'll make it through okay."

Wild waved to the band to continue playing and walked away.

Outside the building, Inspector Eames took charge. The temperature was forty-five below zero and, as he looked over the crowd, most of whom were in their party attire, he noted it made for an odd scene, as all seemed completely insensitive to the cold.

"I'll be quick," he announced. "Doc, you and the nurses had better get to the hospital and get ready for business. Frank and Earl, crank up your radio and get word to Millen at Arctic Red." He then pointed to Bernard. "Round up whomever you can find and bring them here. We're going to need people to carry the wounded man into the hospital."

He held up his hand. "Before you rush off, you have time to get your parkas on. They'll be bringing King in around an hour from now."

McDowell and Edwards, mushing for all they were worth, pulled up in front of the hospital a half hour later. Waiting for them were Eames, Urquhart, and the nurses. There were also three trappers: Karl Gardlund, a young immigrant from Sweden and an expert skier; Knut Lang, a giant of a man at six feet five inches; and Constant Ethier, a former Mountie.

McDowell brought the team to a halt right in front of Inspector Eames and Dr. Urquhart. "King's shot through the chest," he exclaimed, "the bullet went in under his left arm and out his back."

The doctor quickly checked the wound as the nurses placed a stretcher next to the sled. King was lifted onto the stretcher where he was carefully wrapped in blankets.

"Karl, you and Constant take one end and Knut and I will pick up the other," the doctor said. Then they carted King off to the hospital.

That left Bernard and McDowell with Eames. Eames had noticed McDowell's limp, which looked pretty bad, and spoke out.

"Constable, you aren't much good on one pin. Better get yourself to the hospital."

"No, no, I'm not that bad."

"All right, I'll take your word for it. Get off your feet and rest." Eames turned. "Joe, Laz, follow me."

The subdistrict commander hastened to his office and reviewed the list of men available. There were not many. He shook his head, then looked up at his two special constables, Bernard and Lazarus Edwards.

"You men know the Rat River country?"

"Me? Not so much," said Bernard.

"Well, we're going to need you both to go after Johnson. See who you can round up in the matter of dogs and men. I'd suggest Karl Gardlund, Knut Lang, maybe even Ernie Sutherland. He's supposed to be a dynamite expert. That's all for now. . . . And tell Corporal Wild to get over here."

The two Indians left the office.

Eames got up and looked at the huge map of the region on the wall across from him.

Wild showed up in a few minutes and came to attention and saluted.

"Forget the formalities, Corporal," Eames said. "We're woefully low on men for an operation like this." He pointed to the map. "Tell the Signals boys to get word to Millen in Arctic Red. I want him on this posse for one reason: he's the only policeman that has met this guy Johnson. Tell him to go to Blake's post, here." He again pointed to the wall map. "And tell him to wait for us to show up. We should be there in at least four days. If he has any questions, tell him to get the word back to me right away."

"Yes, sir."

"I'm taking command of the posse, and you'll have to run the show here while I'm gone."

Wild nodded. He had been afraid that the inspector would elect to go. Wild wanted the assignment. Anything was better than sitting around an office in Aklavik. If he was ever to get the chance, the time was now. "Inspector, I'd gladly go," he said.

Eames shook his head. "No, Wild. This is my show. I told the specials to round up some of the locals. By my count we're going to need the specials, two members of the force, namely myself and Millen, and three or four civilians from here. You got any suggestions?"

Wild nodded. "Sure, the Verville brothers are in town. They would be good in a fight; they're both crack shots."

"Return men, eh? The Big War . . . Okay, get them if you can," Eames said. "They'll be classified volunteers. Anyone else?"

"Well, Inspector, there's Ernie Sutherland—"

Eames broke in. "I already told the specials to get him if they can."

"That's about it," Wild said, disappointed because he was missing the action.

"That's all, Corporal. Get a good night's sleep."

Inspector Eames sat down at his desk and began to compile figures. He'd have roughly ten or eleven men. They would need supplies, and the dogs to pull them would need food as well. That meant at least six or seven dog teams at five dogs each. This would be roughly thirty-five dogs eating at least a pound a day. And that did not include the staples for the men. It added up to one thing, trouble, if he did not wrap this thing up quickly. He'd always been astute with the budget and now the budget was lower than ever. It would not take much to run over it. Well, he thought, Millen probably could have been tougher with this man. But Eames had found out through working in law enforcement for over two decades that each policeman had a different technique when it came to one-on-one confrontations, and what worked in one situation did not always work in another situation. These were judgment calls, and the last people to understand them were the very people the police protected. Civilians seldom appreciated the fact that often enough a cop had to make a life-or-death decision in a matter of seconds. It was all part of a very tough game.

The silence was deafening for Johnny. He had heard the drivers of the dog teams mush away from the bank in front of his cabin. But he was not sure if it was a ruse to draw him out. What light there was soon dissipated, as the sun, which never rose at all, sank lower below the horizon. He waited hour after hour to make sure they were gone, and then risked going to sleep. The next day when the sun again approached the rim of the earth and cast its ethereal glow over the land, he crawled from the shack and, with snowshoes in hand, circled behind the cabin. Then he donned his snowshoes and, reassuring himself that he was not being watched, he ventured again to the front of the cabin where he soon saw blood in the snow. He knew now that his shot had scored. The blood trail was easy to see. He followed it over the riverbank and spotted where the Mountie was loaded onto a sled and taken away. The trail lay downriver, which made a ninety degree bend to the left immediately below his shack. He guessed that the two parties had left the area and would not be back—at least not for a while. He followed the trail for two hundred yards and spotted something they had left behind. Curious about it he walked to it and saw that it was a sleeping bag. He picked it up and tucked it under his arm. He could certainly use it. He returned to his cabin and pondered what to do. It was no time for recrimination, but he wondered where he had gone wrong. A decade had passed by since his release at Christmas from Folsom Prison. Ten years of freedom, and now he was again in conflict with the law. Well, it was too late now. He'd shot a man, probably a policeman, and if the man was dead, he would hang. Even if the man was only wounded, he knew they would lay a heavy sentence on him. His only out was to run, but where? He had no map, but he did have a compass and he knew that Alaska was to the west. Maybe if he managed to get over there he could hole up somewhere until summer and then drift down the Yukon River and in a year or two book passage for Seattle.

Johnny was sitting on a fortune in gold and he couldn't go near it. He took out the gold he had panned in the British Mountains and sifted it in his hands. It was so near and yet so far. He looked at the little map he had drawn. Could he find the showing again, even with his crude map? Staring at the lines brought everything back into focus. Yes, not only could he recall what the lines stood for, but every little nook and cranny of the creek where his gold deposit lay. Why hadn't he stayed there? If only he had returned to Rat River just to pack up and move back to the lost mine. But it was too late to worry about that now. His only option was to run, and he proceeded to pack his gear and make ready. The odds against him were pretty stiff, but his greatest asset was his stamina, and with luck he might just dodge a posse sent after him.

Johnny knew that his fate depended on the weather. He needed a snowstorm to cover his tracks if he was going to make a run for it. He anxiously looked skyward only to see the stars twinkling brightly and the northern lights dancing across the heavens. It *had* to snow. Two days went by, then three, and four, and still the sky held clear. The stars winked and the aurora flared as though Mother Nature herself was playing a monstrous joke on him.

The burden of what he considered was unfair and unjust weighed heavily on his rounded shoulders and seemed to shrivel his will. He had been a loser, always a loser. And now he had found gold and circumstances were going to keep him from it.

Johnny fought off his depression and used each day of reprieve to prepare for a quick getaway. He decided to take only the bare essentials. He would tote his "new" bedroll, weapons, ammunition, ax, a lard tin used as a tea pail, a frying pan, and his moose-skin rifle cover. The rest would be redistributed in extra pockets he sewed into his canvas parka and his clothing.

He proceeded methodically, placing his choicest possessions—the pearls, money, gold, and map—in a moose-skin pouch. Next he carefully wrapped in tinfoil five gold fillings from his own teeth that had been pulled and stowed them in the same pouch. He would grab the pouch when he bolted for the hills. He knew an even distribution of weight was crucial in making a clean getaway. He stashed a knife he had created from a spring trap into one pocket. He tucked into another pocket an awl he had fashioned from a three-cornered file. He had also hammered a nail into a chisel and stowed that away.

Needles and thread were placed in a pouch. He wrapped nails in tinfoil and stuffed them in the pouch as well. He placed matches in his shirt pocket, as their accessibility was important when the temperature dipped to sixty below zero. He knew he couldn't waste time fumbling through his pack looking for matches if he broke through rotten ice to find himself knee-deep in water. Fishhooks, twine, a metal mirror, compass, candle, and thermometer were also placed with that possibility in mind.

Four more days went by and the Mounties still did not come. Johnny put on his snowshoes and walked several miles in both directions looking for smoke or some sign or sound indicating their presence, but there was none. He was met only by the great silence of a frigid world. Johnny watched eagerly for snow clouds that did not appear. He fidgeted, helpless before nature's whims. He stacked wood in the cabin. He cleaned and recleaned his weapons, again laying out the ammunition where it would be handy. Johnny waited and cursed silently as the long winter night persisted in remaining clear.

The squirrel appeared again and Johnny fed him out of his hand. "Still no snow, Mr. Squirrel," he said to the little animal. "Maybe I'll get lucky tomorrow."

# Chapter 20

# THE CABIN SHOOTOUT

The hospital in Aklavik after four days was not a gloomy place. King was well on the road to recovery, thanks to the professionalism of Dr. Urquhart, a veteran of the war in Europe with considerable experience tending to bullet wounds. Urquhart found that the bullet had missed King's vital organs.

McDowell was visiting King. They were shortly joined by nurse Liz Brown, who was on shift to look after King.

"I told you I would be back for the dance," McDowell offered.

"You sure did," Liz responded.

"Aren't you proud of me?" McDowell chided.

"Who else would come back with a banged-up knee and a friend with a bullet hole through him?" Liz replied sarcastically.

King could not hold back a snicker.

"Constable King, I forbid you to laugh," Liz jibed.

"Hey, Mac," said Alf weakly, "I heard they might get some real nurses up here."

"Yeah, Alf, you're right. I did too, but don't get your hopes up," McDowell responded.

Liz snorted. "Ha! Instead of playing cops and robbers you two ought to try marbles."

"I like her when she's mad," McDowell said.

"Is she ever any other way?" King countered.

"You both be quiet," Liz said slapping a pillow for emphasis, "or I'll call Dr. Urquhart."

"Well, I gotta go," McDowell said.

"Where are you going?" Liz asked.

"To chase Johnson. Where else?" McDowell said.

"Not on that knee!" Liz advised.

"It isn't all that bad, Liz."

Liz turned to King. "Is he serious?"

King nodded.

Liz was worried. "Be careful Mac, really."

McDowell gave her a quick hug and hurried out the door.


Millen had received Eames's message in Arctic Red River and was preparing to leave for Blake's post near the junction of the Husky and Peel rivers. He was at Lydia's cabin, which was neat and clean, with wallpaper and curtains on the windows. Millen was going to put on his scarlet tunic, which Lydia had just washed for him, but then decided against it. Lydia stood next to him with his pistol belt.

"I won't need the tunic on this trip," Millen said.

Lydia ignored his remark. "Why are you going? Send Constable Melville instead."

Millen just shrugged—women wouldn't understand the situation.

"I can't do that, Lydia. The inspector wants me—not Melville."

"Why should it make any difference to him?"

Millen put on a wool shirt and buttoned it up. "I told you before," he answered. "Johnson's my responsibility. Besides, I'm the only lawman who knows what he looks like."

Lydia handed him his pistol belt and he put it on.

"He's no more your responsibility than Melville's. The inspector has got no right to order—"

"Come off it, Lydia," Millen interrupted, "you know the force. God knows your stepfather did. He guided Fitzgerald, Dempster, even my superintendent, Acland."

Lydia picked up his .38 revolver from the table in the small cabin and handed it to Millen. "Oh Spike, why not take a discharge? You were going to anyway," she said.

Millen grabbed Lydia by her shoulders and gently shook her. "Your feminine wiles won't do you any good."

Lydia knew it was a hopeless task trying to dissuade her companion from what he felt he had to do. Irritated, she broke away from his grasp. "I know," she said, "I know."

The Mountie walked over to her and held her tenderly. "Why worry? There shouldn't be much danger from one man."

Lydia started to say something, then caught herself.

Millen looked at her steadily. "Come on, come on, out with it."

"This might sound stupid to you, but father had a nosebleed last night. Someone's going to die."

"That's an old wives' tale, Lydia."

"Not with my people it isn't."

Millen threw up his arms in despair. "If someone died every time a person had a nosebleed there wouldn't be any people in the world."

Lydia reluctantly handed him his mukluks and then stood in front of him with her arms crossed. "Who is this hermit?"

Millen didn't bother to look up as he adjusted his mukluks. "Just a drifter," he mumbled.

"He must be a madman to shoot Alf like that."

Millen finished tying his mukluks and stood up. Lydia reluctantly handed him his parka, which he slipped over his head.

Millen could not resist a little levity. "Either that or he is awful mad at something."

Lydia ignored the remark. "Don't go," she whispered, and put her arms around his neck and hugged him. Finally, he had to break the tight hold she had on him. He walked to the door and turned and looked back, his eyes searching for a lasting impression of her. In doing so, he surprised himself and wondered about it. Then he shook his head. Women tended to make men worry, he thought, and more often that not it was needless. He shrugged the feeling off with a wave and left the cabin. The last item he grabbed on the way out the door was his bolt-action Enfield rifle.

By the fourth of January Eames had put together a posse of seven men and forty-two dogs to go after Johnny. They set out and reached Blake's post two days later.

Millen was waiting for them.

Eames greeted him civilly and did not appear to have any lasting grudges. "How's Melville?" Eames asked, shaking hands with Millen.

"Not too good," Millen answered. "It looks like he's coming down with the flu."

"That's all I need," Eames said.

"He's functional, though," Millen said.

"We'll head up the Rat tomorrow," said Eames. "Could you find a guide for us?"

"Yes, Charley Rat. He says there's a big bend in the Rat River and that we can cut across the bend and reach Johnny's shack from the upstream side."

"Good," Eames said. "That's what I was hoping for."

They set out at dawn—following an Indian trapline trail that Charley Rat recommended. Eames was afraid there were too many places Johnny could ambush them in the tangle of willows that grew along Rat River. The men tramped all day expecting to be met at each stop with the muzzle blast of Johnny's rifle. They camped that night but first posted sentries before they went to sleep.

Charley Rat, their guide, assured them they were only a few miles above Johnny's cabin, meaning they had circled around to come out on the downstream side of it. The next day they tramped six or seven miles and still had not reached the fugitive's shack. Plainly, Rat was either lost or deliberately leading them in circles. They returned to their first night's campground to reorient themselves and figured out they had traveled a distance of twenty-eight miles, and worst of all, had used up most of their supplies. Just what Eames feared had now come to pass. Going through the same motions of the day before seemed to be a waste of energy as far as Inspector Eames was concerned. Consequently, he sent two men on a quick patrol to get the lay of the land. The patrol was a success. The two men found the shack and circled it, noting that smoke poured out of the shack's stovepipe. This indicated the trapper was still there.

The next morning they advanced in force upriver. The temperature was fifty below zero. Under such temperatures trees exploded and the river ice hissed.

The police party wondered if the trapper would stick it out in his cabin for one more night. They reached it shortly before noon. Eames checked a thermometer. It was fifty-two below zero.

Johnny had counted nine days when he heard a musher whistle and a dog bark, and he knew the waiting was over. The Mounties were back. Stoically, mechanically, Johnny placed himself in position in his countersunk cabin. He could kneel and his head would be below the surface of the ground. He had knocked the chinking out of the top of the logs at the surface level, and it gave him a good line of sight.

Eames and his men mushed to a halt under the cover of the riverbank and remained where they were for the time being. There was no way Johnny could get a shot at them without leaving his cabin. The inspector motioned for his men to spread out along the bank. Spruce and cottonwood trees towered thirty to forty feet above them, but there was a clear field of fire in front of the cabin. This would be as equally advantageous to Johnny as it was to them.

Eames and Millen were side by side watching the cabin.

"He must be in there," Eames said. "There's enough smoke pouring out of the cabin to run a locomotive."

"Yes, it's funny in a strange sort of way, but I wonder what his reasoning was in not pulling out," Millen said.

"No snow, more than likely," Eames replied.

Millen knew he was in the doghouse as far as his boss was concerned, so he ventured to take the bull by the horns. "Inspector, I'll rush the cabin if you want me to."

"No, Millen, this is not the time for heroics. I'll see if I can talk him out of it."

Eames cupped his hands around his mouth in order to get the maximum carrying power at fifty below zero. He knew the cold acted like a conduit amplifying the sound.

"Johnson!" he shouted. "Surrender. The man you shot is still alive. You will not be charged with murder."

Johnny heard the voice, but he'd have to serve time, and he could not face the lockup again. Then he was reminded of another situation seventeen years earlier. All of a sudden he was back lying among the rocks between Medicine Lake, Montana, and the North Dakota state line with the county sheriff shouting for him to surrender. Johnny knew he was boxed in and he was going to be captured, but a fog rolled in and he managed to escape. Maybe something like that would happen here if the snow and the elements helped him out. He did not answer Eames and shifted restlessly waiting for something to happen.

Eames figured a few words might save a gun battle, injury, lives, money, and the worst of all, the possibility of endless grief.

So, he tried again, asking Johnny to give up, but to no avail.

The inspector then called the men in. "We'd better start building fires now before we get cold, or the dark will make it that much worse. Lazarus and Joe, build a fire in that grove of trees across the river. And Ernie, start thawing out that dynamite we got from Blake. We might need it."

Eames sent Gardlund and his six-foot-six pal Lang downstream following the dogleg left curve of the river for fifty yards so they could observe the rear of the trapper's cabin.

They returned. "It's open ground, and there's no back door to the guy's shack," Gardlund reported. "He's got a view of the river from front and back."

Edwards and Bernard were posted to the dog watch. Eames knew their job was probably the most important of all. If the dogs got away, the posse would be in as much jeopardy as a cowboy losing his horse. And what disturbed Eames most of all was the infernal cold. He realized, and probably Johnny realized as well, that they were the ones who had to put up with the frigid air. Johnny had obviously stored plenty of wood in his cabin. And he was not wasting his energy cutting wood to build a fire like they were.

Eames was not one to criticize a man in front of the others. Eames waved Millen over to him. "Spike, now you know why I want my men to be tough when they check out drifters in this part of the country. If you'd been a little harder on this guy in McPherson, we might have avoided all this."

Millen realized that this was no time to argue, but what else could he have done—arrest the man for just being there?

"Yes, sir," he replied quietly.

"So be it," said Eames.


Sutherland, in the meantime, had begun unloading the box of dynamite. "This here says 'Dominion Explorers' on the side of it. Hey, Millen! Would you tell me now—how Blake got this stuff."

"The same way Jesse James got his gold," Millen said, smiling. "Dominion's got a lot of caches out here. They fly their stuff in. By the way, have you worked much with dynamite, Ernie?"

"Not up here."

"That's what I thought," Millen said evenly.

"Why, what's the matter?"

"You've got to be awful careful with that dynamite because it's frozen," Millen said. He wondered if Sutherland had really ever handled it in the cold.

"Come on, there's no danger."

"The gelatin crystallizes and if you even look at it the thing will explode."

"Are you serious?

"Yes."

Millen noted that Sutherland's hands had started to shake, and not just from the cold. He walked over and gently took the sticks out of the old-timer's hands and commenced thawing them out by gently turning them over and over in the heat of the fire, which was so encased by the cold, it barely gave off enough heat to thaw anything. He turned to Sutherland. "Here's what you do, put them clear down under your long john shirt. That's the best way to thaw 'em."

Eames realized suddenly that no one was firing at Johnny and it dawned on him the others expected some kind of signal. He finally waved at them and they started shooting. "Knock out his stovepipe," he shouted and he promptly drilled a bullet through it. The posse riddled the pipe and the rest of the shack, but it did not seem to do much good. After a few minutes, the inspector waved them off. He then shouted again for Johnny to surrender. In doing so he exposed himself to Johnny's position, but no shot came.

Millen could not help but smile. If the entire operation had not been so demanding because of the terrible cold, he would have enjoyed it. In the near light he scanned the Rat where the dogs were tied up to trees along its bank. His eyes took in the dancing flames of the posse's fires and the breaths of the men and dogs that hung in the air like so many puffs of smoke from a pipe, and the golden light of a sun that hit the tips of the Richardson Mountains but did not infiltrate the valleys below, and the tiny yet handsome little cabin they were bent on destroying along with the man in it. The whole show seemed to accentuate the folly of Man. Only Man could war in a place like this.

Johnny was safely installed in the pit beneath the level of the ground when the first burst of fire hit the cabin. Slugs from the high-powered rifles slammed through the door and through the cellophane cover of the window to ricochet loudly off a frying pan. And yet another hail of bullets thumped the stove's smokestack. Johnny waited out the storm in one place. Occasionally he popped up to take a look, but the posse did not appear to want to have a go at him. So far, he hadn't fired a shot.

Eames had trouble digesting the fact that Johnson failed to fire back. He couldn't be out of ammunition. Was he even in there?

The inspector voiced his concerns to Millen.

"Well," said Millen, "he could have put a green log on the fire and taken off."

"There's only one way of finding out, right, Corporal?" said Eames, eyeing Millen.

Millen did not have to be a soothsayer to divine the inspector's meaning. "You want me to draw him out?"

"It's up to you."

"Yes, sir."

Millen went up and over the bank as if he were shot out of a cannon. Eames and the others were quick to give him covering fire.

Johnny, who had wondered when the inevitable attack would come, almost immediately spotted Millen and fired five shots so quickly with his lever-action rifle it was almost as if he were firing an automatic.

Millen hit the snow as the withering fusillade whined over his head, pinning him down. He squirmed back over the bank when the shooting stopped.

"I guess that answers your question," he said to Eames.

"Good job, Constable," Eames replied.

Eames took out his pocket watch and looked at it in the firelight. It was only two o'clock in the afternoon yet already the cold was beginning to take its effect. The inspector told Millen to warm himself at the fire, and the others to alternate in doing so. Sutherland indicated the dynamite had not yet thawed out.

Inspector Eames decided to launch another attack. This time he would lead it himself, and take Millen with him. They were the only two professional lawmen in the posse. He would rather not involve the others unless they volunteered to do so.

Eames and Millen wiggled their way over the bank toward the cabin's corners, with Eames taking the east corner and Millen the west. This ruse did not work either. Johnny's keen eyes picked out the two men as soon as they crawled within his field of fire. Several shots sent Eames and Millen scurrying for cover.

They returned to the campfire none the worse for wear, though slightly nervous from their flirtation with death. A few of the other members joined them at the fire.

"Quick," Sutherland commented.

"He's been around guns before," Eames said.

"Firing pistols, maybe," Lang chimed in.

"It is hard to tell in this cold," Millen said.

"Anybody figure out where he's shooting from?' Eames asked.

"Yeah," said Lang, "I'd guess he's in a pit. The whole cabin is countersunk into the ground. A few trappers build them that way—mainly for warmth."

"Or another function," Eames put in.

Lang smiled. "Possibly," he said.


What brief twilight there was disappeared quickly, and as the hours went by, the cold began to register a telling effect on Johnny's foes. The longer the men in the posse were anchored to their positions, the more food they needed to fuel their bodies with heat. The two days lost circling the cabin now became increasingly noticeable as only two days of supplies were left for both dogs and men. They would have to break through Johnny's defenses soon or retreat.

"The dynamite is thawed, gentlemen," Sutherland announced. On Millen's advice he had been thawing it next to his body. He reached under his parka by way of his hood and extracted a stick and handed it across the fire to Millen who reached out to grab it. Somehow the two hands missed connection and the dynamite stick fell into the fire. All of the men scattered, diving into the deep snow—except the old Scot, who calmly plucked the stick out of the fire, muttering at the same time: "What's the matter? There's no cap in this," he said, waving the dynamite.

There was a collective sigh of relief when Sutherland gave them the news and they returned to the warm tentacles of the fire. They figured with the old man working the dynamite they were in more danger from him than they were from the trapper. Millen tucked the warmed-over dynamite in his parka, saving a few sticks that he inserted caps and primer cord into, and in a short time he had two "bombs" ready for use.

"Constable Millen, you once played ball in Fort McMurray, didn't you?" Eames asked.

"That's right, sir. Hit four hundred."

"Well, I hope you can throw as good as you can hit. Let's see how far you can toss one of your bombs."

Millen raked a coal from the fire, applied the primer cord to it until it sizzled, and walked to the lip of the riverbank that gave him protection. He reared back and heaved the bomb at the cabin. It landed up against the structure and exploded with a mighty roar, but when the snow settled and the smoke lifted they saw that it had had little effect.

Johnny was shaken by the sound of the blast, but when he saw there was little damage, he sighed in relief. His luck was holding.

Millen shook his head. "It got there, but that's about it. No damage."

Lang had worked in enough mines to understand the properties of dynamite. "And there won't be," he said and paused.

"Dynamite is about 10 percent effective at forty-five below zero. Right now it's probably colder than that," he said. "Make up a bundle of the dynamite sticks and toss it onto the roof. I'll make a run at the cabin as soon as the charges explode."

"You don't have to, you know," said Eames, "Millen or I could—"

"Nah, you guys have done enough," Lang said. "You're too old, and Millen's the best thrower. Besides I need every one of you, even Lazarus and Joe, to provide me with covering fire."

"I'll give it a try with Knut," Gardlund declared.

Lang and Gardlund then crouched by the sharp incline of the riverbank.

Millen stood between them and threw the bundle using the rope from the package for leverage. The deadly missile arched skyward through the darkness and landed atop the tiny shack's slanted log roof. Millen had added a little more fuse, and it burned longer, sputtering in that deadly interval between lighting and ignition.

Johnny heard the fuse, and dived under his heavy log bunk, flattening himself against the side of the pit.

The homemade bomb exploded with a crack not unlike an artillery round.

Gardlund and Lang ran for the cabin, with Gardlund beating Lang there by three steps.

The tremendous blast caved in part of the roof and knocked the stovepipe askew. The smoke and snow suspended in the air gave the attackers the cover they needed. Lang scrambled for the door while Gardlund fired cover through the window.

Lang reared back with his huge frame and kicked at the log portal. It did not give way completely, but enough for him to squeeze through and get a bead on Johnny whom he could hear underneath the bunk. Through the gloom he saw that the trapper, in his restricted space, could not bring his guns to bear, though he was striving mightily to do so.

Stunned by the blast, Johnny looked squarely at Lang and the vision he got was of a blurry shadow aiming a rifle at him. Johnny figured this time he was surely going to die.

Lang never said a word. He had a split second to shoot the man or not. Though he was deputized, it went against the grain—his grain. He could not do it, and backed off.

Johnny in one fast motion rolled on his side, brought up his shotgun, and let loose with both barrels. The load missed the invader who had jumped back leaving the door ajar only seconds before Johnny fired. Johnny got up and raced for the door, jamming a spruce pole against it, then he dropped again to the floor of the pit, safe for the time being. Luck had been with him again as the second attacker had quit for fear of hitting his associate.

Lang and Gardlund rejoined the others.

"I had a bead on him," Lang confessed, "but I couldn't pull the trigger."

Inspector Eames nodded. "You may have saved us a lot of trouble if you had, but we can't cry over spilt milk."

"It's three in the morning," Gardlund said.

"That means we've been at this for fourteen hours," Lang added.

"Yes, too long," said Eames. "I never figured he'd hold us off like that. It doesn't seem like we can touch him." He turned to Bernard. "Get everyone in. Tell Laz to forget the dogs and keep an eye on the trapper."

To make matters worse for Eames and his men, it had started to snow heavily.

"We could try to get around behind the cabin," Millen suggested.

"Good idea," said Lang, "but there's no cover back there. Karl and I scouted it earlier."

"Suppose we all attacked at once," Gardlund suggested.

Eames shook his head. "If I can help it, I don't want to get anyone killed on this operation."

"Suppose we burn him out," Lang suggested.

"I gave it some thought, but he's not just going to sit there while we're stacking kindling against the shack. We'd be sitting ducks," Eames commented.

"Well, we've got the coal oil flares," Lang said, "If we throw them up against the cabin, the trapper's eyes will be temporarily blinded by the light. That might give us enough time to get him."

"All right," Eames said. "I'm going to lead this sortie."

"Wait a minute," said Gardlund. "I got a flashlight and if we can get through that partially opened door, I'll shine it right into Johnson's eyes."

"Okay, Karl, let's go," said Eames.

The two men wasted no time. The heavy snowfall gave them more cover and they made it to the door before Johnny had even fired a shot. It looked like the strategy might pay off.

Gardlund turned on the electric torch and directed it into the shack. Almost immediately Johnny fired and the light in Gardlund's hand went out. Gardlund flicked the button on the flashlight figuring it had gone dead. At the very least it wasn't working.

"The light has gone out," he shouted to Eames. "We'd better get out of here." The two men ran and pitched themselves over the riverbank as bullets flew past them.

"I never thought my good old flashlight would fail me," he said, and held it up to look at it. Millen grabbed it from him. "Let me see that," he said. Then he held it up to the firelight. "I'll be hanged," he exclaimed. "It didn't fail you." He turned the flashlight upside down and shook the housing over his open hand, and a .22-caliber rifle slug fell into it.

Eames looked at it in amazement and said, "It's dark and snowing. The guy hasn't slept for days and the coal flares are throwing light into his eyes. And yet he can still shoot out a flashlight in someone's hand with a .22-caliber rifle. If anyone ever told me that someone had done this I'd have him committed for being a liar. Well that does it. We're at the end of our resources. We're pulling out. Millen! I want you and Gardlund to stay here and keep an eye on Johnson if you can, but don't take any risks."

# Chapter 21

# ESCAPE!

Undeterred by numerous ruses and raids, Johnny lay prone in his shack confounded that he was still alive. The long-awaited snow had begun to fall, at first lightly, and then heavier. Having been resigned to the fact that he would have to fight to the death, he began to wonder, if by some miracle, he might yet survive. The gunfire abruptly ended after his shot had put out the flashlight. He lay still. An hour went by. Just then he heard the yelps of the dogs, and knew by the degree of the canines' excitement the police were pulling out. The sounds of the huskies faded into the distance in a manner of minutes. He realized that they may have left someone behind to watch him, but he had to take his chances right now while the snow was heavy.

He gathered up all of the grub he had left, and tucked it into his pack with his sleeping robe. He repacked his ammunition, guns, and ax. He then grabbed his snowshoes, and with the stealth of a wolf wiggled past the broken door and slithered into the trees behind his cabin. Once there, he put on his snowshoes and trotted up the Rat River. Johnny was exultant as the swirling snow concealed his tracks. The police could not find him as long as the storm lasted, and every minute so gained was a precious one to be savored in his bid for freedom.

However, traveling at night was not easy. The dark distorted his depth perception, and he frequently fell down while trying to cross patches of ice hummocks that thrust upward as the result of spasmodic freezing and thawing of fast stretches of water. He attempted to avoid them whenever possible, but he dared not take the time to follow any other route.

Also, the intensity of the cold, accentuated by a cutting wind, slowed down his pace. He loped a long distance up the Rat before making camp off river and crawling into his bedroll for some much needed sleep.

When he awoke in the morning the snow had stopped and he realized he had camped too close to the river. His pursuers would find his trail for sure. Exasperated, Johnny hustled straight north following the glare ice of a tributary stream to climb a bench of land above the Rat. Once on the shelf he turned east, doubling back parallel to the waterway, but well away from the rim of the bench, thus avoiding any curious eyes cast in that direction. Johnny went five miles this way. Then, after running a half-mile circle in order to view his back trail, he rested briefly in a willow thicket, and then set out again.

The sun was rising closer to the horizon every day, and he knew it would not be many days before the winter nights were over. His chances of making an escape would lessen as the days increased in length.

But this night was clear and cold. Light provided by the radiance of the aurora and the glistening snow allowed him to pick his way through the bush and descend again to the river. He followed its course until he found glare ice and there crossed to the south side of the stream. From this point he was able to ascertain the position of a cache he had suspended between two trees the previous summer. In it he had stashed some dry meat and biscuits that were now frozen solid. He broke off several of the biscuits and strips of meat and slipped them between his undershirt and skin to be thawed out by his own body heat as he walked. The rest of the food he tossed into his pack.

Johnny knew that a group of trackers as determined as the Mounties and their deputies would cut the trail he made to his cache, so he climbed the bench on the south side and held briefly to an easterly course before swinging around to circle back and again head upriver.

Constable Millen and his associate, Gardlund, were dead tired after the posse left for the long turn back to Aklavik. Realizing that Inspector Eames had given them a little leeway on watching for Johnny, they retreated into the trees during the snowstorm and crawled into their sleeping bags. Even if they had wanted to, it was absolutely impossible to watch Johnny through the heavy snow without exposing themselves to deadly risk. The only thing they could do was to wait for the snow to stop and then look for tracks. Wolves could not evade leaving their footprints and neither could Johnny, no matter how good a woodsman he was.

The next day the snow stopped and they approached the cabin as if they were walking on eggs.

"I think Johnson has flown the coop," Millen said.

Gardlund pointed at the cabin. "You're right. No smoke."

"Let's check it out," Millen said.

A raven suddenly squawked above them and they immediately hit the ground, racking the bolts of their rifles. Seeing the source of the sound, the two men sheepishly climbed out of the snow and resumed their stealthlike pace toward the cabin. When they reached it Gardlund moved up and, standing off to the side, held a bead on the window while Millen approached the door, took a deep breath, and kicked it aside. He peered in and saw the cabin was empty.

"What a wreck. We did more damage than I had supposed," Millen said. "Come on in and take a look."

"Well built though," said Gardlund stepping over the sill and pointing down. "He installed a double row of sill logs."

There was a good-size hole in the roof, and the snow had come down through the opening and covered an area around the stove and stovepipe. The cabin did not look especially cozy.

Gardlund shook his head in disgust. "All that shooting for this?"

"Look at that," Millen said, pointing to the back wall of the cabin, "Snowshoe frames. They must be at least three inches thick. He's a pretty good woodworker."

"There should be no mistaking those snowshoes," Gardlund proclaimed.

The two men rummaged around the area and found a stage cache in the woods to the rear of the cabin, and a canoe.

"That must be the canoe he bought from Abe Francis last summer," Millen observed.

That night Gardlund and Millen built a roaring fire and managed to get warm for the first time in three days. They brewed up some tea and sat upon logs dragged up before the flames.

Gardlund's curiosity was unending once he had become involved in the case, and he knew little if anything about what was going on. Now he saw his chance to find out something and he confronted his companion about it.

"Spike," he said, "What's this all about?"

Millen gazed into the fire, then answered, "I wish I knew, I guess you'd have to ask Johnson."

"All right, but why are you after him? There's got to be a reason."

"Simple and basic," Millen said, "an Indian filed a complaint that Johnson was monkeying around with his traps, throwing them off the trail, and stuff like that. And he may have been trapping without a license. We went to check it out, and King got shot."

"How come he shot King?"

"That's a good question."

"Come on Millen, I'm deputized. I'm a part of this thing. Don't give me that lost-in-ignorance ploy the law uses."

"You're right. Occasionally we do hold back, but Karl, I'm being straight with you. We knew absolutely nothing about the guy before he showed up here."

"How about after he showed up?

Millen grinned. "You are serious. No, we knew nothing that everyone else didn't know."

"Okay. Why didn't he buy a license?"

"Well, it wouldn't have been for the lack of money," Millen said.

"What do you mean?"

"Bill Douglas told me Johnson paid cash for a thousand dollars' worth of supplies and looked like he had several thousand more."

Gardlund whistled. "He had that much! It doesn't make sense."

Millen smiled. "Yes it does."

"It does?"

"Yeah, the money's probably the answer to the whole riddle."

"You mean the fact that he wouldn't buy a license."

"That's right," Millen said. "Let's suppose Albert Johnson was not his correct name."

"Okay," Gardlund said, "go on."

"That being the case, if he gave an alias, in a technical sense he'd be violating the law. In other words he did not want to fill out a form."

Gardlund nodded. "That could have meant many things."

"Correct again," said Millen. "He could have been an immigrant and afraid of being kicked out of the country or an ex-con wanting to start a new life, whatever. He simply did not want to sign a form."

"Do you think he overreacted when you talked with him?" Gardlund asked.

"Yeah, if he'd bought a license, no matter what name he gave, we wouldn't have launched an elaborate investigation," Millen said.

"You wouldn't?" Gardlund asked.

"Not just for a trapper's license. No. Of course, if he did something wrong later we would," Millen answered.

"In other words he snared himself in his own web of paranoia," Gardlund concluded.

Millen laughed. "I suppose you could put it that way. One thing, the inspector isn't going to like this."

"Like what?" Gardlund asked.

"Letting Johnson get away," Millen said.

"Come on Spike, he can't blame us. Last night the snow was thicker than pea soup," Gardlund said.

News concerning the shooting of King had first been released on January 6.

On January 15, word flashed over UZK long-wave broadcasts to the outside world that Albert Johnson was still at large. The fact that Johnny had held out against a larger force tended to bias the public's sympathy in his favor. Called the "Arctic Circle War" by the news media, North Americans remained glued to their radios following its progress, and as a consequence radio fans had a field day second-guessing the case. Newspapers featured the story in headline after headline as the series of gunfights unfolded.

Inspector Eames became irritated at the focus of the stories. Reading the latest one was too much. He slammed down the press report wired to him on his desk. "Corporal Wild!" he shouted. "Front and center."

Wild came through the doorway on the double quick. "Yes, sir," he said, realizing this was no time for informalities.

"Look at what our friends in the media are saying about Johnson," Eames shoved the report across the desk. "If Johnson's demented, I'm John Dillinger."

Wild knew he had better not flag the bull and suggested otherwise. "Maybe they mean it in a different way, Inspector."

"I don't care which way they mean it. Johnson's making me look like an ass. I want the following in my report. Write this down."

Wild picked up a notebook and pencil. "Okay, sir."

"Johnson has shown himself to be an extremely shrewd and resolute man, capable of quick thought and action and a tough and desperate character."

"Are the men ready to go?"

"All set," Wild answered. "By the way, Knut Lang wants to see you."

"All right, send him in."

Lang walked in and Eames got up and shook his hand.

"Nice to see you Knut, pull up a chair," Eames said.

Lang sat down facing the inspector across his desk.

"You're not going with us this time, Knut?"

"That's right."

"You object to telling me why?"

"No, I understand that Bishop Geddes started this whole thing."

Eames, somewhat disconcerted by the remark, replied, "Moccasin telegraph is working overtime. No matter. Yes the bishop told me about Johnson's presence in McPherson, if that's what you mean."

"Well, Inspector, with all due respect, what business was it of his?"

"He's a pretty astute observer, Knut."

"Inspector, do you mean to tell me you sent a special patrol to check on Johnson just on Geddes's say-so?"

Eames shook his head. "Come on Knut, you know better than that. Millen was on his regular patrol to McPherson. He talked to Johnson there."

"If that isn't harassment, what is?" Lang growled.

Eames whirled in his chair and pointed out the window. "Knut, you've been around here a long time. You've heard of the Desteffany brothers. They were Americans. Am I supposed to let every newcomer wander around the country until he almost starves to death?"

"They didn't die."

"All right. Forget about them. How about Nicole and Beaman? They did."

"Someone else complain about Johnson?" Lang asked.

"Yes, as a matter of fact—"

Lang thought immediately who it was. "Nerysoo?" he interrupted. "He's no angel."

"Neither is Johnson," Eames countered. "But that's not the point."

"I don't know, but it looks to me like Johnson got the shaft," Lang said.

Eames got up from his chair and went over to the window in an obvious attempt to control his temper. Then he turned around and spoke out. "Knut, you can disagree. I'd rather have a guy come right out with criticism than talk behind my back. But here's the thing: does Johnson have the right to gun down King because he knocked on his door? You know very well that he doesn't."

Lang was a tough man. He realized Eames had been gracious enough to hear him out, and there was plenty of logic to what he said. But he felt the way he felt, and nothing could change it. He stood up. "I'm still pulling out."

Eames stood up. He didn't offer his hand and neither did Lang. "All right, Knut," he said, "I appreciated your help."

McDowell was recovering in the hospital from his knee, which he had reinjured in his second trip to the Rat. He was trying to hobble, but not doing a very good job of it, while nurse Liz was tidying up his bed.

"I'm missing out on everything because of this damned knee," he complained.

"Oh Mac, they have enough men without you. You've done your share."

"I'm still the odd man out," he said.

"I'm glad," she said.

"You are?"

"You dope. I don't want to see you killed," she said.

The Mounties had lost one of their best men when McDowell injured his knee. Constable Melville's flu got worse and he went onto the sick list as well. Eames was so desperate for help he broadcast an appeal for men over the radio and obtained the services of many on an ad hoc basis throughout the region. However, he only came up with eight men out of Aklavik when the next posse left for the Rat on January 16. These included Hersey and Riddell who had been okayed by the army to join the chase.

Riddell was one of the North Country's great bush men. He was a bridge between the old and the new in that he could take care of anything required in the way of engines, yet also was an expert on mushing dogs and northern survival. Before departing, Riddell constructed several ingenious beer bottle bombs, and made others out of old outboard engine cylinders, in case Johnson barricaded himself in another cabin. The other half of the Signals team was

Staff Sergeant Hersey, a former Olympic marathon runner, excellent in the bush, and obviously a tireless northern traveler. Their principal function was to relay messages for Eames, saving time in shipping supplies and aid when needed. Their equipment consisted of a low-powered transmitter using a 108-volt battery and a 201 tube, and a receiver to use with the battery. The principal problem was to fasten the unwieldy equipment securely enough on a dog sled so the entire rig would not fall apart when they went over the first bump on the trail.

Eames and his men had set up four eight-by-eleven-foot tents at the junction of the Longstick and Rat rivers and had been there four days with no results in the search for Johnson. The inspector had lost track of time. He was sitting on a dynamite box in the headquarters tent.

"Spike," he said, "what day is it?"

"I believe it is the twenty-first, Inspector."

"You had no luck while I was gone?"

"It's a mess up there."

"What do you mean by that?" Eames asked in an even tone.

"You never saw such a tangle of willows, poplars, alders, spruce, and just plain buck brush as you'll see along the Rat," Millen said. "It's bad enough trying to find a person legitimately lost let alone digging out some character who is avoiding you by design."

"You've been up there now with Gardlund, what do you think about getting a plane?"

Millen popped a chunk of dry meat into his mouth. Lydia had smoked it and no one could make it like she did. "It would be a big help. Save us miles and miles of snowshoeing."

Eames nodded in agreement. "That's what I was thinking. It would help me too. We can't keep up supplying this outfit simply with dog teams. It's too slow. I'm going to call in a plane," he said.

"I'm going to Aklavik before we get any lower on supplies. I want you, Frank Riddell, and Noël Verville to keep after Johnson. Go clear up to the headwaters of the Rat if you have to. The Indians tell me he won't try to cross over the Richardson Mountains because it would be too tough. But, I'm not so sure."

Later, Millen walked over to the crew's tent. Oddly, he'd be in command as soon as Eames left for Aklavik. He laughed out loud at the thought. There were literally no Mounties left in his part of the north to draw on. Melville was down with the flu, and McDowell was hindered by a bad knee. King was wounded.

Millen liked the men who were now with him. Riddell was easy to work with, and was not the type to pull rank even though he was a quartermaster sergeant. Gardlund was an intrepid Swede who would never give up on any task he undertook, and Verville, whom he knew only slightly, came well recommended by trappers around Aklavik. Verville had a fine record from the Great War and was a crack shot.

When Millen walked into the tent he noticed that Gardlund was waxing his skis, while Riddell was tinkering with the transmitter on his wireless set. Verville was just sitting there as a spectator, but not an uncritical one.

"Bonjour, Constable," he said. "How are you?"

Millen nodded and smiled. "Okay, Noël." Millen wondered about the Frenchman's accent. He seemed to turn it on and off as the occasion demanded.

"Constable," Gardlund injected, "do you think Frank there can really operate that thing?"

"Just wait until later and I'll show you," Riddell said.

"Why wait, my friend?" queried Verville.

"We only call twice a day, that's why," Riddell said while trying to concentrate on what he was doing.

"Why for only two times?" asked Verville.

"To save the battery, dummy."

"I'm not a man of electricity," said Verville.

"That's for sure," said Riddell.

"Yes, my boy. The electric is crazy like Gardlund's sticks."

"I think he is talking about your skis," Millen offered.

Gardlund was a skier first, last, and always. "I can go anywhere you can go on your *raquettes*," he said mimicking his Quebecer partner by emphasizing the last syllable of the word.

"Not in buck brush, my friend."

"Ha, that's where you are wrong, Mister Verville. Sure I have a tough time in buck brush, but so do you on your tennis rackets. I can go three times as fast as you."

"The turtle argues with the rabbit," Riddell chimed in.

"I hate to interrupt your . . . er . . . philosophical discussion," Millen said, "but let me have your attention for a moment. Inspector Eames wants three volunteers and I nominated you three." He noted the three men looked at each other. "Do I hear any comments?"

"Why do you say volunteer?" Verville asked.

"I agree with Noël. It doesn't sound like we volunteered now, does it?" said Gardlund.

Millen grinned. "Tomorrow we leave for another sweep of the Rat. We've got to check every trail, even a raven's tracks, as we go up the valley."

The next day they set out, and though they had dogs, their progress was slow. Low temperatures, drifting snow, and the short hours of twilight made the task of finding Johnny's trail incredibly difficult. Johnny had the entire vast wilderness to run in and there was always the possibility that one day he might not run, choosing rather to ambush his trackers.

The four-man party, with Gardlund on skis and the others with dogs and snowshoes, patiently worked its way up the Rat River valley. They combed the timber from one side of the valley to the other. From dawn until dark they scanned the snow for any telltale signs of Johnny—a bent sapling, a chopped piece of kindling, his own scat, the impression of a snowshoe, a charred log, chopped ice, the sound of a shot, a depression made by a sleeping bag, the bones of animals eaten, a shell casing—they looked and they did not see anything. It was as if the man had been swallowed up by the wilderness of the Great White North.

Finally they met with a limited success. "By *gar*," Verville reported when he returned to the river after a side trip up a tributary. "I see *une cache*. We go," he said and led the others to the cache.

They carefully checked it and discovered the cache must have contained at least a half ton of meat, mostly moose.

"We'll stake it out," Millen said.

They pitched a tent in a dense spruce island surrounded by buck brush. After two days of sitting around in fifty-below temperatures they gave up the uncomfortable task.

Either Johnny had moved on, bypassing the cache, or he was too sly to approach it. When they left, they took what they needed for themselves and fed the rest to the dogs.

Another frustrating week went by without sight of Johnny's spoor. Each man was hard-bitten to the trail and could trot thirty miles a day behind a dog sled without getting tired. They were Arctic-honed, used to long hours, cutting wood, breaking paths, and stabilizing heavy, laden toboggans over dips and bumps, chopping ice for water, breaking up dogfights—all in temperatures where every movement was an effort. Now even they were beginning to show signs of exhaustion.

# Chapter 22

# THE CANYON SHOOTOUT

By January 28 their supplies were down to a little tea, hardtack, and bacon, and they were almost out of dog food. They had traveled long and far that day and frost collected inside their parkas and froze. They stopped to build a fire and brew tea while on their way back to an outcamp they had established.

Ever restless, the always tinkering Riddell decided to scout around the camp. "I'll be back shortly," he said. "I'll circle our spot here to see if there's any sign of Johnson."

Ridell, the Signals man, strapped on his snowshoes, grabbed a staff he'd cut for balance, and headed out.

"Good luck," Millen called after him.

Riddell had not gone very far when he spotted faint man-made markings on glare ice that looked like snowshoe tracks, but he could not be sure. He latched on to them like a bloodhound. He followed the tracks off the ice and up to the top of a ridge where they suddenly vanished. However, a man with Riddell's experience was not easily discouraged. He widened his circle in an attempt to pick up the sign and was successful coming across the trail again as it wound up a small creek. Making doubly sure it was the markings of Johnny, which he could easily spot because of the thick frames of his snowshoes, he headed back to camp.

"I found him," Riddell said confidently.

"What do you mean by that?" Gardlund queried. "If you found him you'd probably be dead."

Riddell grinned. "I mean his trail. It goes up a creek and then into a canyon."

"How far is it?"

"About a mile, maybe two," he said.

"And how old is it?" Millen added.

"Maybe two or three days," Riddell replied.

"Okay," Millen said, "we'll try to run him down tomorrow."

They stayed at their outcamp, but it was an uneasy night for the men.

The next morning they headed out with Riddell who led them to the point where he had intersected the trapper's tracks. Riddell's sharp eyes had discerned the faintest impression of Johnny's snowshoes.

"See the impression of that portion of the frame?" asked Riddell. "There isn't another snowshoe like that in North America. It's just like the frames you showed me at the cabin."

They were able to follow the trail for several hours, but lost it again.

"Don't worry, I have a hunch he isn't far away," said Riddell.

"Why?" Millen asked. They were low on supplies and he did not have the luxury of extending the search much longer.

Riddell paused while carefully scanning the area. "No great reason, other than he's been avoiding us for three weeks, yet he's still hanging around."

"What do you think, Noël?" Millen asked, deferring to the trapper's experience.

The veteran rubbed rime off his face before answering.

"He don't make sense. Maybe he don't know where to go."

Millen pondered the situation. Then he elected to make one more detour in the direction of the trail Riddell had found.

Johnny was in his own element, and the ease with which he had avoided the trackers for almost three weeks made him confident he could remain in the vicinity of the Rat long enough for the Mounties to give up the chase and possibly veer off in another direction in their search for him. Then he could set out for distant places at his own pace, carefully avoiding trading posts and clusters of trappers and Indians scattered throughout the wilderness, and in that way make a clean escape. He had concealed his trail so well that his pace had been almost leisurely. Yet, he fretted. He did not dare return to his caches as he knew they would now be watched, and his food supply was virtually exhausted. He set snares at night for snowshoe rabbits and squirrels, adding to his rations, but these did not possess enough fat to provide him with the heat necessary to offset the forty- and fifty-below temperatures that he read constantly on his little thermometer. The food situation became so crucial he would have to kill a caribou or moose for the fat he could render from bone marrow. He had to risk the fact that a shot might reveal his position. He even tried snaring a caribou, but the animal broke the snare and darted off.

Another week went by and he could feel his strength waning. The weather was clear and the cold never ceased its punishment, clinging to him like a tenacious bulldog that would not let go. Fighting the cold was like trying to push water uphill. The cold was an all-encompassing mass that flowed around and under and over him. It seeped through tiny apertures of his clothing, his socks, and seams of his sleeping bag. It enveloped his neck and crept under his sleeves and welled-up in his parka. It stung the tip of his nose and burned his cheeks.

Driven by winds, the cold made his eyes water. Tears then froze and formed icicles on his eyelids.

The cold paralyzed his fingers when he removed his gloves, and it so suppressed the fires he built, he had to place his hands in the flames to feel their warmth. The cold numbed his feet, and it squeezed his brain until he could think of nothing else but the cold, the terrible cold.

He knew he must find relief from the cold, and fast, and the only way was to take refuge in a capsule of heat provided by a large fire. To do this he needed to find an alcove closeted from the wind, and where the flames would not be detected. This was his only hope.

Johnny sought out a deep, twisting canyon leading up a tributary of the Rat River. He cautiously made a half circle along a ridge high above the valley, then descended by venturing down the glare ice of a pup that dribbled into the canyon. He wove his way through a jumble of windfall into a dense grove of spruce. He felt so secure there he put up a canvas tarp, hacked spruce boughs for a bed, and chopped firewood. He risked a large fire that night using the tarp to reflect the heat and to obscure the roaring flames.

He strung a rope to hang his mukluks, clothes, and sleeping bag to dry. Johnny took his ax and chopped slabs of ice that he shattered and deposited into a pot to melt for water. When this was boiling he dropped the last of his tea into it and waited for it to leach properly and then drank deeply, and for the first time in weeks he felt completely warm inside and out. A man could get by at thirty below zero with small fires and little food, but when the mercury plummeted to the minus forties and fifties he could not survive without the solace of heat in large quantities.

And this was only attainable by consuming copious amounts of food to heat his insides, and on the outside by nuzzling up to a large fire. Intermediate measures only prolonged the agony. Johnny knew that there were limiting factors involved in gaining both sources of sustenance. Yet, if he did neither and the weather did not break, he would die. Having already risked a fire, he resolved to shoot a caribou or moose if he could find one. Dry and warm, he slept soundly that night.

The next morning Johnny climbed the ice of the stream to emerge on the windswept ridge above the canyon. He circled away from the valley, treading on hard-packed snow that left only the faintest of trails. He recalled spotting caribou tracks on a distant ridge and headed in that direction while keeping below the ridgeline. He soon spotted a caribou bull, and though lean after the fall rut, he was still like gold to a hungry man. He stalked the animal, which was preoccupied with digging through the snow for lichen with his splayed feet. Johnny managed to get within one hundred yards of the creature.

Johnny was squeezing the trigger of his Savage when a wolf suddenly bolted across the ridge in a headlong rush toward the bull. The caribou jinked and avoided the predator, and quartered off at an angle. Johnny could not get a shot. He cursed the wolf and resumed his hunt. He plodded through endless drifts of wind-blown snow patiently scanning the ridges for caribou, and the valleys below for moose. He saw another caribou, but it trotted off, probably skittish from the presence of wolves.

Johnny paused to watch the sun's crescent pierce the horizon long enough to cast a rosette glow on the peaks of the Richardson Mountains, which loomed above him to the west. The bright orb hung onto the earth's rim briefly and then grudgingly disappeared. It was a cheerful sight, but the heat it threw off would be months in coming. He turned to start back to camp. He found himself shivering under his parka and realized that his unfueled body was reacting to the necessity of sustaining a body heat 140 degrees higher than the outside temperature. But it was also a necessity that he continue the hunt. He circled yet again, and picked up fresh caribou tracks and followed them across a bluff. On the other side of the slope the silhouette of a bull caribou appeared like a specter against the dim light. The animal was upwind and did not detect his presence. Slowly, carefully, Johnny approached. When the grazing animal lifted its head,

Johnny stood stock-still until the bull again began to feed. Stealthily, he moved to within range, raised his rifle, took aim, and fired.

The caribou did not move at first and Johnny wondered if he had hit it. The bull walked several paces to the right only to reverse its direction where it stopped and stood still. Then, like a puppet responding to the slackening of a string, the bull suddenly fell back on its haunches. The stricken beast seemed to hold its head up only with a supreme effort. Then its eyes glazed and the gallant head fell back, but not over, propped up in death by its great antlers. Johnny had seen many an animal die but not with such dignity. He wondered about the antlers. Normally caribou bulls did not retain them this late in the winter. When he reached the stag, he quickly cut into an artery and drank the blood feeling its warmth rushing into his body, giving him strength. Only then did he notice an earmark on the animal, and he knew that he had killed a reindeer that had somehow drifted from Alaska across the British Mountains with a caribou herd. It was gelded and that explained why its horns were still on. He quartered the bull and, in relays, packed the meat to his camp. This would provide enough nourishment to last for a month.

Johnny celebrated the occasion by again lighting a large fire in his canyon camp. He broke open the caribou's bones, removed the marrow, and boiled it, skimming the fat off the top. He also boiled strips of meat that he cut into small chunks, and sat before the fire for a long time, thoroughly chewing and savoring the meat and the comfort of his rough bivouac. Finally, drowsy from eating so much, he doused the fire and crawled into his sleeping bag.

The next morning Johnny awoke late with the sun's rays turning the snow-covered hills above the canyon into mounds of pink and white. He built a small fire of dry willows and poplars under a thick spruce tree so that the limbs would disperse what little smoke was given off. He walked a short distance from camp to make sure his precautions were not in vain, and noted that other than an occasional wisp the smoke could not be seen. Johnny whistled a tune while cutting wood. He decided to remain where he was until he regained his strength.

Unbeknownst to Johnny, Millen and his three companions were close above him eyeing his camp.

Earlier that day, Millen and his group had been conferring on which way to turn when an Indian trapper mushed up to tell them he had heard a shot from the vicinity of the Bear River, the point where Riddell had first picked up Johnny's trail. The native trapper figured the shot was fired by Johnny because he knew of no one else who could have been there. So Riddell's hunch was right. In picking up the new trail they discovered remnants of a fresh caribou kill confirming the Indian's report. The trail was spotty and difficult to follow, but they knew Johnny could not be far away. "We got 'im now," said Millen, a little overzealously and slightly out of character. "Let's go down and get him."

Gardlund sensed that the Mountie had one eye on the fugitive and the other on his boss, Inspector Eames. "Wait a second, Spike. I'm about frozen. Why not move back and make camp and get some rest."

"I agree with the ski man. Tomorrow we go after him with a full belly," Verville commented.

Millen saw the logic, and deferred to the majority. "Okay, we might as well go to our old outcamp for the night," he said.

Back in their tent, Gardlund waxed his skis, and Riddell tinkered with the wireless.

"*Mon Dieu*, I still wait for that machine to talk, Frank," Verville teased.

"The main thing," Riddell answered, "isn't that we hear the base. It's that they hear us."

"*Por favor*, how come?"

"*Por favor* ain't French," Riddell snorted.

"I served near Moroccan troops in the Great War, Monsieur," Verville said loftily.

Riddell smiled. "If the base hears us they'll send supplies."

"Supposing the base don't hear us?" Verville persisted.

"Simple, we don't get the supplies," Riddell responded.

"My friend, how will we know we don't get supplies?"

"Easy, they don't show up."

"What do we do then, my friend?"

"Why, we starve, of course."

"*Les anglais* are a little crazy," Verville said, touching his temple with the tip of his index finger.

Riddell laughed. "Crazy? Maybe you've got something there."

Constable Millen was not paying much attention to the banter. Instead he was pacing up and down like a caged tiger waiting for its evening meal.

Gardlund looked over at him. "Calm down, Spike. Johnson isn't going anywhere."

"He'd better not. I can't afford to lose him again."

"*You* can't!" Verville injected, "How about us?"

"Johnson's my responsibility," said Millen.

"Spike's more worried about the inspector than he is Johnson," Gardlund said.

Millen stopped pacing to check the Yukon stove, then spoke out. "That's true in a way. Johnson is my responsibility."

Gardlund shook his head in disgust. "Spike, you know we all create our own problems."

"*C'est vrai*," said Verville. "The trapper digs his own grave."

Millen winced. "It's easy for you guys to say that, but let's be serious. Thanks to me," he paused, "the force's reputation is at stake."

Gardlund shook his head in disgust. "Bah, humbug," he said.

"Hey, fellas, let's get some sleep," Riddell suggested. "Tomorrow's going to be a long day."

"Okay," Millen said. "I'll take the first watch."

Johnny woke up the next morning with the heavy snow pelting the meager canvas that sheltered him. He climbed out of his sleeping bag, kick-started the slumbering fire, and went about his chores, so gladdened by the latest turn of events, that he whistled and even sang while doing his work.

He chopped ice to thaw for water, cut more logs, and even shaved for the first time since he had been run out of his cabin. One good, warm night and the reindeer shanks had brought back his strength. A few more days in his hideaway, and he figured he might bolt for the west side of the mountains, which, in reality, had been hemming him in.

"Another snow dump," Gardlund said, glancing from the tent when the trackers got up the next morning.

"Yes, I figured as much because it warmed up last night," said Millen, "It's only thirty-six below."

"I want you to head over to the canyon and keep an eye on Johnson if he is still there," Millen said. "If he's not there, come on back. In the meantime we'll feed the dogs, and chop firewood, and tend to the rest of the camp chores.

"Anything else?"

"Yeah, make sure he doesn't see you. Crawl, wiggle, or whatever. Keep down. Johnson's got eyes in the back of his head."

"Okay."

"And one more thing. Conserve your energy. It could be a long day."

Gardlund wasted no time getting to the lip of the canyon; he spotted the camp but could not see the fugitive. He realized he could do nothing but lie there and wait for the others to come up and join him.

Back at the camp, the men fed the dogs and themselves, checked their rifles, and made sure they had everything with them they would need if they came up against the fugitive.

Millen deliberated briefly over leaving one of the men to watch their dogs. There was always the chance that the trapper might outfox them in some way and steal their dog teams or turn them loose. As a precaution he had Riddell radio the other Signals man, Hersey, who was now on the way to join them. He told Hersey to keep a sharp look out for Johnson just in case.

When Millen, Riddell, and Verville approached the lip of the canyon, they could see Gardlund lying ensconced behind a tree with his head turned slightly to the right. The intensity of his gaze indicated Johnny was still there. Smoke confirmed it.

"I can hear him, but damned if I can see him," Gardlund whispered.

"We'll have to go down and have a look," Millen said. "Karl, you and Frank go first, but watch your step. Any noise and we'll give ourselves away."

Gardlund had removed his skis and put on snowshoes. He followed Riddell, depending on the signalman's keen eyes to look for trouble. They made it down the sharp, tree-lined slope all right. Riddell then waved for Millen and Verville to begin their descent.

The two men angled down the precipitous slope. One of the great problems of navigating such an incline was the possibility of launching a tiny avalanche. This happened to Verville. One minute he was standing upright and the next he had plunged twenty feet into a tangle of windfall, breaking a host of frozen branches on the way down. Anyone hearing the sound would be immediately alerted that some large creature was in the vicinity.

Such was the case with Johnny, who had no sooner heard the noise than he leaped for his rifle, levered a cartridge into the chamber, and fired all in one motion.

Verville, in turn, rolled behind a tree just as a rifle slug whined over his head and hit a rock and ricocheted into the forest. Gardlund, Riddell, and Millen all dropped to the ground and fired on Johnny.

Johnny saw immediately that he was in deep trouble where he was, and to improve his position he jumped across the campfire and flung himself behind an overturned spruce.

Gardlund was ready for the move and snapped off a shot at Johnny as he jumped. Gardlund was certain he scored a hit because Johnny appeared to fall in a heap behind the fallen tree.

"Shoot up his camp," Millen yelled. "I want a bullet hole in every pot and pan he's got."

The four men pumped shell after shell into Johnny's camp with pots and pans clattering and finally Millen waved to them to hold up, saying: "He'll never eat out of them again."

Johnny burrowed under the fallen tree like a wolverine digging for a squirrel. The odds had caught up with him again and this time he did not have the advantage of a cabin's bulwark. He realized that he may have been too careless in shooting the reindeer and building the fire. There was only one way he could ever break out of the box he was now in, and that was to stay alive until nightfall, and hope the snow kept falling to cover his tracks. Johnny had been in jams before, and his years of living like a wild animal told him he must remain motionless. He was the prey this time and the predators were stalking him. To outwit the hunters he must outwait them. He had one advantage, though. He judged there were three or four men stacked against him by the amount of shots fired. Well, they would have to ferret him out before darkness. In addition, they might figure he was wounded, and if so, they would assume he was dead. They might get careless, and when they came for him he would be ready. So he lay there and waited, and waited. An hour went by, and an hour at forty or fifty below was an eternity. He realized now that something would have to happen.

The one drawback to his scheme was the infernal cold that knifed through him as he lay immobile in the snow. He thought of a marten that can freeze almost immediately in a trap at forty below zero because its movements are restricted. Of course, the Mounties, too, would slowly freeze to death if they could not move. Being less desperate, they would more likely break the stalemate than he, and that was to his advantage. Luckily he was in a good position. The fallen tree he had leaped behind angled up the side of the canyon. He saw that the diameter was thick enough to conceal his movements, and long enough to enable him to wiggle higher up the hill. He inched his way along the furrow of the log, and came across a small vent he could use, undetected, to survey the area slightly below him. It was not much in the way of an advantage, but every straw was worth grabbing on to.

So he waited in the cold. It bit at his cheeks like a weasel nibbling a bone. It seeped through his mukluks, encasing his toes in a frigid canister, which at first burned and then numbed them. His muted breath created ice crystals that settled around his nostrils and eyebrows. Cold was the invisible enemy that governed all movement in the North Country. It descended silently, like an eagle swooping down on its prey, and was just as unforgiving and uncompromising. It played no favorites and gave no warning and was unparalleled in its capacity to inhibit and finally destroy.

Silence overwhelmed the scene, which moments before had reverberated with the roar of gunfire. The wind moaned through the trees. A chickadee chirped intermittently and a raven squawked somewhere up the valley. The snow continued to fall, powdering the forms of the men as they played out this deadly game on the roof of the world.

Another hour went by, then two. The sun, obscured by the falling snow, dipped below the horizon, leaving only a murky twilight in the deep valley.

The wind continued its siege stirring up a snow devil that whirled and wobbled, ghostlike among the spruce trees. Finally, it danced across Johnny's position and disappeared in the gloom of the darkening forest.

Verville, who was closer to Millen than to the others, spoke in a low voice. "Spike, did you see that?"

"See what?" the Mountie asked.

"The snow devil."

"Yes, I saw it."

"You know what that means?"

"Sure," Millen replied. "It means a whirlwind picked up some snow and carried it off."

"That is not what the Indians say," said Verville, dropping his accent. "They say he's a spirit from another world."

"Here? Why?"

"Just visiting, that's all."

"What are you telling me for?"

"I thought you would like to know."

The chirps of the chickadee ceased, and the cry of the raven dwindled off until it was heard no more. The trackers were covered with snow. Complete darkness was approaching, and Millen knew he would have to act. If he did not go in and rout Johnny out of his hole, the trapper would get away again. Johnny was the monkey on Millen's back. He had to get him out even if it meant risking his life to do it.

The constable reached from where he lay and tapped Verville on the shoulder. Pointing to a cutbank, he spoke softly, "Let's work our way over to the others."

The heavy snow continued to fall. They joined Riddell and Gardlund and discussed the strategy under the safety of the bank.

They knew it was Millen's show and let him talk.

"I'm going in after him," he said. "More than likely Karl got him, but if not, I'll need covering fire."

Verville spoke up. "Spike, I don't like this. I've kicked around these parts a long time, and I figure Johnson is playing possum. If you go in there, he'll get you for sure."

"If I don't dig him out, he'll get away in the darkness," Millen replied.

"I'd wait," said Verville. "If he's dead he won't go anywhere. If he's alive, he's cold, maybe even colder than us. He won't be able to go far."

Constable Millen could not very well express his inner thoughts to the deputized Quebecer. Millen was thinking of Inspector Eames. If he let Johnny out of this jam without even trying to get him, he knew, or at least he thought he knew, Eames would read him out of the force. Millen was between the devil and a hard place. But he was a brave man.

"I'm going in," he said simply. "Noël, you climb up a little higher and cover me." Nodding to Riddell and Gardlund he said, "Same with you Frank, and you, too, Karl. Give me some cover."

The two men looked at each other. "I'll go in with you," Riddell said.

"Same here," Gardlund added.

"Okay, spread out and follow me," Millen said.

Verville climbed to the place Millen had indicated, and waited, vainly trying to spot Johnny in the shadows, but could see nothing. With great foreboding, he watched as his companions climbed over the bank. None of them had ever been in the trenches like he had, and consequently did not realize just how vulnerable they were.

The three men, gingerly, slowly, moved toward Johnny's hiding place while Verville covered them. They had walked only about three paces when Riddell suddenly shouted, "Watch it!"

The Signals sergeant ran and dove headlong over a nearby embankment just as a shot thundered and a rifle slug buzzed through the trees above his head. Accentuated by the cold, the ear-splitting blast of the rifle resounded through the canyon. Gardlund sprang for cover. Millen, who was parallel to the log on the hill and slightly behind Riddell, saw the movement of Johnny's rifle barrel, then dropped to one knee, aimed his Enfield and fired. Then Millen wrestled with the rifle trying to rack the bolt back to eject the cartridge. More time was lost pushing the bolt forward to thrust another shell into the chamber. Finally, he lifted his rifle again and fired.

Johnny retorted in kind with his Savage. Both men missed. Johnny moved to a sitting position. His lightning speed with the lever action came to an advantage as he snapped off two more shots so quickly the muzzle blasts seemed to come from one fast burst.

Millen suddenly rose up from his kneeling position as though trying to fire at Johnny, whirled, and fell face down into the snow.

When Verville saw what happened he scrambled down to join the others. He had not even had time to fire a shot. Riddell laid down a barrage with his rifle while Verville and Gardlund crawled to Millen, tied the constable's legs together with laces from his mukluks, and dragged him over the cutbank.

Verville opened Millen's parka and felt his heart. He looked up at the others, and said somberly, "He's cold already. It was a heart shot."

"He's dead?" Gardlund asked.

Verville nodded.

It was too dark for them to do much against Johnny now.

Darkness quickly enveloped the site.

With Riddell covering their back trail, they toted Millen's body out of the canyon figuring any minute they might be ambushed by Johnny. However, all was quiet. They finally reached the lip of the canyon.

"We'd better get the word out," said Riddell. "It's too risky to try another attack on that wild man."

"What about Spike?" Verville asked.

"We'll put him up in a stage cache until we can bring a dog team down here," Riddell said.

Gardlund and Verville went to work building the cache to keep Millen's body out of reach of predators, while Riddell made his way back to their temporary camp. He met Hersey who had just arrived with fresh supplies.

"You look beat," Hersey said.

Riddell nodded. "I am. Johnson killed Spike in a shootout with us. The radio's dead so I'm heading down to the inspector's camp to let him know. Take charge here while I'm gone."

"One thing," said Hersey. "You've got to go to Aklavik. That's where he is right now. Take my team if you want."

"Thanks, but my team is well rested. Will see you in a week or so," Riddell replied.

Soon afterward Verville and Gardlund returned to camp, exhausted from their long hours in the cold.

"Well, he killed Spike," Verville informed Hersey, and flopped down by the fire Hersey had kindled in the camp stove.

Hersey nodded. "Yeah, Frank told me."

"It makes you wonder," Gardlund sighed, "Why? What kind of hatred does this guy Johnson have against the world?"

"A big one I'd guess," Hersey muttered. He was a man of few words.

# Chapter 23

# TRAPPED?

If indeed Johnny had killed the last Mountie he had shot at, as the silence of the enemy indicated, the moral aspects of the slaying never entered his mind. It was as if he were fighting a war where such ethics take on a different meaning. It was either kill or be killed. The odds were up for grabs and the man who was the quickest, the sharpest, won. If he was captured now, it would be to face the hangman. The thought of it only firmed up his resolve not to be taken alive.

As darkness descended, the tension in Johnny's body eased like the string of an unstrung bow. He remained behind his bulwark, straining to see whether anyone was attempting to outflank him, but all was quiet. A twig snapped somewhere off to the side, and he jerked his weapon in that direction, but held his fire. If he could not see in the dark, neither could the others. If he pulled the trigger, the sound and the flash would reveal his position, and if the ruse was a thrown stick, he'd be set up for the kill. He had not heard the men leave. However, after an hour, to make sure, he grabbed a dead branch and hurled it toward his camp. If anyone was watching they might bite at the bait and shoot. The branch hit with a clatter, but no shot came. Either they had gone, or sentinels were set up blocking escape both up and down the canyon. He dared not venture in either direction. That left him but one alternative: to climb the cliff behind.

Holding his rifle across his forearm, Johnny crawled down to his camp. There he fumbled for his gear, now covered with snow. He found his ax, sleeping bag, and snowshoes, which he thrust into his deep packsack. Every few seconds he would stop, lift his head, and listen, like a wary gopher feeding close to its den. Johnny gathered in frozen slabs of meat he had hung from a tree branch and stuffed them into the pack like so many boards. Next he crawled to the base of the cliff and lay there studying its slope. To his relief, he saw it was not absolutely perpendicular, though it rose sharply for several hundred feet. A few trees even grew out of its wall and a natural furrow, faintly discernible, seemed to run up the slope like a wrinkle in an old bedsheet. The furrow was not much to follow but it would do. Feeling along the stock of his rifle in the dark, his fingers found the takedown screw and he detached the barrel. He removed the ax from his pack, replacing it with the two rifle parts. He would not be able to use the rifle when he was climbing the cliff, but he could use the ax. He tucked the ax through a loop in his pack.

Johnny slowly inched his way up the face of the cliff by keeping to the foot-wide fissure and holding onto saplings and outcroppings of rock. His feet were numb from the cold, making it that much more difficult to feel his way along the shelf. He reached a tree about one-third of the way to the top and paused to get his breath. He had been relatively safe negotiating the first segment of the cliff, but from the tree on, it not only got steeper, it exposed him to anyone posted in the canyon looking in his direction. Johnny again started upward, his body leaning against the mountainside. He felt his way with his hands and feet while moving up at an angle. With every step he went farther out from the cover provided by the trees, and though it was dark Johnny was afraid if a sentinel was posted at the bottom of the canyon, he might spot his presence not so much by distinguishing his human form, but by sensing a shadowy object out of place.

Inch by inch he ascended until he reached a point where he put his foot out and there was no fissure. Johnny brushed the cliff in a sweeping motion with his mukluk and realized that he had run into ice. A sweep with his right foot confirmed the presence of a tiny glacier that had formed, probably from a spring, and extended across the furrow. Snow had covered the treacherous ice, which he estimated to be about six or seven feet wide. Should he attempt to cross it? He could go back, but he knew it was much more difficult descending than ascending a cliff. If he went down, he'd be taking his chances that someone would be waiting in ambush. Yet, if it stopped snowing, trackers might not think about his attempting the cliff—a tactic that could delay their search for a while. Johnny took the ax from the loop and with his right hand chopped toe- and handholds in the ice. It was a noisy job, and if anyone was around, he would probably be discovered. He wondered if they waited to nab him at the rim of the canyon. It would be a clever strategy if they did.

Johnny kept at the task, pausing frequently to rest. Finally he reached a point only two feet from spanning the glacier. He hacked a toehold and placed his forward foot in it, then chopped at the ice for a handhold. His grip was loose and the blade of the ax turned so that the handle slipped from his hand and the ax fell away. Johnny quickly extended his leg and wedged the tool against the cliff face, holding it there with his foot. He removed the mitten from his right hand using his teeth and slowly reached down and grasped the handle of the ax and retrieved it.

Moving quickly now with his hand exposed to the cold, he cut his way the remaining two feet and gained the furrow again. Shaking from exhaustion and tension, he tucked the ax under his arm and thrust his hand into the mitten and rested. He carefully studied the remainder of his route, which looked fairly easy. Johnny set forth once more and cautiously climbed until he was immediately under the rim of the cliff. Here he waited, listening for any movement or sound. He held his ax, ready to use it if he had to. He peered upward trying to tune in on any unusual sound, yet all he heard was the wind coursing through the trees. Slowly, he pulled himself over the lip of the canyon's rim and crawled away from it, half expecting someone to pounce on him. A minute went by, then two, and he realized he was alone. Johnny had escaped the trap.

He removed the rifle from his duffel and put it back together, then returned the ax to its place in the pack. He took out his snowshoes, strapped them on his feet, then circled warily, looking for the trail of those who had ambushed him. He found it dimly outlined under the falling snow, noting that one of the men was on skis. The tracks went back the way they had come. He had won! The joy over this spurred him to a tireless effort and he trotted for four hours before he stopped for a break.

Inspector Eames, back at headquarters in Aklavik, knew he would have to get a plane after hearing the news of Millen's death. He called Corporal Wild into his office.

"Dick, Constable Millen's death is the last straw. We're not going to catch up with Johnson by the usual means. Wire Superintendent Acland and request an airplane."

"Yes, sir," Wild responded. "How about the Arctic Red River detachment? It's wiped out."

Eames had not thought of it exactly in that way, but it was true. One man killed, one wounded, and one down with the flu. "Send Melville back there. I understand he's walking around a bit," Eames replied.

"What about Millen?"

"If we can get an airplane, King can fly out with the constable's body. We're going to need a replacement for King. Ask for the best rifleman Superintendent Acland can spare. He can come up with the plane."

"All right, Inspector."

"And Corporal, I can't wait for answers. I'm heading out with another posse. This man has got to be brought in."

"One more thing, Inspector," said Wild.

"Yes?"

"Knut Lang wants to come back. He says Spike was a friend of his."

"That's fine, we need him," said Eames.

The course of events weighed heavily on Eames's shoulders that evening as he walked to his home in the government housing complex at Aklavik. He brushed past his wife on entering the door and threw his hat onto the divan.

Mrs. Eames realized there was something wrong. "What's the matter, dear?" she asked.

"It's Spike. He was killed two days ago."

"Oh Alex, no," she exclaimed.

"It's true, and I can only blame myself. I pushed him too far."

Arctic Red River had had its share of bad news and now there was more. An old Indian dressed in a parka and beaded mukluks walked out of the police station with a message of some kind in his hand. He stuffed it into his pocket, put on his snowshoes, and walked up the hill. He passed several cabins until he came to a structure near the top of the hill, and, following custom, he took off his snowshoes and opened the door and walked in.

Lydia Ladoucer was sewing a button on Millen's tunic.

"Father," she asked, "what brings you up here on so cold a day?"

Lydia's stepfather was a tall, lanky man of regal bearing. He stood for a minute and then sat down opposite Lydia.

"I bring bad news," he said.

Lydia studied her father's eyes as though searching for anything but what she truly expected.

"Yes?" she said.

"It is about Constable Millen."

Lydia's hands clutched the tunic. "Oh, Father, tell me he is just hurt or very sick."

"My daughter, it is worse," he said.

"Spike's dead?"

"Yes, Lydia," he nodded.

Lydia pressed the tunic to her breast and walked to the window, looked out, and wept.


Reverberations from the "war" in the northwest corner of Canada were being felt in G Division's headquarters in Edmonton, Alberta. And the pressure was not internal, it was external. Superintendent A. C. Acland heard all about the "Johnson problem" on the radio and read it in the newspapers often before he received the information via official channels. Standing in front of him was Constable William Carter, the man he was going to send north along with the plane, which had approval from all the way up to the Canadian cabinet in Ottawa. Acland held in his hands a folder from the personnel file, and he read it out loud.

"It says here 'Constable William Carter, age twenty-six. He's a veteran of northern service. The best rifle shot in G Division.' Constable, I guess you already know why you're here?"

"Yes, sir," Carter replied standing as straight as he could.

Superintendent Acland got right to the point. "Constable, not only is our failure to capture Johnson a Canadian story. It's all over North America."

"The Rat River area is rugged country, sir."

"I know it, Constable. I walked over every inch of that ground in the summer of 1910."

"I wasn't aware of that, sir," Carter said with some surprise.

Acland picked up a bundle of newspaper clippings that lay on his desk. "Let me read you a couple of clippings, not from our newspapers, but the *New York Times*. January twelfth: 'Routs Mounties in Arctic Battle: Trapper Thought Demented, Holds Cabin on Yukon Trail After Two Attacks.' That isn't all. Here's another. February first: 'Mad Hunted Trapper Kills Constable: Outlaw Pursued for Month by Canadian Mounties in Arctic, Again Repels Attacks.'"

Superintendent Acland put the clips back down on the desk. "Constable, I want you to find out what in the hell is going on up there, and send your report directly to me."

"I will, sir."

"You'll be flying north tomorrow with pilot Wop May and his mechanic."

On February 2, the same day that Carter left Edmonton on the flight to join the posse, Inspector Eames set out for Rat River with some of the veterans of the chase and three new men recruited because they were pals of Millen's. As luck would have it Eames and his men ran head-on into a howling blizzard that deposited several feet of new snow on the trail and delayed their arrival at the main camp on the Rat. Once there, Eames found out the situation had gone from bad to worse. No one had the slightest idea where Johnny was.

"He's somewhere between here," said Hersey, "and there." He pointed to the Richardson Mountains, which were about fifty miles away.

Eames decided not to leave any stones unturned to get Johnny. That meant bringing in Mounties from the Yukon side of the Northwest Territories border.

"Earl," said Eames, "I want you and Riddell to get word out by radio to Old Crow. Tell them to send a couple of men over here. I've got a hunch Johnson might bolt across the mountains. Be sure you advise them to keep their eyes open on the way."

Constable Sid May and Special Constable John Moses of the Old Crow detachment had been making their regular winter patrol and knew nothing about the pursuit of Johnny. First they had traveled up the Porcupine to the Bell where they checked on the welfare of Paul Nieman, a German immigrant with many years of trapping experience under his belt. After that visit they mushed up the Eagle River to call on two trappers, Phil Branstrom and Bill Anderson, both of whom used skis on their traplines and were located about thirty miles apart. Their next destination was the camp on the Whitestone River.

May and Moses struggled through miles and miles of buck brush wherein every few yards the dog harnesses were caught in the stringy willows. When they finally reached the Whitestone River and the cabin of Willoughby and Reuben Mason, they were tuckered out. These brothers had been in the north since the days of 1898, and it was said they were among the first men to ever take a gasoline-driven boat down the Mackenzie River. They were progressive and hard-working and even had a radio in their cabin. When not trapping, Will and Reub were perpetual prospectors searching for gold or any other mineral that could produce financial gain. They had even searched for the famed Lost Cabin mine. In fact, their friend Sam Scottee recommended that Johnny contact the Mason brothers for information about the mine. Inevitably, the subject of the mine arose again when May and Moses visited the Masons. The men were gathered around a table in the Mason's spacious cabin having coffee.

"I'm tellin' you, Sid, there's gold at the headwaters of the Bell and Porcupine rivers," said Will, the more talkative of the two brothers.

May was a slender but tough Mountie who was no *chechako*. He'd seen it all in his many years in the north. He laughed good-naturedly. "Sure, Will, but why are you here if the gold is up there? We're a hundred miles south of it."

Reub broke in. "It's winter and trappin's good here. That's why."

Will spoke, ignoring his brother. "We found colors up there. Besides we're hot on the trail of the lost mine."

"But you haven't found any big pay?" said the Mountie.

Will shook his head. "No. We gotta find the cabin first."

"It's three-sided. That's where the gold is," Reub pitched in.

May turned to his special constable, Moses, who was from Old Crow and had lived in the region all of his life.

"John, have you ever heard of it?"

Moses nodded. "Yes, white man find gold somewhere near the head of the Driftwood River long time ago."

Mounties, too, were trappers and prospectors and always on the lookout to improve their flow of earnings.

"Exactly where was it?" May asked.

"Only Lord knows," Moses replied with a twinkle in his eye.

Will and Reub were all ears, as they, too, would track down any information they could find about the mine.

"Yes," said Will, and added, "Well, he knows everything."

May laughed. "He doesn't mean that Lord."

"He don't?" asked Will.

"No, he means Peter Lord of Old Crow," said May.

Will's eye squinted craftily. "Then why don't he go get it?"

The twinkle came back into Moses's eyes. "Lord knows," he said and laughed heartily at his own joke.

They all laughed with him.

"The Driftwood River, eh?" Will said.

Suddenly, the Mason's radio crackled behind Will and their ears collectively tuned in to listen.

"That's KNK out of Fairbanks," commented Will.

Mounties are close on the trail of a trapper named Johnson who killed Constable Edgar Millen, acting commander of their Arctic Red River Detachment, in a shootout on a tributary of the Rat River. He is believed to be somewhere in the vicinity of the Northwest Territories–Yukon border. Johnson is about five feet eight inches tall, has light brown hair, blue eyes, and speaks with a slight . . .

"The Yukon border," May exclaimed, "that's us. John, we'd better hook up the dogs."

"Need some more men?" asked Will.

"It sounds by the radio like we do. You're hired. Ten bucks a day," said the Mountie. "Get your gear and dogs and we'll head out."

# Chapter 24

# CRACK SHOT AND PLANE JOIN POSSE

Constable Bill Carter had just stowed his duffel on the plane, a Bellanca, at the Edmonton airstrip. Jack Bowen, May's mechanic, went to the propeller, grabbed it, and asked, "You ready?"

"Yeah," answered pilot May, distinguished by his black beret.

Bowen gave the propeller a spin and the motor kicked in. The mechanic scrambled around the spinning blades and climbed aboard with May and Carter. "Well," he said, "here we go."

The flight took two days of bucking headwinds, pancaking into patches of snow for fuel stops, worrying over carburetor icing, and making conversation.

Carter was not much worried about his assignment. He could handle anything on the ground—the air was another matter. He knew Wop May was one of the best bush flyers in the business, but as far as he was concerned, the sooner he was out of the plane the better.

"Mr. May, you're a return man, aren't you?" Carter asked.

"Yes," said May, "flew in France."

"He did more than fly," Bowen chimed in. "He shot down eleven planes."

"Mr. May," Carter asked, "weren't you in on the Baron von Richthofen thing?"

May shook his head. "No," he said. "He had me in his sights and Roy Brown came up behind him, gave him a burst, and that was it."

"It wasn't planned?"

"No," said May, "I don't know where that rumor got started. He had me. I flew low trying to get away. Aussie ground gunners may have gotten a piece of him as well."

"Mr. May—"

"Call me Wop," the pilot said.

"How'd you get that name?" Carter asked, since May brought it up.

Wop laughed. "When I was a tiny kid I'd walk around saying something like that, and the folks started calling me by what I was saying. Something like 'wop, wop, wop.'"

"Did the superintendent give you any special orders for me when we get to the Rat?" Carter asked.

"Not really, other than to put you down in the main camp."

"You going to stick around?" Carter asked.

"Yeah, they want me to pack supplies, scout for you guys, and whatever. Must be a tough guy they're after. You ever run across anyone like that?" Wop asked.

Carter smiled. "Yes, all the time. Most of these trappers are a rugged breed. They might not have the fighting skills of Johnson, but they're tough physically."

"Anyone you can think of in particular?" Bowen asked.

"Sure," said Carter. "When I was patroling the Nahanni area, Gus Kraus was one. Another was Gus Liefee, a Finn. They were absolutely tireless."

The plane flew on and on down the Mackenzie River. They landed at just about every little settlement along the river, many of which Carter had served in with the Mounted Police. Fort Providence, Fort Simpson, Norman Wells, Fort Norman, Fort Good Hope, Arctic Red River, Fort McPherson—all of the forts represented the Hudson's Bay Company's predilection for naming them.

Eventually they came in over the Husky River, and pilot May was concerned about his fuel. "We've got a dump at Aklavik, so I guess we'd better go there first. Frankly, I'm not sure where the main camp is on the Rat," he said to Carter.

A blizzard hit Aklavik the next day canceling any flying. It was not until the following day that they took off for the Rat and made an uneventful landing at the main camp.

The stage was now set for the ultimate thrust against Johnny.

Johnny's stamina began to fail him after the canyon shootout. He had to leave most of his precious food behind, and with the posse closer on his trail, little time was available to hunt and even less for rest. The bone-chilling cold was taking its toll.

He crossed a range of hills to the Barrier River, camping at night in willow thickets. During the day he climbed to the high hills where his trail could not be so easily seen because of hard-packed snow and winds swirling through the ridges and slopes of the Richardson foothills. He frequently circled back to reappear on his own path, and in such a way hoped to disguise the fact he was heading for the Yukon Territory, which was directly west and on the other side of the mountains. Once there, he would make a feint toward distant Alaska, then bolt directly south for the central Yukon and familiar country.

Johnny struggled for a week to reach the source of the Barrier River on the east buttress of the Richardsons. It was seven days of unparalleled cold. He had lost his thermometer in the canyon, but he knew from the constant chill that the temperature seldom warmed up to forty below zero and was more likely ten degrees colder than that. The cold plagued him. It irritated him. And he knew if the cold spell did not break it would destroy him. And it did not break. The cold forced rodents into their holes and browsing animals into their beds. It froze the sap in trees, expanding and splitting them into pieces. It stopped water from flowing, and its long tentacles reached down into the depths to freeze solid pools of water and the fish in them. It settled on the land like an invisible gas, sinking into every nook and cranny of the wilderness to clench man and animal alike in its deadly grip.

The ugly persistence of the cold galled him. Ordinarily a warm spell could be counted on, but it failed to come, and as the cold persisted, Johnny became weaker. The little food he was able to snare was not enough to sustain him, and the fires he made were too small to effectively warm him and to dry out his gear.

He was cold from the need of shelter. He shivered from the want of a fire. He was tired from the lack of sleep. His body screamed for a supply of energy, which he could not provide. Each day was the same litany. He set snares at night only to find them empty in the morning. He melted snow to drink and then shaved with ice forming on his beard. And now his clothes no longer fit him. They hung on his frame like an overencumbered scarecrow. He knew his weight was down, maybe twenty, thirty, or even forty pounds. And there was no respite as he tramped across this dry and bleak arctic desert. It was the hell of cold and ten times worse than the hell of heat.

Yet in spite of it all Johnny believed he still might make good his escape. He did not know the date, but he figured from rough calculation it must have been at least a week into February. He bivouacked in an oasis of trees on a high bald plateau just short of the pinnacles of the Richardsons. The day was clear, but the winds tumbling down off the peaks churned the atmosphere into an impassible frigid air mass no man could penetrate. Johnny remained among the trees where he was temporarily protected from the blasts of the arctic zephyr.

Johnny gathered wood in the little copse by snapping dead branches off the trees, and while so occupied heard a distant whine as though the wind had picked up another notch in velocity. It was a strange sound, and the strangeness of it caused him to stop what he was doing in order to listen to it. The weird noise grew louder and came toward him from the north. He turned in that direction and moved instinctively to stand against the trunk of the nearest spruce. The whine increased in decibels until it became a drone and finally a roar. Then Johnny realized it was a plane, and the men in it were looking for him. He knew immediately it would spell his doom. In a matter of minutes all his work setting up blind leads, back trails, and dead ends would go for naught. A sickening feeling of loss and helplessness overcame him as he watched the plane slowly circle over the headwaters of the river below him to head back down the valley. It was ironic that he should suffer the humiliation of first being tracked down by telephone, and later by men in an automobile, and finally by an airplane. It made him feel no better when he recollected that Delker had warned him of all three possibilities. The presence of the plane meant there would be no possibility of chancing barren, open ridges to occasionally drop down into the tree line for warmth unless he traveled at night when temperatures were the most extreme and visibility the worst. He had no other option but to run for the Yukon Territory and the forests of the Porcupine River watershed.

Johnny walked to the west side of the small cluster of trees and scanned the Richardsons. The highest peaks of the mountain range were immediately above him. There was no pass here, but there was a slight gap made by one of the many tributaries that fed the Barrier River. Under the piercing cold, the stream had glaciated until it was nothing more than a green ribbon of ice, dusted clean by the winds, stretching into the seemingly infinite snowfields of the high peaks. His eyes roved the panorama from south to north and back again searching for a lower notch in the mountains but found none. The narrow gap of the creek in front of him was the only crack in the giant buttress he faced. He studied it carefully, gauging its course as it descended from a saddle between two peaks. This was where he would cross.

Johnny saw that his ascent would not be a cliff climb. However, he judged he would have to scramble to four thousand feet to get over the ridge. If there was no wind the elevation would work to his advantage, as the higher he climbed out of the valleys, the warmer it became. There could be as much as thirty degrees' difference in temperature between the floor of the river valley and the crest of the saddle he planned to cross.

The decision to pass over the mountains was an easy one to make, as he had no other choice. The plane had changed everything. Johnny would wait for a storm, and when it blew up, run for it. He ambled back again to the other side of the copse and looked out over the Barrier River. He estimated the trackers were several days behind him, as he had seen no sign of their presence, other than the plane.

Johnny spent the afternoon piling wood and making his camp ready. At darkness the wind died down and the stars came out to hover over his shelter like so many twinkling diamonds. He would remain in camp one more day. If by the second day it did not snow, he would chance crossing the pass anyway, as snow drifting before the winds probably would cover his trail.

That night Johnny risked building a large fire and dried out his clothes and sleeping bag. When he unhooked his suspenders, he noted that his pants hung around his hips; his shirt fell loosely over his chest, and his parka now seemed several sizes too big. He had long since finished the slabs of the reindeer meat he had taken with him after the canyon battle. Now he was trying to survive on rabbits, squirrels, whisky jacks, and ptarmigan. These barely staved off his hunger. The looseness of his clothes brought forth the stark reality that he was starving. He put snow into a pot and kept cramming it in until it was full and the water boiling. He thawed out a squirrel he carried in his pack and two whisky jacks, then skinned the squirrel and patiently plucked the feathers from the birds. He cut them up and dropped the pieces into the boiling water. He cooked them for a half hour and then ate the stew. Instantly, he felt strength surge through his body. He would need all he could muster for the climb ahead.

Johnny woke up the next morning to see gently falling snow dusting his camp. Though overcast, the clouds were high and visibility good. He carefully studied the sky and made his decision. He would go. Johnny stowed his gear in his pack, then filled every extra space in it with kindling wood. Crossing the mountains he would need wood, as there was no timber of any kind at that altitude some sixty miles north of the Arctic Circle. Laden with his snowshoes and the takedown rifle he had left in his pack, he hoisted the load onto his back. The pack settled heavily on his spine and the straps bit into his gaunt shoulders. Then, with a deliberate effort, he launched himself toward the wall of mountains ahead. His weariness seemed overwhelming and he was stiff from the cold. He trudged slowly toward the buttress that rose up in front of him. He estimated it would take him eight hours to reach the summit. Once there he would have to crawl into some niche among the rocks to make camp. There, he would wait for dawn, aware that there was nothing more dangerous for a climber than to descend the blind side of a mountain never before trod.

Johnny reached the gap provided by the stream easily, but here the ascent almost immediately became steeper. Using boulders for handholds, he painstakingly made his way up the small canyon. He slipped frequently, sometimes losing hard-gained yardage because of the ice. Then, using his ax to cut footholds, he inched his way up again. Thus, methodically he wended his way higher up the great mountain.

The ribbon of ice ran up the narrow defile to a gentler slope. Here the passage widened and walking was easier, but for him it was still a struggle. He stopped to rest and scanned the plateau and valley below, but saw no signs of pursuit. His rest break did not help him much. He had to drive himself to shoulder his pack once more and start up the mountain again. He followed the creek, which was really now only a streamlet, then the mountain steepened and he was forced to leave the path of the stream. Now it grew darker and the snow thicker. A breeze sprang up blowing the flakes ever so gently at first, but just before twilight the breeze became a gale and Johnny found himself in the middle of a mountain blizzard.

The storm caught Johnny three-quarters of the way up the mountain and engulfed him like a tidal wave. Luckily, the wind was at his back and he was able to "feel" his way up the slope. He continued his ascent, but more slowly, the cold and fatigue weighing him down like a ball and chain. There was no shelter from the great drafts of air that pounded him. He stopped to rest, but the frigid air pierced his clothes so quickly, he was forced to keep moving. On and on he went, zigzagging upward through the icy blasts and pelting snow. He would have quit but the thought never entered his mind. Almost by instinct, he kept walking. As long as there was a spark of life in his body he would fight to retain it, but the monstrous effort to climb four thousand feet was too much for a body already gaunt and emaciated. The demands on it accentuated the physical breakdown of his now skeletal frame, until he was propelling himself solely on his sense of purpose, that of staying alive. The snow swirled and stung him, and it caked up on his clothes and on his pack and weighed him down even more, but he plunged ahead.

The incline was now so sharp he could put his hands out in front of him and touch the slope. He traversed the last precipitous leg of the climb and finally reached the crest of the saddle. Scattered boulders lay along the ridge. He took his snowshoes out of his pack and, using one as a shovel, dug out a spacious chamber between two huge rocks and made camp. Thus he obtained refuge from the thrust of the gale that lashed the ridgetop. He pounded his frame with his fists and arms. And he stamped his feet and rubbed his cheeks to prevent frostbite. And now thirst was added to his woes as his mouth became increasingly parched from the lack of water. His tongue swelled up and his throat contracted until he began to gag on his own saliva. In order to obtain water, he would have to make a fire, which he had purposely held off doing as long as he could. Once he burned his precious wood there would be no more fires until he got off the cursed mountain. If the storm did not quit he could be stranded there a week and die of thirst. Dogs and wolves could obtain ponderous amounts of water from eating snow, but humans couldn't because it dried out their throats. The insanity of the whole thing plucked at his imagination—it was like a man dying of thirst on a raft in the middle of an ocean of water that he couldn't drink.

Johnny explored his pack with his partially numb fingers searching out the kindling. He removed the sticks and stacked them into a pile. He brushed back the snow in his little refuge and placed a small pot on the pile of wood. Then hacking ice chips, he filled the pot. He removed matches and half a candle from his shirt. He lit the wick and held it under the kindling until it caught fire, then blew out the candle and deposited it again in his pocket. The fire's heat reflected off the boulders surrounding his refuge and gave him some warmth while it melted the ice and snow in the pot. He drank the water and melted more and kept on drinking until the fire dwindled down and was no more. In twenty minutes it was out, but the sustenance of the fluid was enough to partially restore his strength. He looked out from the ridge and tried to ascertain what lay ahead, but visibility was nil. Then he unrolled his sleeping bag and crawled into it and went to sleep.

During the night the wind and snow abated and the sky cleared.

Johnny slept heavily and when he awoke the sun was nicking the horizon to the southeast. Its rays diffused over the peaks encasing them in a scarlet glow, as though the whole range had suddenly caught fire. Reluctantly, and with some trepidation, Johnny crawled out from his refuge between the boulders and looked down the west side of the mountain. He saw, to his relief, that the slope below, though steep, was navigable. He scanned the landscape he planned to travel over and carefully plotted and memorized the route. He knew that once he dropped down off the summit his eagle's perspective would be lost. Farther westward he could see what he figured was the Bell River and its tributaries, the Rock and the Eagle, both appearing as thin, white ribbons winding through the blackness of the spruce forests that lined the waterways.

Johnny decided to make for the Bell, and follow it to the Eagle, and then head up that stream to its source where the forests were thicker. He knew that a plane's capabilities were not unlimited. For one, the pilot could not land in the middle of a thick forest, and for another the pilot could not see beneath the forest's canopy. This plan might give him some chance of hiding from the aerial patrol. However, in order to do this he would have to stay many miles ahead of the men chasing him.

Johnny turned and stared northward. He could see the length of the Barrier River and more distantly, the Rat. He was unable to discern any signs of activity, but he knew somewhere in the vast patch of snow-covered hills, men were looking for him. Their purpose was to make him pay the ultimate price for his transgressions of the law.

Like a bolt out of the blue Johnny suddenly wondered if he might be enjoying this battle of wits. There was no intricate web of alternatives to confuse him in this confrontation. The Arctic was his element. He was good at living and fighting in it. The savagery was a part of him. So far he had won, and with each victory came his own personal redemption.

The vast snowfield that descended below him was hardpacked and he realized he could slide down the steep slope. The only real threat he foresaw was the possibility that the slope ended in a cliff, but he would take that chance. Johnny strapped on his snowshoes, shouldered his pack, and then sat down on the snowshoes. Making himself as comfortable as possible, he stretched his long arms forward and grabbed the tips of the webbed shoes with his mitten-encased hands. Then he leaned forward, shifting his weight downward. As he did so, his makeshift toboggan started to slide. It quickly gained momentum until he was rocketing down the incline.

Steering by yanking the tips of his snowshoes in the direction he wanted to go, he veered into a natural chute that went over a blind hill to plunge wildly down another chute. This took him for a mile before he came to rest in a swirl of snow at the bank of a small creek. He stood up and looked back. It had taken only minutes compared to many hours of backbreaking toil in climbing the mountain the day before.

Johnny resolutely set off in the direction of the Bell River. He did not waste time trying set up decoy trails now that the airplane was in the chase. He walked in a straight line, but his stride was shorter, and his rests were more frequent. The cold persisted, and game continued to be scarce. He set snares at night, but to no avail. He took to carrying his stockless, sawed-off 16-gauge shotgun in his parka pocket so that it was quickly available for any small game he might be fortunate enough to encounter. The days ran together, and he walked on through the cold, ever weakening in the process. Another blizzard descended on Johnny's now stooped form. This time it blew out of the southwest. Stinging, blinding ice crystals rendered his face into a blackened, turgid, frostbitten caricature of a human being.

Starvation and dehydration stretched the skin so tightly across his cheekbones that his countenance took on the appearance of a skeleton. What little fat had been on his muscular frame now was used up by his body's need for fuel. The result was an exaggerated projection of the rib cage. This stood in sharp contrast to his stomach, which had collapsed into a cavernous maw against his backbone.

Fatigue, starvation, frostbite, and scurvy turned Johnny's physique into a debilitated shadow of his former self. Legs that had once been sturdy and strong were pin sticks that barely supported his run-down body. His arms, now thin, were no more than bony appendages barely able to tote the weight of his rifle. His once bull neck was now incapable of supporting a seemingly oversized skull. The fact that the "thing" called Johnny Johnson was capable of movement was nothing short of miraculous. His brain, fogged by the manifestations of cold and starvation, fought a losing struggle to reach rational decisions. Basically, Johnny was no more than an automaton, a walking corpse that moved instinctively. Flashes of brain activity spasmodically overcame the incessant battering of the cold to reveal a flicker of life in eyes mummified by the lack of food. In such a state, he made his way southward until thirty-seven miles up the Eagle River he came upon ski tracks. Bleary-eyed, and not knowing they were Phil Branstrom's, he looked at them, dumbfounded by what he saw. He recalled that one of his pursuers wore skis. Somehow the posse must have gotten in front of him. With the last bit of his strength he climbed a tree looking for his pursuers, but saw nothing. He turned around, and reeling like a drunk he staggered back to the river. That evening he camped on a sharp bend of the Eagle. The storm abated and the stars came out. Several hours later the aurora appeared in all its glory. And, as the waves of color saturated the heavens, Johnny gazed up at them, reminded of the Sami legend in which a youngster ignored his older brother's warning and teased the northern lights. Were the Lapp gods telling him something? He wondered if, on the morrow, the tentacles of light would find and destroy him like they had the little boy that his brother, Magnor, had warned him about so long ago. Maybe he had pushed his luck too far.

# Chapter 25

# DOWN FOR THE COUNT

Inspector Eames sat in his headquarters tent on the Rat River. A huge map lay in front of him on a makeshift table of empty food cases. For once everything appeared to be in order. He had the plane he'd asked for, and now at his disposal was another badly needed Mountie, Sid May. With his arrival and the men accompanying him Eames now was commanding roughly nineteen men. He had asked for two, and May had brought five. That part was appreciated. May sat at his side on another box also looking at the map.

"You brought five good men, I hear," Eames said. "What were their names again?"

May nodded. "Will Mason and Reub Mason, Jim Hogg, Frank Jackson, and John Moses, my special constable. I'd better write them down for you for when you make out the payroll," he said.

Eames thought everything was going too smoothly and now he knew why. "What payroll?" he said with his voice on a rising note.

"For the men I brought over, sir," May said with all confidence. "Your appeal on the radio asked for all the men we could get, within reason, of course."

"Constable, I asked you. What payroll?"

Constable May saw that his favored status was rapidly plummeting. "Well, Inspector, the ten dollars a day I promised the volunteers. That doesn't include John Moses; as you know he is already on the payroll."

Inspector Eames stood up.

Constable May knew when the inspector stood up it meant bad news for anyone in his immediate vicinity, and other than a man who was waxing his skis, he happened to be the only one in the tent besides his boss.

Eames reflected on his position. One thing about commanding a group of young men in their twenties and thirties was the fact that you never knew what they were going to do next. Maybe that's what Eames liked about the job. There were always plenty of surprises. Sometimes they were good surprises, but of late they seemed to be balancing out in the other direction.

"Constable May. Do you know what it took to get that damned plane you see out there?" he said.

"Well, sir, I can't see it," May said honestly. "It's quite dark out."

"Constable, you don't have to see the thing to know it's there!" the inspector huffed.

"Yes, I guess you're right, sir."

"The point I want to make," said Inspector Eames, "is the cost involved. My request had to go through Superintendent Acland in Edmonton. He passed it on to General McBride, the chief of the department in Ottawa, who in turn had to get the okay of the minister of justice. From there Parliament had to approve the appropriation."

"I'm sorry, Inspector," May injected, "I don't get the connection."

"I sent word to your NCO in charge, Thornthwaite, to send over two men, not five!"

"I get you, sir. I brought too many. I'm sorry about that," said May. He was still puzzled by the long way around Inspector Eames was taking to tell him something.

"Let's start again," said the inspector. "You offered them ten dollars a day."

"That's right," said May. "That's only four men."

Inspector Eames threw his hands up in the air. "The point I'm trying to make is the deputized men here joined on a voluntary basis."

"Well, so did mine," said May.

"But Constable, I am not paying my deputies."

Then it dawned on Constable May. "You're not?"

"I was not, but I am now," said Inspector Eames. "No thanks to you."

"I never thought—" May started to say.

"Forget it," Eames broke in. "Right now I have more important things to worry about. I guess you heard that Johnson passed you somewhere in the mountains."

"Yes, sir," said May, "Trapper Peter Alexi told us the Indians have seen him around Lapierre House."

"I don't know how he did it, and no one else does, but the bugger made it across the highest part of the Richardsons in a blizzard," Eames commented.

May nodded. "My special, John Moses, said only a wolverine could do that."

"All right," said Eames, "I want you and your men to stock up on grub for yourselves and your dogs, and turn around and head for Lapierre House. I'm going to fly over there with Carter, Gardlund, and Riddell. That will be our main camp. That's all," he said abruptly. "I have to get going."

Walking out of the tent, May saw a man waxing his skis.

"Skis?" he said, staring at them.

"That's right."

"You must be Karl Gardlund?"

Gardlund nodded.

"You know Phil Branstrom?"

"No."

"Traps up the Eagle River. Swears by 'em. He can really go," May said enthusiastically.

Inspector Eames, Gardlund, Riddell, and Carter boarded the Bellanca with Wop May. They took off easily and in a short time were flying over the Richardson Mountains.

Eames looked down at the rugged appendage of the farthest north extension of the Rockies and half shouted to be heard over the roar of the engine. "Johnson crossed here?"

"Yes," said Wop. "He's a tough man. He must have been raised on nails." He then pointed to the north. "It looks like we've got another storm blowing in."

Eames turned and stared in the direction the pilot pointed to and shook his head. "Just what we need," he said sarcastically.

They landed at Lapierre House, the trading post run by the Jackson brothers. The Jacksons helped unload their gear and what supplies Wop May had squeezed aboard.

"I'm going to try to make it to Aklavik right now," Wop said, "before that storm hits."

Shortly afterward he took off, and almost immediately he was back again. "Looks bad that way," he said.

Inspector Eames had another task for the flyer. "How are you fixed for fuel?" he asked.

"Got some," Wop said.

"All right, you and Carter fly over the Bell and the Eagle, and see if you can find this character."

"Will do," said Wop.

"One more thing," said Eames. "There's a couple of trappers pretty far up the Eagle, and at least one of them, Branstrom, is on skis."

"Gotcha," Wop replied as he and Carter boarded the plane.

They took off and in a matter of minutes saw where Johnny had taken the long way around a bend in the Bell and had headed up the Eagle River. They lost his trail there amid several thousand caribou tracks.

"Maybe I'll get a shot at him," Carter said. He had principally been sent north because he was a crack shot and wanted to use his expertise if he could.

"I'm sorry, Bill, but I can't let you do that," said Wop.

"Why not?" Carter asked. "One shot and it would all be over."

"I agree with you there," Wop said, "but I can't risk this plane. If I get him in range of us, it also means we're in range of him, and from the evidence at hand, he is one hell of a rifle shot."

"I see what you mean," Carter said. "You're the pilot."

"It looks like a dead end here right now and it's getting dark," said May, "I'm heading back." Shortly thereafter he landed the plane back at camp and tied it down for the night.

The blizzard Wop feared swept in on the main camp that night and grounded the Bellanca the next day. The same storm lambasted Sid, Hersey, and the others mushing to Lapierre House via Rat Pass, one of the few navigable notches in the Richardson mountains. By the time they reached Lapierre House the mushers were exhausted and immediately rolled up in their sleeping bags and went to sleep.

The next morning Riddell greeted his fellow Signalman, Hersey, who was "boxing" the ears of his lead dog, Silver.

"Well, you made it, Earl. How was the Pass?" Riddell asked.

"Rough, but we led the whole way . . . eh, Silver? Last night was the worst blizzard I've ever seen. It stopped us in our tracks."

"Makes you wonder how Johnson can do it," Riddell commented.

"A will of iron," Hersey replied.

Lapierre House was now a large encampment bursting at the seams with trappers fleeing the wilderness to avoid Johnny and lawmen and deputies. There were also the regular residents consisting of Old Crow people, Gwitchin, who were related to McPherson residents. They spent the trapping season there. The result of all this activity was a rapid depletion of supplies that was further accelerated by the arrival of Constable May and his group.

Wop managed to fly to Aklavik that day and came back with food supplies, ammunition, gas, and oil. While he was in the air a ground party of eleven men set out after Johnny. Thanks to aerial guidance from Wop and Carter, the posse cut short a bend on the Bell and reached the Eagle that evening where they made camp. In the meantime a heavy fog settled in over the entire region, grounding the Bellanca.

The men gathered in one tent and Eames went over plans for the next day.

"First of all," Eames said, "as is fairly obvious, the Bellanca can't get off the ground in this soup. Therefore, tomorrow morning we'll cut down a few trees and mark out our direction with an arrow in the snow. Presumably this will save Wop May a little time when he comes looking for us.

"Lazarus, here, noticed Johnson's stride has shortened considerably. He's weakening, so don't stick your necks out." He pointed to Hersey. "Earl, your team with old Silver there, is the fastest one we have. I want you to lead off tomorrow, and keep alert because more than likely we'll be running into this guy."

The next morning the first thing Inspector Eames did when he emerged from his tent was to look skyward. The fog was gone and he knew the Bellanca could take off. The men laid arrows made out of spruce branches and trees indicating the direction they were taking.

Johnny saw the sun for the first time it seemed in weeks. It was February 17, 1932. By now he was a man in a daze, running on nothing but instinct and the powerful urge to survive. His life was coming to an end and he knew it—whether at the hands of the posse or from plain physical breakdown. He had turned again to walk upriver, but by a strange quirk of fate and a twist in the river, his steps were taking him in a northerly direction. When he looked back into the sun, he thought he saw someone, but could just barely make out the individual. It had to be the posse. They must have cut across a bend in the Eagle to get in behind him. Using his last ounce of energy, he ran to the thirty-foot-high riverbank and tried to climb up it in his bid for sanctuary among the trees.

No sooner had Hersey cut across the river's bend than he spotted the fugitive climbing the east bank of the Eagle. Hersey grabbed his rifle, flipped the sled over to stop the dogs, and kneeled and shot at Johnson. The bullet went into the trapper's pack and glanced off a pan.

Taking a cork from the muzzle of his Savage, Johnny levered a cartridge into his .30–30 and, aiming instinctively through eyes partially snow blind, snapped off a shot at Hersey.

The slug from Johnny's rifle ripped through the kneeling Hersey's elbow, then ploughed through his knee to penetrate his chest, and send him reeling into the snow.

By now the rest of the posse of dog teams and men had reached the scene of the action and split, bolting for both sides of the Eagle. Two men grabbed Hersey and pulled him to the bank of the river.

Adrenalin pumping, Johnny ran away from the posse, actually gaining a few yards on them, but tiring quickly, he turned and dumped his pack into the snow, throwing himself behind it.

Inspector Eames, who was next to Sid May, shouted, "You have one last chance to give up, Johnson!"

Johnny's answer was a wave of his hand and a bullet that sailed by Eames's ear.

The posse raced into position.

Moses aimed and fired from his place above and to the left of Johnny.

Verville's brother, Joe, a sniper in the big war, squeezed off his Enfield at Johnny, now prone in the center of the river.

Sid, the Mountie from Old Crow, stood next to Eames in the middle of the river and coolly leveled his Enfield on the fugitive, racked a shell into the chamber, and pulled the trigger.

Carter, the best rifleman in all of G Division of the Royal Canadian Mounted Police, darted up the west side of the waterway, knelt down, and shot.

Constant Ethier, a former Mounted Policeman, was right behind Carter, and he, too, leveled his Winchester and sent a bullet in Johnny's direction.

Frank Jackson, the trapper and trading post owner at Lapierre House, trotted to the east side of the Eagle, and dispatched his weapon at Johnny.

One of the first shots hit ammunition in Johnny's hip pocket and then exploded. Johnny jerked violently as a big chunk of his thigh disintegrated.

Another shot pulverized his shoulder.

And still another slug ripped into his arm.

Johnny now recognized the specters of light from the muzzle blasts. Magnor was right. The northern lights had caught up with him. But he would not die easily, not while there was a flicker of life left in him. He raised his Savage to fire again, but only lifted the weapon halfway to his wounded shoulder when a sniper's bullet struck his spine and shattered the sciatic nerve. This initiated a shock wave that surged through Johnny's nervous system immobilizing his brain and plucking the soul from his tormented body. He grimaced in death, and his upper body crumpled as it fell forward, facedown into the snow.

Wop landed his aircraft immediately next to the dead man and signaled to the others. "He's dead," he shouted.

The men warily approached Johnny's position. Sid got there first and turned over the body with his rifle barrel.

"He's dead all right," Sid confirmed.

Eames and the others looked down at the body while Sid searched the dead man's clothes for any sign of identification.

"No wallet," Sid said, "Only a pouch."

He opened up the moose-skin bag and took out a vial of gold, a thick wad of money, and what looked like a packing slip.

"Will you look at this!" Sid exclaimed, and rifled through the bills and hefted the gold, which he handed to Eames. But Sid held on to the piece of paper.

Eames looked at the bills. "And he wouldn't buy a trapper's license. There's over two thousand dollars here!"

Sid handed Eames the wrinkled slip.

"What's this?" Eames asked.

"I don't know," Sid replied, "Some lines, a triangle, nothing written. It doesn't make sense."

Eames scanned the paper hurriedly. He scowled and then extended his hand to give it back to Sid who missed it, and it fell between them. The inspector did not notice the descending paper because he had turned to the pilot.

"Come on," he said. "Wop, we've got to get Hersey to Doc Urquhart in a hurry. Let's go."

Eames turned to Sid. "Load Johnson's body onto your sled and take him to Lapierre House. Tomorrow we'll fly him to Aklavik for the coroner's examination."

"Yes, sir," Sid replied. Sid glanced at Will Mason who had just arrived on the scene with his dog team. "Will," he said, "how about giving me a hand?'

"Sure thing," Mason replied.

The rest of the posse moved to the plane in order to get the wounded Hersey aboard.

Sid and Will were alone. They slid Johnny's body onto a canvas tarp and wrapped it up, and then placed it onto Sid's sled. The dogs comprehended that something was askew and howled their lament.

Sid was ready to pull out. "One last thing, Will," he said.

"What's that?"

"You'd better pick up that scrap of paper."

"Where is it?" Will asked, puzzled.

Sid nodded in the direction of the paper, hardly visible in the snow. "Right there," he said, pointing to it.

Will stooped down and picked it up and studied it closely. "This is a map. There, a triangle. Hell! It marks the Lost Cabin mine!"

Sid winked at Will then turned to his dogs and shouted, "Mush on, you mutts."


"The pastor isn't wasting any time getting through this funeral, Liz," McDowell whispered.

Nurse Liz Brown nodded. "I can't say I blame him. It must be forty below. By the way, why is Mr. Johnson being buried clear across the plot from the rest of the graves?"

The policeman grimaced. "That's easy to answer. Technically he is a murderer in the eyes of the law and the Anglican church. He shouldn't be buried in the cemetery at all."

They watched as the box containing Albert Johnson was lowered into the grave.

"Look," the Mountie whispered, "by the length of the ropes used in lowering the box, the grave must be pretty shallow—no more than three or four feet."

"It's all so sad," Liz said softly.

"He's lucky. It could be worse."

"How so?"

"When a man is classified as a murderer they usually forget the box and dump a bag of lime over his body."

Liz looked at her Mountie friend to see if he was serious. "Why would they do that?"

McDowell shook his head. "I really don't know. Possibly the custom began in old England."

They watched as blocks of frozen soil were pushed into the grave.

Then, with the others who had been in attendance, they walked slowly away.

McDowell turned to Liz. "Did you ever read Robert Service?"

"Yes," she said.

"Do you remember the last verse of 'The Men That Don't Fit In?'" He did not wait for an answer. "It goes like this: 'He has failed, he has failed; he has missed his chance; he has just done things by half. Life's been a jolly good joke on him, and now is the time to laugh. Ha, ha! He is one of the Legion Lost; He was never meant to win; He's a rolling stone, and it's bred in the bone; He's a man who won't fit in.'"

"Right on target, Mac. I didn't realize you knew any poetry," Liz commented. "It certainly fits the image of Mr. Johnson."

McDowell nodded. "Yes, it's almost as if Service, who wrote it years ago, could see into the future."

# AFTERMATH

Today the plot at Aklavik has filled up and Johnny is no longer alone. His grave is marked by a tree stump that is painted with "A. J.," the initials for Albert Johnson.

Ironically, Johnny, like Butch Cassidy, has become something of a cult hero. This is not specifically because of his actions, which after all were transgressions of the law, but more for what he represented. It would appear that Johnny wanted nothing more than to lead an independent life in the wilderness. Millions of people today would like to pursue the same course, but the opportunities are vanishing along with the wilderness. The solitude they search for is no longer there; if not gone materially, it has certainly disappeared metaphorically. Snow machines, outboard motors, jet boats, motorbikes, ATVs, helicopters, pontoon planes, motorized hang gliders, and a proliferation of all other types of machines have virtually erased the wild as a sanctuary known to old-timers.

Perhaps stories of individuals like Johnny will encourage us to pursue a more self-controlled lifestyle in regard to the waste of our planet's natural resources.

Or have we already gone too far?

We probably won't be long in finding out.

## The Lost Mines

Though the treasure map mentioned at the end of this story is fiction, the rest of the information about the Lost Cabin mine is true. Willoughby Mason took a fling at looking for the mine, but apparently was unsuccessful. Mason, however, did find a small amount of gold on the upper Driftwood River, which drains into the Porcupine near its confluence with the Bell. According to Stephen Frost, a resident of Old Crow, a boiler that Mason lugged into the area is still there and marks the spot of his discovery, but it is definitely not the Lost Cabin mine. For those who read this and are packing to go look for it, hold up! The first rumors of the cabin began shortly after 1900. That means the cabin marking the spot probably has long since collapsed, making it almost impossible to find.

The Lost McHenry mine may or may not have been found. Much depends on how one interprets the information about it. Some people believe McHenry actually stumbled across the Bonanza gravels that sparked the 1897–98 gold rush long before that rush. Even so, no workings were found indicating his success.

The Lost Graveyard mine, too, is elusive. The pay streak could be just about anywhere, though it would be confined to the Nass River, which only narrows down its location to a couple of thousand square miles. The trail to it commences at a trapper's cabin located next to an Indian fishing camp and graveyard along the Nass River. The path to the pay streak supposedly follows a tributary that narrows down to a canyon that can be crossed by felling a tree. Following this creek to a spot shortly above the timberline one may find a site where the creek crosses a vein of quartz loaded with stringers of gold (not to be confused with placer gold).